What if

I don't want to invite my cousin's three kids?

I do want to invite my father's second wife?

Some of the guests are vegetarians?

I'm a vegetarian?

My in-laws are threatening to boycott the wedding?

My mother keeps calling me at work to discuss centerpieces?

*The best man loves dirty jokes
and I'm terrified of letting him give a toast?*

*I really need to talk about my doubts and fears, but everyone looks
crushed if I even hint that I'm not the perfect, happy bride?*

One of the bridesmaids is making life difficult for everyone?

I'm on the verge of tears?

"Covers everything the traditional to the offbeat bride needs to custom-design her wedding. Want to learn how to register for camping gear, hold the reception in a firehouse, buy a wedding dress off the rack, get unique deals on flowers, food and photos? It's here. There are even pointed questions to ask each expert before signing any contracts. When all the planning is done, [brides] can find hints on how to relax and deputize an assertive friend to make sure all runs smoothly on 'the' day while they're busy enjoying themselves."
                                                                            —*Booklist*

How *to* Have *the* Wedding You Want

(Not the One Everybody Else Wants You to Have)

CHRISTINE EGAN

BERKLEY BOOKS, NEW YORK

THE BERKLEY PUBLISHING GROUP
Published by the Penguin Group
Penguin Group (USA) LLC
375 Hudson Street, New York, New York 10014

USA • Canada • UK • Ireland • Australia • New Zealand • India • South Africa • China

penguin.com

A Penguin Random House Company

Library of Congress Cataloging-in-Publication Data

Egan, Christine.
How to have the wedding you want : (not the one everybody else wants you to have) / Christine Egan.
pages   cm
ISBN 978-0-425-26968-8 (pbk.)
1. Weddings.   2. Weddings—Planning.   3. Wedding etiquette.   I. Claro, Danielle.
How to have the wedding you want.   II. Title.
HQ745.C56   2014
392.5—dc23   2013033251

PUBLISHING HISTORY
First Berkley trade paperback edition / February 1995
Berkley trade paperback edition / January 2014

PRINTED IN THE UNITED STATES OF AMERICA

10   9   8   7   6   5   4   3   2   1

Cover photo of "Wedding" © Roc Canals Photography/Getty Images.
Cover design by Diana Kolsky.
Interior text design by Laura K. Corless.

*Penguin is committed to publishing works of quality and integrity.
In that spirit, we are proud to offer this book to our readers;
however, the story, the experiences, and the words
are the author's alone.*

Thanks to all the brides and grooms who shared their stories

Contents

How *to* Have *the* Wedding You Want

Introduction

*S*o you're getting married.

Suddenly the world treats you differently. Coworkers find you intriguing; strangers in elevators offer congratulations; your aunts and uncles have a newfound respect for you. But what exactly have you accomplished? Is it that you've "bagged a man"? You're a little puzzled, a little annoyed. What's going on? You're getting a whole lot of weird attention, and you're not sure you like it.

But that's not all. You're only up to the C's (cutlery) in a ten page single-spaced Word doc of wedding details, so you're wracked with anxiety. Your father is talking about ice sculptures for your reception, and you're looking for a nonviolent way to set him straight. And you and your boyfriend have started fighting, so you're wondering why you're going through any of this in the first place. On top of it all, since you're not completely joyous and glee-ful, you feel guilty. When does that glow start, you're thinking, that dewy, placid look you see in wedding gown ads?

Don't worry, you've got it. But it comes and goes. This is supposed to be the happiest time of your life, but it also might be the toughest. And confidentially, the models in those bridal magazines aren't really getting married anyway.

You see, a wedding forces people to deal with all the touchiest topics: commitment, priorities, religion, money, dysfunctional family habits. It brings out the extremes of every relationship and every personality type, including your own. (You didn't realize you had a personality type? Neither did I. You do.) It can spark explosions or bring people closer, sometimes simultaneously. It is an apt prelude to a marriage; if you can get through this, you can get through just about anything.

While you're planning, all your loyalties are forced into competition, and your past and present become disturbingly merged. You know how some people don't like to mix different groups of friends? Imagine mixing every single person in every disparate aspect of your life. Your old boyfriend's sister and your future husband's mother. Your boss and your out-of-control college roommate. It's like inviting your father to eavesdrop on an intimate conversation between you and your best friend: "Hey, everybody, this is my life! Take a look!" Feeling a little vulnerable, perhaps?

Not to mention a little torn. *Your* mother wants this, *his* mother wants that, and you want something else completely. That's why you'll be in the best shape if you go at it with a mix of assertiveness and adaptability: the strength to fight (if necessary) for what you really care about and the discretion to know when to compromise.

You're not on some amusement park ride gone haywire. You *can* be in control of your wedding. Getting past what people might think of you is your first step toward wedding-planning empowerment, if you'll pardon the term. There's incredible social pressure to do this "the right way," and you just have to say, "To hell with it." There can also be pressure to *not* do it the traditional way, depending on who you are and who your friends are. Whatever you decide, there'll be someone who begs to differ. Being in the bridal spotlight is hard. People are going to gossip about you, criticize your choices (maybe even your choice of husband), bombard you with unsolicited suggestions. Now you know how Kate Middleton feels.

Everyone wants to give you advice about your wedding. Everyone. This book is *full* of advice, from people you don't even know. But you can close or open it whenever you want, which is more than you can say about your cousin/sister-in-law/coworker's mouth. Another thing, this book is always on *your* side. Not that your friends and family are necessarily against you, but even the most well-meaning among them can provoke in you daily fits of hysteria.

And when it comes to the practical stuff—flowers, a dress, invitations—the people who traditionally offer the most advice are the ones whose names follow "Pay to the order of" on the checks you write. The florists, the caterers, the photographers who tell you, "This is the way it's done." Please! Remember that ad for the diamond industry that said, "Is two months' salary too much to pay for something that lasts a lifetime?" Thanks for your input, guys, but last time I looked you were trying to make a profit off me.

No, that's not where you want to get your advice. You want to hear from people like you, who have been where you are about to venture and who have the scars to prove it. This book is your BFF, It will tell you stories and try to make you laugh. It will help you think about wedding stuff you haven't dealt with yet and maybe don't want to deal with. It will support whatever it is you want and give you lots of new ideas. "Wow! What *won't* it do?" you ask. Well, it won't detail the traditional financial responsibilities of the groom's great uncle or tell you the proper way to address invitations to members of Parliament. We're talking about real life here:

It's not 1950, you don't have Jennifer Aniston's wedding budget, and Cinderella isn't your role model. Having a wedding is about much more than checklists and pretty pictures. Maybe the reason people like bridal magazines is that they're so full of . . . fantasy (what did you *think* I was going to say?).

The first question I asked the brides I interviewed for this book was "If you had it to do again, what would you do differently?" In fact, sometimes that was the *only* question I asked. Everyone had tons of advice. The names have been changed to protect their marriages and their relationships with their respective mothers-in-law. Almost all the advice in this book is from regular people—brides, grooms, opinionated guests. But I also talked very frankly with a few "wedding professionals" about some cost-cutting options and about the misconceptions some clients (that would be you) approach them with.

There are so many things I wish someone had told me about before I got married. I came away full of "should've" and "could've." I hope this book helps you deal with parts of the planning that other books don't talk about and makes you aware of some new options. And that by reliving gut-wrenching psychological, emotional and practical wedding-planning experiences with us, you'll emerge stronger, smarter and better armed with a sense of humor for the planning of your own excellent bash.

Anything Goes

*F*irst things first. Before you get anywhere near the details of planning, you'll have to make some big-picture decisions. Loosely speaking, what kind of wedding do you want to have? Not to be confused with, what kind of wedding do you think you'll *probably* have? Different issue. Here we're talking fantasy. What would be fun? What would be different? What's in your head, before you consider what's expected of you? The brides and grooms whose stories make up this book are a creative, resourceful lot. Their choices were based on the same things yours will be: visions of a dream wedding tempered by the harsh reality of financial constraints. But forget about money for a minute and think "mood." There are as many types of weddings as there are couples. Here are a few variations on the traditional theme.

The Cocktail Party Wedding

"When I'm at a wedding, I hate the dinner part," says Celia, who likens table assignments to prison cells. "You hate who you're sitting with, you're separated from your college friend who you haven't seen in five years, and dinner won't work because it's chicken or beef, and you're a vegetarian." Celia didn't want to put any restrictions on her guests in terms of movement or menu. She considers the cocktail portion of a reception to be the fun part, so she made her wedding all cocktails. "It was a real party the whole time, because you could move around, you could dance, you could sit down for a while with your boyfriend or meet new people." Making a meal out of hors d'oeuvres is easy to do, and it's a lot less expensive than serving dinner.

Celia and Peter kept their whole party very free-form. "The only downside to that," says Celia, "is that people left early." Not all guests are creative about filling up four hours without ever being told, *Go here now, sit there now, dance now.* But if you like, you can have a cocktail reception and still make use of some of the structural elements of traditional wedding receptions (i.e., have a time when toasts are made, a time when the bulk of the food is passed, and a time when the music is specifically geared toward dancing). And you can always create a sense that dessert—whatever it is—is worth sticking around for.

The Surprise Wedding

Ruth and Bob didn't want to make a big deal out of their wedding. It was Bob's second, and Ruth had never felt the urge to be the center of that kind of attention. "We didn't want gifts or any fuss," she says. They decided to spring it on their friends as a surprise. Everyone received invitations to a Christmas party. "We throw a casual one every year," says Ruth. "We asked people to RSVP so they wouldn't bring extra friends, which we usually encourage." Ruth hired someone to work the door and check invitations, so they'd know when all the people closest to them had arrived. In the middle of the party, the iTunes playlist switched from holiday tunes to "The Wedding March." The music grew louder till it silenced the puzzled crowd. Ruth called for everyone's attention, and a minister began the very short ceremony. "Everyone was stunned," says Bob. "They were totally taken off guard." After much hugging, crying and congratulating, the party music came back on, and the celebration continued.

The Micro Wedding

A lot of people dream about a small, intimate wedding. *Dream* is an apt term. It's a fantasy many brides-to-be are forced to give up. Once you face the reality of planning (the fighting that would ensue within your immediate family if you excluded certain relatives, the genuinely hurt feelings of friends you couldn't invite, not to mention the in-laws blaming this "small wedding thing" on you), you're often forced to rethink. You've really got to be able to accept the fact that some people are going to be hurt and are likely to stay mad forever. If you think you can handle it, I'm right there with you. (I was ready to go for it, but my husband nixed the idea immediately.) But make sure you're okay about dealing with the consequences. Can you isolate this guilt from your joyous occasion? Will it make you miserable in the long run? If having people "mad at you" is your most feared form of punishment (some of us never work through that junior high thing), here's another alternative: a *really* small wedding. If a few friends or relatives get huffy because they feel left out, you can take comfort in the fact that they're being unreasonable and will probably get over it.

Amy and Brad had saved about $10,000 to spend on their wedding. "We figured we could have a low-budget party with all our friends and relatives, or we could make it really tiny and very luxurious," says Amy. So they got their immediate families to come to San Francisco, where they live, had a ceremony in Golden Gate Park, took the whole bunch to an outrageously glamorous restaurant for lunch and stayed in a fabulous hotel. And then they went to Italy for a week.

The Do-It-Yourself Wedding

Some people take on one or two elements of a wedding and instead of spending the money, do the work themselves or with friends. A brave few go whole hog, often out of necessity.

Josie was lucky. She worked at an exquisite rustic floral shop, and her boss offered the place to her as a wedding present (not to keep, just to use for her reception). Finding an affordable location that has all the necessary elements for entertaining and feeding a crowd is tough. Josie and her husband, Tom, did all the cooking themselves. They baked two turkeys in their, un-air-conditioned studio apartment on a ninety-degree June day. "If we'd realized how bad that would be, we would have asked to use somebody else's kitchen," says Josie.

They planned their downtown Manhattan wedding for the day of the annual Gay Pride Parade because the neighborhood is so festive and lively that day, and as they walked through the streets from the church to the reception with their 80 guests, they soaked up the party atmosphere.

Josie's advice about doing it yourself: "Have lots of helpers. If anyone asks for something to do, give them a job." There are myriad details involved in even the simplest homemade wedding, so if nothing comes to mind when friends offer their services, ask if you can think about it and get back to them. "One thing I forgot to do was assign someone the task of taking our presents home for us," says Josie. "You can't believe how many people will show up with gifts." She and Tom had to do it themselves. That was a lot of trips up and down five flights of stairs in a pink linen suit (Josie's).

When you're doing it yourself, you really have to respect your own limitations and the limitations of the space. Because their wedding was at a flower shop, Tom and Josie had lots of refrigerator space and a big sink, but no stove or oven. "That meant all cold food. And the shop was small, so we made foods you could easily eat standing." If you have a little money to spend, a few cases of wine and a few cases of champagne or a cleaning crew might be a good place for it to go. The prewedding work is fun and exciting, if exhausting. But after the wedding, says Josie, the last thing you feel like doing is grabbing a broom.

Joni and Fred did a major amount of work for their wedding for 180. Joni found that the stress of about a million last-minute tasks didn't mix well with being a relaxed, fun-loving host. "We thought it would be so fun to have our friends around us all weekend. There was the rehearsal dinner Friday and a picnic all day Saturday. But that doesn't work if you're doing everything yourself. You can't be the hostess with the mostest the whole time."

Joni found herself in the throes of a prewedding frenzy, not peculiar to do-it-yourself brides. "The day before my wedding I was still ordering food—the club soda and the bread. I ordered a loaf of bread for every single person and enough rolls for everybody also. I was thinking, *Oh hell, it's not that expensive.* They delivered it to our apartment that morning, and we filled up a whole SUV with it." At the end of the wedding, the couple was left with 120 extra loaves of bread. Joni handed it out as guests exited. Says Joni of her over-ordering, "I guess I was a little out of my mind."

The Guests-as-Staff Wedding

Having a wedding in which all the guests help out is not easy. According to the brides, grooms and guests I spoke with, the way to make it work for everybody is to keep expectations very low and flexibility way high. Otherwise, there's lots of opportunity for resentment. If you think you can keep the spirit of the party light and fun and not be a stickler in any way, you might want to give it a try. If you're a control freak, figure something else out. You're not paying these people. And you want them to like you when it's over. The happy-go-lucky, like-water-off-a-duck's-back types are the ones who succeed here.

When Nina and Jeremy got married, they had very little money. They asked all their friends to chip in with food and their time instead of bringing gifts. "Our only expense was the wine, the flowers and the rental of the loft," says Nina. "I think we spent $5,000 for the whole wedding." It worked because Nina and Jeremy didn't have any preconceived notions about what the wedding would be like. They let it define itself and didn't worry about making it "feel like a wedding." Guests were excited to be a part of it. "We were the first of our friends to get married, so it wasn't like everybody had been through so many weddings. I think it was a bit of a novelty."

Generally speaking, lack of organization would be a liability, not an asset. But kismet was with the couple, and the fact that the plans weren't spelled out created a great spirit of cooperation. "Everybody sort of spontaneously took charge," says Nina. "Whoever comes to that naturally—you know, the people at a party who are always cleaning up—they took care of things." Some friends heated up food, some served drinks, others made sure there was always music in the background. Whoever was left at the end helped clean up, including the guests of honor, so it was a pretty quick job.

Nina and Jeremy's only hopes were for a fun party. They were not worried about making it weddinglike, and there was no pressure for any element to be perfect. They couldn't be disappointed, so they weren't. They were delighted, and their guests/helpers felt appreciated, because everything they did was met with surprise and gratitude.

Vanessa and Eli *did* have expectations for their larger-scale pitch-in wedding. Vanessa worked on the wedding full-time for four months, making each invitation by hand, and cooking all the food with her mother. She had a very specific design for every aspect. More important, due to the stress of the massive undertaking, the couple was in pretty bad emotional shape immediately before. Both broke down and cried at the rehearsal, aware that what they were attempting was too ambitious. Family tensions rose and created a general atmosphere of doom. So the preparations did not have a "let's all help out" feel. The members of the wedding party felt they had been unfairly sentenced to a weekend of hard labor. Lots of resentment ensued. One groomsman described the whole ordeal as "emotional root canal."

Vanessa and Eli were aiming for the smoothness that comes with painstakingly planned, heavily financed weddings. If you want to exert that kind of control, you need either a whole lot of money or a very short guest list. You can't expect your friends to be as meticulous as Martha Stewart when they're arranging flowers. They're doing you a favor, so whatever they can do has to be okay. Otherwise you'll drive yourself nuts, and you'll piss people off.

The Dessert Wedding

Where does it say that lots o' food equals a good wedding? Even if it does say that somewhere, or if that's what your relatives believe, so what? The concept *wedding* is yours to develop and define. Ginnie and Chris are from large families. "We're close with our cousins, and we didn't want to exclude anyone," says Ginnie. One way to eliminate the "more heads equals more dollars" problem is not to worry about feeding people. "We kept it simple, just one big flower arrangement, lots of balloons, very good champagne and three kinds of cupcakes." Making plans was incredibly easy, so there was no pressure on the couple or on their families and friends. "And we invited everyone we wanted to invite." Of course, they said on the invitation that it was a cake and champagne wedding, so guests knew to arrive with a full stomach.

Eloping

If you're looking at this book, you've probably pretty much eliminated this alternative. But believe me, at least once during the wedding-planning process, eloping is going to start looking mighty tasty. You'll fantasize about chucking the whole thing and sneaking out in the middle of the night. Or disappearing for a week with your two best friends to an island in the Caribbean. When you return, your mother will be so glad to find you alive (she spent the whole week filling your voicemail with dozens of panicked messages) that she won't even be mad!

Laura and Hollis were together for six years when they started planning their wedding. They had their hearts set on an eighty-year-old beachfront hotel that they visited every summer. A year later, they were still waiting for the hotel to finish its renovations. "I was so frustrated. We couldn't really make any plans until the work was done," says Laura. "We just lost our momentum, and planning became such a chore. It was not fun at all anymore." So Hollis suggested they forget about the wedding and elope. They went to Jamaica and came back hitched. Their parents (each had two sets) were very understanding about it—there had been a couple of tense divorces among them. If they were at all disappointed, they kept it to themselves. But Laura's best friend felt gypped and angry. "She was probably looking forward to our wedding more than we were. I was kind of shocked that she would dare be mad at us over such a personal thing, but people get weird."

Some couples can look into their familial crystal ball and see a scenario they would do anything to avoid. Darren watched his mother interact with his two sisters as they planned their weddings, and he knew he could never put himself through such hell. He tried to picture telling his mother that he and Hillary were not going to get married in a Catholic church. The prospect of such a conversation made his spine tingle. So they eloped. They got a few friends together on the spur of the moment and drove from L.A. to Las Vegas one night. Occasionally, Hillary feels a little sad that they never had a wedding—it would have been on the beach at sunset in shorts and T-shirts. "But," she says, "what we did was so fun, and we never had to deal with the family stuff, which I think might have ruined it for us."

The One-of-a-Kind Wedding

Ricky and Sibyl *did* have a beach party. It was a clambake on a summer night. "The only thing I was worried about was my mother, but she loved it," says Sibyl, who wore a flowy white dress (and a chiffon cape) just for the ceremony, then changed into more comfortable clothes so she could play volleyball and dance.

Liz and George are, in Liz's words, "not wedding types." So they booked their favorite bar for the night (a Sunday—the owner said he couldn't close on a Friday or Saturday) and had hors d'oeuvres brought in from the restaurant next door. The jukebox provided music, and friends dropped in and out all night. "We invited everybody by phone," says Liz. The ceremony took place at midnight, two hours into the party. "One of our friends sent away to the Universal Life Church to get his license so he could marry us." The party lasted till four A.M., then the last few guests and the bride and groom went out for breakfast.

· · · ·

What these couples have in common is that they did pretty much what they wanted to do. That's the whole point—not to have a beach wedding, or a bar wedding, or a dessert wedding, or a destination wedding, but to have the kind of wedding *you* want. Maybe you're not quite sure what that is yet because you've been slightly brainwashed into limiting your imagination. So open your mind, and try to relax. You've got a lot more options than you might think.

PHASE

1

· ·

The Politics of Planning

*Y*ou have a certain kind of wedding in mind and so does each of the players in your newly expanded cast of characters. If everyone was thinking the same thing, life would be grand. You'd all work together toward your common goal in peace and harmony. But that's not the way it goes. (And would you really want it to? I mean, what would you bitch about to your friends? What would you have to feel relieved about when the whole thing is over? What would you look back on and laugh about twenty years from now?) If you've ever considered running for office, think of this as practical experience. You've got your own agenda, but you've also got a whole bunch of constituents to keep happy. And each of your constituents has an agenda. You can't just forge ahead and ignore their concerns, because you'll need their support in the future.

The early part of planning is where these political concerns seem most intense, partly because you might not have been expecting them. But they're steady throughout, right till you're safely in a car and off to your honeymoon. Oh, and then they continue for the rest of your life.

This section is about communicating without fighting, and getting what you want without making the people close to you miserable. You'll never be able to make everyone happy, so as a general rule, try to guard the happiness of the two most important people—you and your husband-to-be.

Diplomacy is key here, but sometimes things are out of your hands. You might find support where you least expect it, but you'll also run into difficulties you never anticipated. People are at their most volatile when a wedding is a-comin'. You can't predict the buttons this event might push. But having a sense in advance of what you might encounter can mean the difference between slamming a door and saying calmly, "Hey, let's sit down and talk about this."

Think of the Boy Scout motto: *Be prepared.* I also have another motto for you. Maybe "mantra" is a better term, because you'll probably have to keep repeating this one over and over to yourself: *Choose your battles.* Some things are just not worth crying over. Keeping a nice clear focus on your priorities will help you stay in control. And although everyone I interviewed for this book had different wedding priorities, there's one that should be universal: protecting the relationship you're preparing to celebrate. *Duh*, you say, but only if you haven't gotten into planning yet. Because if you have, you know that the strain of the situation is unlike any you have so far experienced as a couple. "Getting married is like a big crisis in your life," says Nina. "And it brings up so much garbage. Just because it's a joyous event doesn't mean it's not stressful and not without its negative, difficult parts."

It's easy to get mad at people and feel slighted, but it's a lot more productive to realize when the problem is coming from you.

Then you can actually do something about it. "I felt very uncom-fortable about the whole gift-getting aspect of a wedding," says Gabi. "I guess I was uncomfortable with the attention in general, which is weird because I'm an actor, and I like to perform. But getting attention for getting married made me squirm." At the time, Gabi didn't think of it as *her* problem; she thought of it as her mother's problem for fussing too much, and her mother-in-law's problem for suggesting things Gabi wasn't into, and her hus-band's problem for not understanding.

The "I'm not worthy" thing is hard to overcome, but it will get you nowhere. If you're going to have a wedding of more than two people, accept the fact that you're going to get attention. It doesn't matter that you didn't "earn" it. Attention is not always about achievement. This time it's about happiness; giving you attention is everyone's way of getting in on the joy. And if it helps, the attention—though it seems to be directed at you—is not all *about* you. It's about weddings in general, and even rites of passage in general, and life. There. Feel better?

Daphne, another reluctant princess, was "flipping out" over the way her family was treating her, over the magnitude of the event, and over having to be in the spotlight. She decided to go to therapy to try to work it out. She went for ten sessions, and about a month before the wedding, her anxiety started to lift. It was a rough time for her, but the therapy helped her lighten up, and she managed to have a great time at her wedding.

Understanding yourself and handling your own anxiety is im-portant, but having the confidence to know what you want *and to say it* is just as crucial. Alexa got bullied by her boyfriend's wealthy family into the wedding *they* wanted to have. "I felt outclassed," she says. "I didn't know all the 'right' things to ask for, so I didn't ask for anything."

If you can dispense with the concept of what's "right," you'll be able to identify what's "right for you" a lot sooner. You're probably in for a little more drama than you're used to, and maybe even a couple of confrontations. So keep some tissues in your bag.

Okay, enough about you. Now on to the people in your life and what *they* think about you.

Mr. Wonderful and You

I think the word "boyfriend" is nice. It connotes youth and pleasant companionship. I don't like "fiancé." It reminds me of *Love, American Style.* How many men do you know who seem like fiancés? I can think of one, and I wouldn't want any friend of mine marrying him. So if you don't mind, I'm going to stick with "boyfriend." Maybe if we all did that, expectations would be lower, and there'd be less trouble.

Fighting and tension are, ironically, an integral part of the wedding-planning experience. If I had it to do over again, I would make a general resolution not to fight with my then boyfriend/ now husband. It's not just that there are a lot of details to quibble over, it's the details *plus* the intensity of the situation. It's choosing flowers when you're half in shock over the impending major life change. Every stupid disagreement between you and your boyfriend has the potential to escalate to the "Why am I marrying this jerk?" level, because you're both a little out of your minds.

You see sides of your boyfriend you've never had an opportunity to see before. Unless you've worked together on other projects, you might be surprised by the way he handles his share of wedding responsibility. Maybe he'll be a dream, and you'll love him even more. Then again, maybe he won't.

Kimberly's work takes her out of town a lot, so she and Gene began scheduling monthly wedding "production meetings." At one early meeting, Kimberly briefed Gene on the location scouting she'd done and e-mailed him a list of places to check out. "I was amazed at how organized he was about it. He was in medical school and was incredibly busy, but when I got back the next week, he'd seen all five places I'd asked him to go to, and he had prices and his own assessments written down in a little notebook." Kimberly had just assumed she'd have to do the bulk of the footwork, but she and Gene planned everything together and "if anything, Gene did more running around."

Lois, however, was not so thrilled with Michael's approach. The wedding was to be in his hometown, and he seemed to think it would come together fine without his participation. "I needed him to contact people, but just getting him to talk about the wedding was a chore," says Lois. "The worst part is that I was forced to nag him: 'Call your mother. Call your mother. Did you call your mother?' We were like Ralph and Alice Kramden, and we weren't even married yet."

In a New Light

Watching your boyfriend deal with his parents in terms of his wedding can be eye-opening. Sure, you're already familiar with the way they communicate. But when wedding plans begin and there's any kind of conflict between what *you* want and what *they*

want, it's the guy in the middle who will have to take action.
Or not.

Kelly and Matt had been living together for eight years when
they started planning their wedding. Kelly's from a Catholic family, Matt from a Jewish family. Says Kelly, "I'd always said to him,
'I want to be married by a judge. Is that okay with you, Matt?'
And he'd always said, 'Fine.'" Everybody's happy, case closed,
right? Uh, no.

It became clear to Kelly as the wedding approached that Matt
was getting flak from his parents. The topic of who would marry
them came up again and again. He asked about having a cantor
perform the ceremony, and Kelly said no. He kept saying things
like, "A cantor is not really Jewish." "As some sort of concession to
me," says Kelly, "he suggested we be married by a woman cantor."
Kelly's reaction: "No. Why don't we find a Jewish judge?"

"Matt's not religious at all, so this took me by surprise," says
Kelly. "I was shocked that we were even discussing it again. I
thought, This is an issue? You're kidding, right? I just tried to ignore it, but it kept coming up." Despite Kelly's position, Matt
urged her to meet a cantor he had found. "I felt like, well, okay,
who am I to not want to meet someone? But no, she won't be marrying us. So we met her and I said she was very nice, but no, she
can't marry us. And I thought that was the end of it."

A couple of weeks later, Kelly went with Matt's mother, Marilyn, to try on her wedding dress. Afterward in the car on the way
to dinner with Matt and his father, Marilyn said that she was "so
thrilled" Kelly had agreed to let a cantor perform the ceremony.

"First I was shocked," says Kelly. Then she realized that Matt
had lied to his parents, or simply had not been brave enough to
tell them the truth. He was letting himself be manipulated, and
Kelly decided she wasn't going to participate. She said to her

mother-in-law-to-be, "Marilyn, this is very awkward for me, but that's just not true. In fact, I've decided absolutely no, and I never really considered it in the first place." Matt's mother floundered for something to say. Finally, in desperation, she echoed Matt: "But a cantor is barely Jewish."

At dinner that night, the issue came up. Matt was mute during the whole discussion. Says Kelly, "I just thought to myself, 'I am marrying a two-year-old.'"

The conflict became a negative undercurrent that ran through their relationship. Matt refused to discuss it, and Kelly refused to discuss anything else until it was settled. "He had clearly decided that this was worth pushing to the point where it was not pretty to come home at night." Kelly felt betrayed by the fact that suddenly this person she'd loved for eight years was not standing up for her wishes or what she believed were his own.

Kelly was never surprised that religion was an issue for Matt's parents. What threw her was the fact that Matt seemed totally unprepared for the problem and ill-equipped to deal with it. "This was something that he could only resolve when it became very tangible," she says.

To make a ridiculous sweeping generalization, men and women approach the future differently. It seems men have a harder time projecting into the future, imagining what they might want, picturing what might be important to them somewhere down the line. Until they get there, some men simply do not know what they want. This childlike wonderment can be charming and sweet. It can also be irritating and extremely inconvenient when you're planning something that will not come to fruition for almost a year. *You* may have thought through a whole bunch of wedding-related issues as soon as you decided to get married, or maybe even before you decided to get married; he might not know what he wants until he has agreed to something else and realizes he's un-happy.

Obviously, it's not fair and not productive to condemn your beloved simply because he has not thought something through. Instead, sit down together one night with a list of wedding topics and perhaps a bottle of wine. Do this before your families become too involved and you'll save yourselves a lot of grief.

In the olden days, weddings were for girls. Not anymore. For this book, I spoke with some men who had more to say about their weddings than their wives did. Even if you feel you know more, give your boyfriend a chance to voice his opinion on every single subject. That way you'll discover what's important to each of you. Of course you'll disagree a little, but then you'll make compromises; it's a microcosm of the coming months and years. And it can actually make things easier. When you're swamped at work and you haven't been to the gym in three weeks and you've spent every Saturday since you can remember with your mother, you'll be grateful to have a boyfriend who wants to meet with a photographer while you take a day off.

Nice Touch

Regina and Ted had been together for eleven years when they got married. They figured out how many days that totaled (a whopping 4,207) and produced a batch of funny keepsakes for their guests: heart-shaped buttons that read "4,207, but who's counting?"

Big Stupid Fights

"The first year we were together," says Lindsay, "we never fought. Then we got engaged." I heard this same old story again and again. I think when the concept of permanence becomes a reality, some people worry that every concession they make is going to set a precedent, so they compensate by being much more assertive. Paul and Krista disagreed about the typeface on their invitations. A little argument became a major battle of wills. "We both have pretty strong ideas about what we want visually," says Paul. "I got mad because she wouldn't let me pick the type, because that's what I do [he's a graphic designer], and she got mad that I was being so stubborn and stupid." They didn't speak to each other for two days. "That's never happened to us in the six years we've been together. We never fight to a point where we don't speak."

Kathleen felt pushed around by what her boyfriend, Jonathan, and his mother wanted. At one point, his mother was lobbying for them to register for gifts. Kathleen didn't want to. Jonathan came home one night with advice from someone he worked with: "Tyrell says we *have* to register. She says we'll get so much crap otherwise." And Kathleen threw a fit. "I was screaming and crying and stamping my foot. I was so angry about being told what to do by someone who doesn't even know me. Really, of course, I was angry with Jonathan and his mother." These scenes were not out of the ordinary for the couple. "I was on the verge of hysterics during most of the planning." When reminiscing about their wedding, Jonathan refers to the registering argument as Fight #14.

Stand By Your Man

You're on the same side, even if that's sometimes hard to see, and this party is supposed to be about celebrating your love. Be the big one, the one who doesn't start the fights. You'll be so glad in the

Too-Cool-For-School Bride (or Groom)

Remember the episode of *30 Rock* when Liz Lemon and Criss Chros got married? Sure they loved each other and had decided to make it official, but they were on slightly different pages when it came to how their actual wedding day should unfold. Criss was happy to help plan the traditional white-dress affair with a sit-down dinner for two hundred or so guests, but Liz was much too terrified to buy into that whole concept. She said she wanted it to be just the two of them at city hall, but when they met at the marriage bureau she felt self-conscious and commented on how she expected more people to be wearing gym clothes and carrying grocery bags of toilet paper. Now, Criss was happy to accommodate Liz's wishes (however conservative or unorthodox), but he just wanted to make sure she was accommodating her own wishes, even if they were in keeping with accepted societal traditions she abhorred. (In the end, they compromised by having a city hall wedding with Tony Bennett performing live. Not bad.) The point is that if one of you doesn't share exactly the same level of interest in or excitement about the planning stages as the other, it doesn't mean one of you is less into the marriage, so don't go reading too much into it.

long run. Take a step back, and look at what your boyfriend is going through. He's getting married! He's being pushed and pulled in all directions. He's terrified and overcome with joy. He *needs* you.

"If I had to give one piece of advice," says Julia, "it would be that it's your marriage that matters." She and Barry fought nonstop about their families during the wedding planning, and it nearly ruined their relationship. "Ultimately you're not going to be living with your mother-in-law or your sister, and you'll resolve a lot of that stuff in time as long as you have a relationship where you can talk to each other. Keep going back to your relationship and don't get too focused on other, external things."

Mother, Can You Spare a Dime?

*N*ow, how does it go? The groom's family pays for the rehearsal dinner, the cuff links and two-thirds of the salmon mousse, and the bride's family covers everything else, right? Wrong. The only rule is that there are no rules. And that makes it tough. Money can be a nightmare—talking about it, coming up with it, asking for it, spending it. It can make people feel guilty or angry. It can keep you awake at night. It can come with all sorts of strings attached. And it's the very unromantic starting point to planning a wedding.

Tradition!

Think of where the custom of the bride's family financing the wedding originates. It's rooted in a time when it was worth money to get rid of daughters. Their value decreased in inverse proportion to their age, they had no earning power, and there was always the possibility that they would produce more mouths to feed. Well, thankfully things have changed. So right off the bat, assume (or pretend) the financial burden lies with you and your boyfriend. That way you won't approach the issue of money with an unhealthy sense of entitlement, and you'll be grateful for anything anyone offers you.

It might be hard for you to talk about money with your parents, and the idea of broaching the subject with your prospective in-laws probably has all the appeal of oral surgery. But if you need help, you have to sit down with them and speak frankly. If you just assume your parents are going to be okay with certain arrangements and never bother discussing them, you could be setting yourself up for a bone-crushing fall. And making assumptions about your *boyfriend's* parents' intentions can be worse; tradition is on the side of them opting out, financially speaking.

Let's Communicate Here, People

"My mother had offered to put money toward the wedding," says Jason. "But when the four of us were together, I realized she hadn't discussed it with my father." Jason brought up the subject like it was a done deal and was shocked when his father actually laughed at the notion. "I launched into some prices, and suddenly I realized my father had no clue. So I immediately started trying to protect my girlfriend from the awkwardness, and my mother tried to protect my father." The walls went up and never came down. "We weren't able to say, 'Okay, there's been a misunderstanding. Let's start over.'" Dealing with only one of your parents when the issue at hand involves both is obviously risky. "But I never talk to my father," says Jason. "I always deal with my mother." Yes, but chatting about work or about how your high school gym teacher was on some reality show is different from making major once-in-a-lifetime financial requests.

Rick and Alice figured Rick's family would participate in the wedding costs. "We just assumed they would because his parents have money, and my mother is a widow," says Alice. Rick's parents had always been "extremely generous" with him, so Rick didn't spend a minute thinking about whether or not they'd want to contribute. The couple booked a restaurant, a band, a photographer, a florist, all under the impression that their parents would split the bill. Time passed and Rick's parents never offered to help. Rick hinted, talked around it, and finally flat-out asked them for money. There was no response. "Actually, my mother tried to change the subject, and when she realized that that wouldn't work, she hurried off the phone," says Rick. "She said she'd call me back in an hour, but three days later I still hadn't heard from her."

Rick hadn't taken into account the fact that his mother had some serious resistance to his getting married. She couldn't stop the wedding, but she could decide not to facilitate it. Rick was aware of her disapproval, "But I didn't want to fight with her about it. I thought if I ignored it and just acted normal, maybe she would too."

If Rick had managed to force a conversation with his parents early in the planning, he would have discovered that his mother never had any intention of giving him money for his wedding. The fact that her position was tied to unspoken mother-son stuff that had been brewing for thirty years crippled Rick completely. "We had to discuss it eventually," says Rick. "I just wish I'd been able to confront it before the financial damage was done."

Conditional Contributions

Elyse's father offered to pay for her wedding. Great, she thought, and told him what she had in mind—something small, about sixty guests, at a restaurant. But that's not what he was thinking. He wanted *his* friends—golf buddies, coworkers, barber, you get the picture—and all the relatives to be invited. Two hundred people at the country club. Elyse said she didn't want that kind of wedding. Her father said that was the only kind he'd pay for. "It was so controlling of him to insist on those conditions," says Elyse. "He just wanted to have his party for two hundred that would happen to also be my wedding." Elyse didn't give in. She and her boyfriend threw a small wedding themselves. Her father came, and a year later gave her a "wedding present" that covered almost the whole cost.

Elyse's father's position is not so unusual. Some parents want to pay for what they can enjoy too. And many see their child's wedding as a chance to show off and compete with friends. (Whose kid had the better band? Whose kid had the fancier menu?) If it's a matter of their money or no money, you might be forced to compromise.

An Offer You Can't Refuse

On a smaller scale, a lot of couples find themselves faced with offers that are simply impossible to refuse. Parents present money that's earmarked for certain expenses and, like a cheap plane ticket, is nontransferable. It doesn't matter that you need a photographer, they want to pay for a rehearsal dinner. So what if you don't want them to spend $1,500 on a formal portrait of you?

THE POLITICS OF PLANNING

That's what they want to spend it on and, no, they wouldn't rather buy you a wedding cake.

Sylvana paid for most of her wedding. Living at home and working, she had saved up a good chunk of money. But she and Reed had no apartment and no furniture, so they were in for lots of additional expenses. Reed's parents wanted to give the couple some money toward the wedding or toward setting up their home. But instead of offering, they quietly paid off $2,000 on Reed's new low-interest car loan. The couple was grateful, sure, but a low-interest loan was the last place they would have put cash at that point. They needed a couch and a bed and a security deposit.

Then Reed's parents said they were planning a rehearsal dinner. Sylvana didn't want this for the simple reason that her parents do not speak English, and an intimate dinner at a restaurant with the Cleaver family would be very awkward for them. "It was a big expense that nobody would enjoy—not me, not Reed, not my family," Sylvana says. Reed tried to explain this to his parents, hoping the money could go to better wedding use but, says Sylvana, "I'm not sure how far he actually got. His parents really wanted to have a rehearsal dinner, and they made that clear." Ultimately Reed didn't push it. He felt he couldn't combine his purposes—explain why Sylvana didn't want a rehearsal dinner while requesting that the money be rechanneled—without coming off as a jerk.

I'm not going to pretend it's easy to tell your loved ones just how to spend their cash on you. You don't have a right to be assertive about someone else's money. That's known as looking a gift horse in the mouth. And in many of these situations, "gift" is the operative word. Parents offer what you consider a luxury— something they can wrap with a nice big emotional bow and hand to you, saying, "Here, this is for you." It makes them happy. Helping out with necessities may not be as gratifying. So if they're not acknowledging the fact that you have to choose between hiring a band and paying your rent, well, it's up to you to either make them understand or to realize it's not worth it.

The rehearsal dinner comes up again and again in these situations, maybe because it's a traditional opportunity for the groom's parents to be the hosts, and they get into that. You have to tread carefully. You know your parents; your boyfriend knows his (although you might have some insights that can help him out). If hurt feelings are a more likely outcome than, say, a response like, "Take the money and use it for whatever you need," you might be best off graciously accepting what's offered.

Imbalance of Power

"My parents are middle class, and George's mother has a lot of money, which she wanted to spend on our wedding," says Erika. "She also wanted to plan it for us, which was fine because we lived a thousand miles away from where it was being held." Erika's parents wanted to contribute. They told Erika they could give her $3,000. George's mother had in mind a wedding for about seventy-five at a restaurant. The total cost would be about $18,000, which she was happy to pay the bulk of. But she decided to offer George and Erika the option of taking the money instead of having the restaurant wedding; then she would throw them a small party at her home and the couple would walk away with a bundle of cash.

Erika was worried about how her parents would feel if the wedding was at George's mother's house. "They always step to the side anyway, because they don't have the stuff, they don't have the money." Erika didn't want that to happen here. "I chose to have it at the restaurant, because I really wanted the wedding to be on neutral territory. I didn't want my parents to feel like guests at their daughter's wedding, just because I was marrying someone whose mother has more money."

"Help" That Isn't Green

Jed and Lauren paid for their own wedding. They took care of everything themselves. "At first I didn't realize that I was leaving my mother out and hurting her feelings," says Lauren. "She felt bad about not being able to contribute financially, even though I didn't ask her to." If your parents want to be involved, give them opportunities that don't involve a checkbook. "My mother is an artist, so I asked her to take care of arranging the flowers. It was a big job, and I wasn't sure she'd want to deal with it." But she did, and she was happy to help. "I know she was especially glad to save us money on a florist—the money thing was a big deal to her."

A portion of our parents' generation continues to believe that the bride's family pays for the wedding, and that if they can't, they've somehow failed. That puts a lot of pressure on people who don't have a spare $50,000 or $100,000 laying around.

If you believe your parents should pay for your wedding, you probably have a reason to: *They* believe it, and taught you to. I'm not going to try to convince you otherwise. I'm not going to suggest you break the chain of crazy expectations. I'm not going to ask, "Isn't it enough that they sacrificed for you for so many years?" I'm not going to appeal to your enlightened side and say, "Come on, you're a grown woman." No, I'm not going to do any of that. I'm just going to say that some people wish their parents *wouldn't* try to pay for a wedding they can't afford.

We Insist!

Tracy and Doug wanted to pay for their own wedding. They have far more money than Tracy's parents have, but Tracy's mother was insistent: "We want to pay for it. We've been saving for this for years." Tracy's parents had worked hard and lived carefully all their lives. Even if they had managed to put aside that kind of money, the last thing Tracy wanted was for them to blow it on her wedding. "It was killing me to think of it all going to one day. I wanted them to use it for themselves," says Tracy. After much prodding, Tracy's parents agreed to let the couple cover the cost of Doug's relatives. But they insisted on including Doug's parents among their guests. To them, that's the way things are done. They expected to throw a wedding for their daughter from the minute she was born, twenty-six years before. Even splitting the bill, Tracy's parents spent "a fortune. But the only way I could have stopped them was to not have a wedding at all, and that would have made them so unhappy."

Easing Your Way into a Budget

You're going to see in bridal magazines (if you don't buy them for yourself, someone will buy them for you) and on wedding blogs lists of all the elements involved in a traditional wedding and what portion of your budget should go to each. Interesting idea, but no one can really make that decision for you. The two of you have to determine what's really important, eliminate items from the original list (the sterling silver napkin rings, perhaps?) shop around for some ballpark figures, then figure out what portion of your budget you want to allocate to each feature.

Maybe your wedding is going to be outside in a beautiful yard, and you want to forgo flower arrangements. Maybe you're wearing a dress that's in your family, and you don't have to worry about spending money there. Or your friend's band is going to play at your reception. Before you get yourself worried about what you *can't* afford, find out what you already have or what you can get a deal on. Talk to anyone and everyone about your wedding. (Oh, you're already doing that?) Just start asking around. You'll need referrals for everything, and people love to help with weddings, hence all the advice in this book.

If you start by knowing approximately how much you want to spend, you'll do a lot better when you go out into the field to do research. Once you've scouted around, come back and retrench. *Then* it's time to come up with a budget. But don't let those first prices you hear scare you. By cutting out some unnecessary costs and occasionally working around the wedding industry, you can have a great wedding even without pawning your extensive collection of gold stacked rings.

Think of it as a challenge, a puzzle with a variety of solutions. And don't bum yourself out by imagining what you could do if you had unlimited funds. Three weeks before her own wedding, Marie went to a very lavish affair thrown by a wealthy family. "It was at this farm," she says, "which is, I think, their third home." The ceremony was held on a hilltop; guests were shuttled up there in SUVs. The bride (a second cousin of Marie's husband) arrived in a horse-drawn carriage, her hair and dress wound with dainty strands of real miniature English ivy. She held a huge cascade of fall flowers, which somehow magically wrapped around her and trailed behind like a train. For the reception, there was a fifteen-piece swing band with a singer who sounded like a young Sinatra. Surrounded by such grandeur, Marie sat and moped about her relatively plain upcoming wedding and how her husband's extended family would be recalling both in the same breath for the rest of her life.

What can you do in a situation like this? Well, you can avoid it or, if that's not possible, take comfort in the multipurpose response of so many wise aunts: "Rich people have problems too. Look at the Kennedys."

Money Isn't Everything

So you have no money. Okay. You've thrown parties before, right? A wedding is a party, so you can throw a wedding. First you have to abandon some preconceptions. People is conditioned to think that what makes a wedding "special" is all the trappings. Consequently they feel pressured to take the same special measures everyone feels compelled to take, and they end up having the same wedding as everybody else.

There's an industry of people out there who make their money because regular folks like us think what we can do on our own is not special. What makes a wedding special is that two people are celebrating their love with their friends and family. There. That didn't cost a penny. The second section of this book is filled with inexpensive wedding options and suggestions on how to redefine the word "wedding" to fit your personality and budget.

Spending money you don't have on your wedding turns an already stressful situation into a threat to your sanity. It's not hard to see why. The wedding's over, you're coming down off that high, you're feeling a little depressed and empty . . . and you're heavily in debt. What a joyous way to start your new life together!

Paul and Krista planned and paid for a wedding they couldn't quite afford. Because there was no money (or space on their credit cards) left for a trip, Paul's friends at work chipped in and gave the couple cash designated for a honeymoon. They went to Florida for a few days. "When we got home, there were three messages from the phone company warning that they were about to disconnect us, and one from the student loan police," says Paul. So instead of luxuriating in their first days of connubial bliss, Paul and Krista worried about next month's rent and argued about which was more important, groceries or electricity.

Not for the Faint of Heart

Jodie and Brett discovered that the kind of wedding they wanted would cost a fortune they didn't have. After getting some prices, they gave up planning for a while, dejected. By the beginning of the following year, they couldn't wait anymore. They decided they wanted an April wedding and went out again in search of reasonable prices. They had practically no time. After looking at a number of spaces that were booked solid for the next year and a half, they happened upon one with an April cancellation. "When the house wedding coordinator told us the price per head, we were sure she had made a mistake," says Jodie. It was half what comparable places had quoted them the year before. The cost of the band and the photographer were also much lower than anything the couple had anticipated, all because the wedding was only three months away. Restaurants and other wedding vendors would much rather make half of what they're used to making than have an income-free Saturday.

Just for her own amusement, after the wedding was over

and done with, Jodie's mother called the restaurant unidentified and asked about having a wedding there a year in the
future, in the wintertime (off season). The price was double
what Brett and Jodie had paid. Score!

Now, I can't tell you to wait till the last minute and then
see what's available, and that you might end up with something you love and could not have afforded normally. No, I'm
not suggesting that. Okay, maybe I am. But I'm addressing
only the risk-takers, the mavericks, those willing to look the
industry in the eye and say, "Go ahead. Make my wedding
day." If that's you, imagine wielding such power over these
masters of overcharging. In this scenario, they need you
much more than you need them. Doesn't that sound like fun?

Mama Bear and Papa Bear

*T*he other day my friend Melissa called to tell me she's getting married. My response: "That's great! Have you set a date?" She sounded irritated. "Everyone keeps asking me that, especially my parents," she said. Well, no kidding, Melissa.

Some people want to be engaged but don't want to associate that state with planning a wedding. And of course that's fine. But if that's where you are, you'd better make it clear to your parents.

Eva says her parents were "very well-behaved" throughout the planning of her wedding. "But their initial reaction to our engagement freaked us out a little." They sprang into action, immediately shopping for reception halls and looking for bands. "We weren't prepared for how fast things started to happen."

If you're ready to be engaged, but not to start planning a wedding, tell your parents right off the bat. (i.e., "We want to let you know we're engaged, and we'd like to have a wedding in about x years, when Elmo here finishes his thesis/when I get promoted/when we win the lottery so we can pay for a huge, lavish wedding.")

Parents get excited. They've been thinking about their kids' weddings forever. And most of us (our generation, I mean) take a lot longer to decide to get married than most of them did. A "simmer down" attitude in you won't tame their zeal and will probably make you seem like a brat.

Let me say something hokey that might help. You're lucky you have parents who care enough to be too enthusiastic about your wedding. It's a hassle to be bombarded with opinions, but why not listen to everyone's ideas and then do what you want anyway? Just talking about the wedding is an end in itself, a way of participating and sharing in the excitement. So let them talk.

When Nicole announced she was getting married, the wedding became her mother's full-time occupation. "I didn't want it to, but since she retired, she's had all this time on her hands," says Nicole. On the only day she counted, her mother called her at work sixteen times with wedding-related questions. "I had to do something about it, but I didn't want to hurt her feelings." So Nicole told her mother that she was getting pressure from her boss not to make wedding plans on company time (a lie, but a necessary one that didn't hurt a flea). "I said she could call anytime if she'd just call at home instead. I promised I'd check my voicemail every hour and if anything was really pressing, I'd get right back to her." It worked fine, except there were a couple of days when Nicole's mother filled up her voicemail with messages.

"Particularly because it was the first wedding in my family, my parents were just so excited, and they got so overly involved in the planning," says Pam. "I kind of felt like I was losing control, and they were taking over." Whether you like it or not, it's their day too. You don't have to agree with what they say, but you do have to respect their right to say it. "Now that I'm a parent, I finally understand what they were feeling." Pam's parents were covering a large portion of the costs. "I realized I had to let them control certain things, but it was okay because we agreed on a lot. Once I made that decision, I relaxed."

But what if you don't agree? At Lori's wedding, her mother kept apologizing to guests for the location. "We argued about it for months," Lori says. "She wanted it to be at a much more formal place, and the spot we chose was a renovated picnic house in the middle of a public park. I know it was killing her that a crowd of dusty little kids with baseball gloves was standing around watching the ceremony. But the place meant something to us." Throughout the wedding, her mother could be heard mumbling, "This is what they wanted. I don't know why, but this is what they wanted," her voice cracking with embarrassment.

When They Presume

Your parents might make some assumptions about the big decisions (that you'll invite all forty-six of your first cousins, or *any* of your cousins, for that matter) and the tiny details (that you'll wear shoes to the wedding and throw your bouquet). You have to head these off at the pass.

One day at lunch Karmen and Ethan told Karmen's mother that they were getting married. The first words out of the joyous woman's mouth were, "Oh, you have to call that lovely church your brother used! It gets booked way in advance." Ethan squirmed, but smiled, figuring they'd discuss that later. Karmen, not thinking ahead, said, "Well, Mom, Ethan doesn't want to get married in a church." Ethan kicked her under the table because she didn't say, "*We* don't want to get married in a church." But taken off guard, it was all Karmen could do to stand up to her mother. In fact, she was proud of herself. "But I realize it was a mistake," the wiser bride says now. When you're talking to your parents, don't separate your boyfriend's wishes from your own, especially when you're likely to encounter resistance. If you cast him as the difficult one, you're giving your parents permission to complain about him to you. Bad idea. It could create a dangerous sense of "us" (you and your parents) against "him" later on. Think of presenting a united front. (This is a good tip to pass along to your boyfriend, especially if he's a little on the spineless side when it comes to confronting his folks.)

"We didn't want any of the schmaltzy stuff at our wedding. We just wanted to throw a great party," says Sandy. Her father was disappointed to discover that he would not have a formal dance with his daughter. He'd been to so many of his friends' kids' weddings, and now it was his turn. Sandy realized that it really did matter to her father, that he truly was looking forward to that traditional dance. And though it struck her as a little silly, she decided to go along with it. But they danced to *her* choice of song ("Young at Heart"), not his ("Daddy's Little Girl").

It's All Relative

Once you get a taste of dealing with your boyfriend's mother, your own mother might start looking pretty good. No matter how difficult she might be, you don't have to worry that she's evaluating you.

"The beauty of my own mother is she knows what to do and what not to do," says Kelly. "If she suggested something I didn't want, I could tell her. I didn't have to be worried about offending her." It's so true. And the contrast between dealing with the unknown quantity (mother-in-law-pending) and the familiar can sometimes bring you closer to your own mother.

But for Mika the opposite was true. She found solace with her boyfriend's mother and got "a lot of insanity" from her own. "My mother pressured me into having a church ceremony in a big white dress, because she wasn't satisfied with her own wedding," says Mika. "She got married outside in a light-blue suit with the din of traffic in the background." Mika wishes she'd done it her own way, but her mother was so insistent. "It was as if her feelings were just so much stronger than mine that I couldn't say no." This is manipulation. Mothers are good at it. It's their responsibility to utilize their powers for good instead of evil, but sometimes they don't. When you and your mother are completely at odds, you have to weigh the pros and cons. If your inclination is to give in and let her have what she wants, think about the fact that this is your one and only wedding. Are you going to let yourself be miserable? It might be worth making a list, just for yourself, of elements *you* want and elements *she* wants. If you're giving in on a major component—like the structure of the wedding—be firm about having the details your way. Acquiescing completely in order to avoid confrontation will make you resentful forever.

Now You Have *Two* Crazy Mothers

If you were to draw a little illustration of you, your boyfriend and the two sets of parents, you and your boyfriend would be in the middle. The middle can mean many things. It can mean the center around which things revolve. It can signify neutrality. Unfortunately, it can also refer to a no-man's land where you're in danger of being blown up by both sides.

Never, ever get between the two sets of parents. If there's some reason they need to speak to each other regarding the wedding, I suggest you get out of town well in advance. There are few things freakier than having your parents and your boyfriend's parents relating about you. And if money is one of the subjects at hand, well, you might want to leave the country.

Katie and Jim tried to stay out of the way, but they came away from their wedding with a wealth of stories about the tension between their two mothers. When Katie's mother was picking up the dress she was to wear to the wedding, Jim's mother showed up at the shop's dressing room to sneak a look at the price tag. At the wedding, they fought over who would stand to the right of the couple for the group photos; Jim's mother wanted her corsage to show, and Katie's mother was determined to have the "good side" of her expensive dress visible. Later, following a toast by Katie's mother, Jim's mother got up, shouted drunkenly into the mike, "Equal time! Equal time!" and tearfully rambled about her son's sixth-grade graduation. The climax was the rehearsal dinner, at which the two women had an argument about the seating arrangements that turned physical (this was the one time Katie and Jim got in the middle).

When People You Love
Hate Each Other

*T*elling you to seat feuding family members far apart is pretty pointless; you'll figure that out all by yourself. But even a carefully wrought seating plan can't address serious discord. In an effort to make their weddings something other than a test of emotional endurance, some brides and grooms I spoke with took more drastic measures.

"Peter's family and my family are both very divorced," says Celia, "so instead of trying to create this artificial gathering of both divorced sides, we had two parties." Four months before their wedding, they had a party in New Orleans with Celia's mother's side of the family (her mother had died years earlier) and invited Peter's father and his wife. And at their New York wedding, they had Celia's father and his side, and Peter's mother and her side. There were some hard feelings. "Peter's dad pouted for a few days even though he wouldn't have wanted to be in the same room as his ex-wife. And my uncle, who told me it was okay with him not to come to the wedding, complained behind my back. But Peter and I did not want to play divorce court at the wedding. And that's often what happens to the bride and groom."

When you're in this type of position, it's especially important to remember that the wedding is for you. If doing the conventional thing is going to make you a nervous wreck, you owe it to yourself to find an alternative.

Jack didn't. He never considered excluding members of his immediate family from his and Kerry's wedding. "It was the first time my father and sister had seen each other in eighteen years. And my mom was flipped out in a corner because she was terrified of having to meet my father's new wife. She never left her seat." Jack spent the evening looking back and forth between them. "You have to realize that you're gonna be a mess if you've got two parents in the same place who have not gotten along for twenty years."

Katrina's wedding brought her relationship with her father to the breaking point. "It was a total disaster," she says. "At the time, nobody in my family was talking to my father but me. When I announced I was getting married, my mother said, 'Of course you want your father at your wedding, and I understand.' But I knew I couldn't have a fun wedding with him there." What she and Ray came up with was having just a ceremony in Montreal, where Katrina is from, with their immediate families, "and then I would let my mother do whatever she wanted, and my father could do whatever he wanted." The real wedding would take place in Chicago, where Katrina and Ray's friends were. "And everyone but my father would be invited to that one."

For the Montreal event, each of Katrina's parents decided to throw a separate party, her mother a small one, her father a more elaborate one. "A week before the wedding, my father started pulling all this garbage with my mother, fighting with her about alimony payments," says Katrina. "I mean, my mother didn't have money to put food on the table, and he was rich." Katrina confronted him. She said, "I can't take this party from you while you're torturing my mother. I won't be able to live with myself." He told her, "If you cancel the party, I don't want to ever see or speak to you again." Katrina wrote him a note asking him to stop giving her mother such a hard time. She tried to help him understand her point of view. He replied by disregarding the content of her letter and restating his ultimatum. She didn't see him for eight years.

* * * *

You can't ignore serious family stuff when it comes time to have your wedding. But you do have some control over how much it's going to color the event. Katrina and Ray have great memories of the wedding they had in Chicago, and Katrina has no regrets about her decision not to accept her father's party. Celia and Peter loved their wedding too. If you're in an extreme position, sometimes you have to take extreme measures. This wedding is for you and your boyfriend, and you might have to make some tough choices to ensure it's a happy day.

The Son Worshiper

When you hit a certain age—maybe fourteen or fifteen— you start thinking about how different a mother you'll one day be from your own mother. And when you begin to plan your wedding, you make another promise to yourself: that you will be a very different mother-in-law from the one you are about to inherit. To be fair, some women have great relationships with their mothers-in-law. But the bad ones are so bad, they spoil it for the rest. (Because the position has such a rotten reputation, my own mother-in-law asked me never to refer to her as such.) I think maybe each generation gets better at it—like there's this evolution of mothers-in-law. That's because every mother-in-law was once just a regular married woman with a mother-in-law of her own. She too swore she would never inflict the kind of suffering her mother-in-law did. And in a way, she kept her promise, but she unintentionally came up with her own tiny tortures. You see, there are so many ways to offend, annoy and hurt the wife of your son, that it will take millions of years before the species mother-in-law is properly socialized. Meanwhile, if you have a sense of what you're in for as you prepare to become a daughter-in-law, you'll be in better shape. So take this handy quiz and see.

What Kind of Mother-In-Law Are You Getting?

(Circle the icon next to each answer you choose.)

1. When she learns you're getting married, the first thing you hear is

   ■ "That's wonderful. Should we go look at dresses tomorrow?"
   ▲ sobbing, then the slam of the bathroom door.
   ● "Great! I'll do my very best to be there."
   ◆ "I hope my son realizes how lucky he is."
   ★ "Why are you doing this to me?"

2. She considers her son

   ● just one of her kids, who she loves equally.
   ■ a smart guy with good taste.
   ◆ her greatest joy.
   ★ the messiah.
   ▲ sexy.

3. She considers you

   ◆ one of her own.
   ■ a peer.

- ● a puzzle.
- ▲ too pretty.
- ★ the Antichrist.

4. Her idea of a good time is

- ★ junior moving back home.
- ● a day to herself.
- ■ lunch and a movie with just you.
- ◆ having her whole family together for dinner.
- ▲ gazing into her son's eyes and reminiscing about his prepubescent years.

5. She is often seen wielding

- ■ a credit card.
- ◆ a digital camera.
- ● a gym bag.
- ★ a handkerchief.
- ▲ pictures of her younger self.

6. She enjoys

- ● debating hot political topics.
- ◆ cooking for you.
- ■ talking to you.
- ▲ talking *about* you.
- ★ plotting against you.

7. You show her your very cool, untraditional wedding dress. Her first response is

- ◆ "Only you could get away with something like that."
- ■ "It's perfect."
- ★ "If I'd known that was what you had in mind, I would have told you to look in the trunk in my garage."
- ▲ "I don't think my son goes for that style."
- ● "Now what should *I* wear?"

8. It's a week before the holidays. You and your boyfriend have always spent them apart, to avoid mother guilt. But now that you're engaged, you want to be together. So this year, the two of you are going to *your* parents' house. His mother

- ■ says it's fine, and maybe you can come for dinner next week.
- ● already has plans to go skiing that week.
- ▲ tells him if he wants to let a woman run his life, that's okay with her.
- ◆ calls up and cries, but apologizes a few days later.
- ★ puts a hex on you and your family.

9. You, your boyfriend and his mother are shopping together. You and your boyfriend are silently fighting. His mother

- ◆ walks ahead and looks in windows to give you a little privacy.
- ■ walks between you and addresses only you.
- ★ walks between you and addresses only him.
- ▲ walks between you and holds his hand.
- ● says, "I've had enough of this. I'm going home."

10. Your mother-in-law-to-be is religious, but you and your boyfriend are not and have decided to be married by a judge. She

- ■ recommends a nice one she met at a party.
- ● shrugs it off.
- ♦ is disturbed, but forces herself to say, "whatever you want."
- ▲ says that if she and her son were the ones getting married, they would definitely choose *their* house of worship.
- ★ rends her garments.

Scoring

Mostly ■s. Fate is smiling down upon you. You've got **The Buddy**. She loves you and has no need to smother or control you. You'll be able to talk to her about the occasional unreasonableness of your husband, and she'll understand. When you're around her (often, by your choice), you won't have to watch your language or worry about the fact that your bra strap is showing.

Mostly ♦s. **The Doter**. She's fussed over your husband for decades, and now that you're joined at the hip, she'll fuss just as much over you. You'll never leave her house empty-handed—food, clothes, a necklace of hers you admired. You'll do okay. She'll want to take you on vacations with her and always try to get you to sleep over. But get used to letting your voicemail take her calls; she'll call every night.

Mostly ●s. Feel like she has trouble remembering your name? Her kids' names too? She's **The Mom-sicle**. Fond of her son, but glad he's gone, she always has a funny story and a full schedule. She's too busy to dislike you, so don't even think about that. She never calls but is always happy to hear from you, as long as you keep it short. You'll realize how truly blessed you are soon enough.

Mostly ▲s. You've got a problem. There's another woman in love with your husband, and she's his mother! **The Other Woman** will cut you down when you're not around and will go to great pains to set up those situations. She thinks it's okay to kiss her son on the neck and say to him stuff like, "I would wuv a hug." The only solution: Have a baby. A grandchild is the one thing that will take her mind off "her little man."

Mostly ★s. **The My-Way-or-the-Highway Mom.** Her mission is to make your life a guilt-fest. You took her boy away; you changed his way of thinking. Now you must pay. If she can't control you, she'd like to drive you away. Imposing her beliefs, traditions, schedule and priorities on you is her birthright. You can't make her happy, but eventually you two will figure out how to peacefully coexist or, at the very least, how to stay out of each other's way.

Now that you've reduced your mother-in-law to a ridiculous stereotype, read about some flesh-and-blood m-i-ls and the d-i-ls who love to talk about them.

Friendly Force (The Buddy)

You know you're getting a cool mother-in-law if you've never, in these past few months, thought about the fact of *having* a mother-in-law. It's nice if she shares your interests, sure. But what really matters is that she's warm, rational and not competitive with you.

Victoria's future mother-in-law was a new friend, a comrade in arms, while Victoria and Luke were planning their wedding. "She served as kind of a reality check for me," says Victoria, who was dealing with a lot of tension in her own family, "and helped put my own mother in perspective." She was there to support Victoria's decision not to register for stuff she'd never use (like china and silver), and to listen while Victoria was grappling with bigger issues. "I could always bounce the insanities of my mother's plans and gripes off of her. She was just a very calming presence."

"Let Me Make You a Plate" (The Doter)

It's almost always nice to have someone doing for you and giving you stuff, but there's a downside to the doter. Naomi's mother-in-law to-be was very generous with her. A couple of months before the wedding, she gave Naomi a string of pearls to wear with her wedding dress. That was really nice and all, but pearls weren't Naomi's style. "It was as if she'd put my hand in a bear claw and asked me to walk around my wedding in it," says Naomi. "I was horrified by the whole notion." But she was not quite as honest with Ned's mother. "I couldn't say anything, and Ned refused to handle it for me, even though I begged him to." What Naomi decided to do was pretend she forgot the pearls on the day of the wedding. It was fifty miles from her home, so there would be nothing anyone could do, and she would come off only as flaky, as opposed to ungrateful and inconsiderate. The big day came and went with no thought or mention of the pearls (except on Naomi's part). Her mother-in-law forgot. She had other things on her mind.

Would You Like Some Ice With That?
(The Mom-sicle)

What's great about the Mom-sicle is that over time she might turn into a buddy. It's really the initial shock that's the hardest. When it comes to making wedding plans, she'll do what she's asked to do, and she won't have time to poke around where you'd rather she wouldn't.

Mia describes Robert's mother as "hands-off to the point of being cold." She never calls. Ever. But Mia has learned not to take it personally. "At first I was hurt and insecure. I kept wondering, Does she hate me?" But she doesn't. She's just busy with her own things and not very expressive about her feelings. "My family is all emotional," says Mia. "My grandfather cries at the drop of a hat. So getting used to Robert's mother was hard." She travels, works long hours, hangs out with her husband. She has a very full life of her own.

But just because she doesn't say she loves you, don't assume she doesn't feel it. "When we announced we were getting married," says Mia, "Robert's mother said to me, 'We think of you as a daughter,' and I thought, Well why didn't you say that before? I could have used that." When Mia's mother came to visit, after a year during which she and Mia hadn't spoken, "there was this really freaky competition over who I would belong to." At lunch with both mothers, Mia saw this for the first time. As Mia's mother talked about taking Mia on wedding-related errands, Robert's mother grew colder and colder, until she was barely speaking. "I could see that she felt threatened by my mother's presence." It made Mia realize that Robert's mother not only cared about her, but was vulnerable enough to feel hurt by the prospect of losing her. "It was a real turning point for me," says Mia.

You Against Her (The Other Woman)

Maybe you figured that quiz earlier in the chapter was a joke. Okay, a lot of it was. But Julia's mother-in-law *did* hold her twenty-nine-year-old son's hand while walking down the street with him and Julia. No joke. Of course, her son, Barry, didn't stop her. That's what the pros call "enabling unhealthy behavior" in a big way. When it came time to plan their wedding, the problem worsened. Barry's mother was so resistant, so downright combative, that Julia had no choice but to confront Barry. "I think you have to be aware that if you're marrying a son who the mother's in love with, you're going to have trouble," says Julia. "She's going to take it out on the bride. And just remember that it's not about you, it's about them and their relationship changing."

But it *is* about you if you have to be the bearer of the bad news, the one who has to say, "Honey, your mother's got a thing for you." Barry and Julia began to resolve their situation with the help of a counselor. "It was too sensitive an issue for us to talk about without help. It just turned into one screaming match after another."

Julia had even considered eloping, to protect her getting-married experience from the gust of negativity that is her mother-in-law. "I guess that looks like the obvious solution," she says, "but I had a friend who eloped because of similar problems. It took a year for her mother-in-law to get over it. And during that year, she went through the same stuff I did."

Julia and Barry's problems didn't start and stop with the wedding. Getting married just forced them to deal with an issue that was present from the beginning. Eventually, Barry acknowledged the fact that something was wrong. And at some point Julia forgave Barry for not having defended her to his mother, for not having been able to stand up for them as a couple better.

But that first part—admitting there's a problem—is critical, as trite as it sounds. Because when it comes to men and their mothers, there's very little objectivity (okay, women and their mothers too). And if a guy can't admit that maybe his mother is wrong or a little nuts or anything less than saintly, things get sticky for the person trying to convince him of that (that's you, you suspicious, paranoid bitch).

Wendy's boyfriend, Ben, did not think there was a problem. But Wendy felt that his mother's attachment was way over the top. "He's an only child," says Wendy, "and his mother was very manipulative with him, calling up in tears over nothing every so often, just to get some attention." One night about a month before their wedding, Ben's mother took him out to a fancy, romantic place for dinner without inviting Wendy, because "it was the last time she'd see him alone before he got married." "I mean, how was I supposed to take that?" says Wendy. Ben was thirty-three when he got married, but his mother had not really gotten used to the idea of him not "belonging" to her anymore. "Because he hadn't had any really long-term relationships before," says Wendy, "the reality of it was kind of new to her and consequently, ours was the relationship during which she had to work this thing out." Over the two years the couple's been married, Ben's mother has made a real effort, and "the situation has definitely improved." The lesson here is that what you see now is not necessarily what you get forever. Your relationship with your mother-in-law will evolve and will probably improve as you become more comfortable with each other and as she becomes used to the fact of you.

Can't Live With Her, Can't Kill Her
(The My-Way Mom)

This character is a little like the traditional TV mother-in-law of our youth. Interfering, openly rude, spouting opinions all over the place. But sometimes these mothers-in-law are perpetually cheerful, which makes it a bit hard to tag them at first.

Jocelyn's new mother-in-law follows her frequent barbed comments with a smile and qualifiers like, "I wouldn't have it any other way." (i.e. "Ever since you've been together, he's been broke. I guess he's been buying you lots of nice gifts . . . but I wouldn't have it any other way.") Jocelyn, always caught off guard, comes up with many stinging comebacks hours later. "I wish I'd told her, 'Yeah, he's broke now because I finally convinced him to start paying back his student loans instead of hiding from bill collectors.'" Such fantasies make life worth living.

A common manifestation of the "My Way" personality disorder is Imposition of Religion. Regina was raised loosely Catholic. Her boyfriend, Ted, is Jewish. "We had a very hard time during the wedding planning with his mother. We would want to do one thing and she would always want something else," says Regina. "And she had no qualms about voicing her opinions on how we would *have* to raise our children Jewish or she would die." When Regina agreed to be married by a rabbi (because it was important to Ted), the mother-in-law started in on something else. "She insisted we have a kosher reception, but that would mean we couldn't use the caterer I wanted. And it was a lot more money." Regina said no, but Ted's mother continued to bring up the subject on a regular basis. "She called and left a voicemail with a list of the relatives who wouldn't come to a nonkosher reception. I was so stressed out over the problems that woman gave me, it really made my wedding difficult." Regina's advice is to make sure you and your boyfriend stick together in the face of mother-in-law–induced adversity. "Because if you don't, it can really tear the two of you apart."

That's something you have to be careful about. Remember, you're on the same side, even when it doesn't seem like it. Jill, who was on the receiving end of much disrespect and rudeness from Ronnie's mother on a variety of topics—from religion to the way she dressed—turned to Ronnie for help. "What was frustrating," says Jill, "was that I wanted him to stand up to her and, at that point, he just couldn't." Jill feared she'd be persecuted by her mother-in-law forever. But once the wedding was over and the pressure had subsided a bit, Ronnie was able to deal with the problem. "He had to wait till after the wedding. It was just too much stress to handle at once."

Mixed "Bag" (Get It?)

The fact is you'll probably end up with a mother-in-law who's a combination type (dry on the cheeks, oily T-zone). And sometimes when you become more than that girl her son's been living in sin with, or whatever she likes to refer to you as, a change of attitude can occur.

When Terry and Emily got engaged, Terry's mother started behaving very differently. "She'd always treated me pretty much the same way she treated all of Terry's friends," says Emily. "She's not a very emotional person. I've never heard her talk about her feelings." The day after the couple called their parents to announce the news, Emily received a dozen roses. "I assumed they were from Terry," she says. But they weren't. They were from his parents (really his mother). The card read: "Emily, We love you too."

Sometimes the transformation is more radical. At first, Greta wasn't even allowed in Stuart's mother's house. "His mother disapproved of our relationship because I wasn't Jewish," says Greta. "And then we lived together, so there were major taboos all over the place." During that time, Stuart's mother would have parties to which Greta would be expressly not invited.

After a couple of years, his mother started to soften. Then, when the couple got engaged, she sent Greta a Miss Manners etiquette guide. Next came a series of phone calls during which she'd say to Greta things like, "I don't really know who you are."

"She came to New York to 'get to know me better,' and she made me stay in her hotel room for the weekend, without Stuart." They went to fancy restaurants, where she'd order for Greta ("things I couldn't bear, like lobster sandwiches"). Greta wanted a "short normal dress" to wear to her wedding. Stuart's mother took her shopping and bought her one.

"When she started coming around, I had to milk it," says Greta. "I have to admit, now I kiss up to her. At this point I genuinely like her and I find her kind of intriguing and funny." They don't have a lot in common. Stuart's mother is from France, she's never had a job, and she has lots of money. "And she's really a character. But she's got a generous heart if you're on her good side, and I would prefer to be there, because she made me miserable when I was on her bad side." Now Greta's mother-in-law calls her every day at work, "bar none," and often leaves slightly wacky, sentimental voicemails like, "I just want to let you know that in a land far away, somebody loves you very much."

Clash of the Clergy

*W*ho will perform your ceremony? Does this question make the veins in your neck pop out? Does it inspire you to throw your arms up and let loose a crazed cackle? Well then, let me ask its companion question: "But how will you raise the kids?"

There. All the cards are on the table. Now let's talk. Remember Kelly and Matt and the judge and the cantor? That story had many tense moments, but a nice happy ending. The couple was married by a judge, and a cantor came and sang as part of the ceremony. Some scenarios are less well resolved, and in those cases, one half of a couple often brings to the marriage a suitcase full of resentment.

Religion is king of all touchy subjects, and when you're in a position of religious conflict with your boyfriend or his family or your family, you start to wish a wedding could really be about cotton-candy subjects like flowers and dresses.

First of all, when people ask you how you're going to raise your children, you can tell them that you'll raise something else if they don't get out of your face. Really, you don't have to be able to answer that question right now, no matter what anybody says. And your wedding ceremony does not have to be a power struggle that foreshadows the years to come. For now, if there's a religious discrepancy, think of it as a logistical problem that manifests itself in one way: a question about who will perform the ceremony. You can't figure out the next fifty years the moment you discover you and your boyfriend have different officiants in mind. You love each other. You want to be together. You're getting married. That's plenty of "future" to deal with right now.

There's a lot going on here—the obvious stuff (parents who have an agenda), and the less predictable (rites of passage prompt some people to return to religion). For some couples it's a cut-and-dried matter of two vying religions; for others, it's the stickier issue of one religion versus no religion. This is no fun to talk about, but someone's got to do it.

Choose a Rabbi, Save a Life

Andrea and Curt were together for ten years when they got married. All that time Andrea had been made painfully aware of Curt's mother's heartache over her non-Jewishness. "We got married by a rabbi," says Andrea, "because it was important to Curt." Not to mention the fact that his squeaky wheel of a mother wouldn't have had it any other way. Says Andrea, "She would have thrown herself in front of a train if we didn't." Needless to say, Andrea didn't want her mother-in-law's death on her shoulders. At the time, Andrea didn't think she cared about who performed the ceremony, and Andrea's mother said it didn't matter to her either.

"If I had it to do over again, I would have a priest there with the rabbi. I think my mom was a little upset that I didn't, and because she would never presume to tell us what to do, I didn't really think about her feelings."

A Stand-Up Guy

"When my Jewish boyfriend proposed to me, his father threatened never to speak to him again," says Gail. Charlie responded by not responding; he simply ignored his father's threat. Then the father changed his position. "He announced that it would be okay as long as I converted to Judaism. He even offered a bribe of some expensive jewelry if I converted. I'm not kidding." Charlie and Gail continued to disregard his proclamations. Then he said he would come to the wedding only if the ceremony was performed by a rabbi. Gail did not convert; the couple did not get married by a rabbi. They were married the way they wanted to be—by a judge. Charlie's father was there, "But the wedding would have taken place even if he hadn't been," says Gail.

A Lie-Down-and-Roll-Over Guy

In order to marry Michael, Lois had to agree to a Catholic ceremony. There was no argument to be had. It wasn't worth it to Michael to go against his mother's very strong wishes, because his own were pretty vague. In fact, for five years before they were married, the couple lived together and lied to Michael's mother. (The story was that Lois and her sister—their third, fictitious roommate—shared the double bed, while Michael slept on the couch.) About the ceremony, Lois says, "I did it, and I lied." She doesn't feel good or bad about it, but the how-are-you-going-to-raise-the-kids issue is creeping up on her rapidly. Says Lois, "If Michael won't handle that with his mother, I will."

Bullied Into Submission

When Alexa was married the first time, she was twenty-one. It was a spur-of-the-moment thing—the wedding happened a month after the couple decided to get hitched. Her in-laws instantly took over the plans. "I didn't really say anything, because I was marrying into a family that had a lot more money than mine," says Alexa. "I had no self-confidence then, and so I sort of let them do whatever they wanted. My family is Jewish, and they're Catholic, with a capital 'K,' I might add. So I was informed that we were getting married by a priest."

"My mother, who hadn't been in a temple in thirty years, all of a sudden got religious on me," says Alexa. "She was really upset." So upset she called her daughter crying every day for the two weeks before the wedding. She went so far as to utter the cliché, "How could you do this to me?" Alexa's father, whose new wife was Christian, had no problem with it.

Alexa was worried about her mother. "So I cut a deal with the priest and some other people at the church when I went to meet with them. I said, 'I'll do this, but it's gonna be really offensive to my family, and I don't want any mention of Jesus. You can say God if you want, but I just can't do the Jesus part.' So they said, 'Okay, we promise.'" Toward the end of the ceremony, it happened. "The priest said, 'And do you promise to raise your children in the house of our Lord Jesus Christ?'" Alexa looked at Joe;

they both paused for a second, then said, almost in unison, "No." The priest brushed right by it and went on with the ceremony. "I mean I don't want to offend anybody, but, no, I'm not gonna do that. And I'm not gonna stand in front of everybody and lie either."

Double Wedding

Stephen's parents did not attend his and Liza's wedding, which took place in a Russian Orthodox church. Stephen's parents are Jewish, and they refused to see their son married by a priest. (When the couple had first met, in high school, Liza had added an "O'" to the front of Stephen's last name, so her parents would think he was Irish-Catholic. Little did she know that six years later she'd be marrying the guy—and that four years prior to that she'd get caught in her sitcom-esque lie.) So Stephen's parents didn't come to the wedding. Neither did any of his other relatives. But Liza's family didn't go to the Jewish wedding that Stephen's parents threw two weeks later. Oh, maybe that was because they didn't *know* about it. Liza's siblings were not told about the Jewish wedding either. She didn't want to put them in a position of having to lie to her parents. This insane little caper went off without a hitch, because the families lived two states apart. Only four friends attended both affairs. Three years later, Liza doesn't complain. She paints it as a positive experience and claims to be glad it "worked out. Everybody got to go to the wedding they wanted to go to," she says. Excuse me, can you say "denial"?

Grooms Who Find Religion

"If somebody asks, I consider myself a Catholic," says Kevin. I don't go to church on Sunday, but I was brought up Catholic. I don't agree with a hundred percent of what the church represents, but I don't agree a hundred percent with what anybody represents, so that doesn't mean that I leave the church behind." A little defensive? You would be too if you were trying to justify your wishes to be married in a Catholic church to someone who would never set foot inside one. "Gabi is completely nonreligious—actually anti-Catholic—so she wanted anyone *but* a priest. Actually, she said she might be okay being married by a priest, but not in a church. So I made a series of phone calls, which are probably made once in the life of many lapsed Catholics, and was told that a priest cannot marry you outside the four walls of a church." Then Kevin began to search for another type of spiritual person to perform the ceremony. He found an Episcopalian minister he liked. By this time he and Gabi had talked a lot more about what the ceremony should contain. Gabi was happy to have Kevin choose the officiant, if that was important to him, but she had specific requirements about the content. Says Kevin, "She didn't want Jesus, any of the saints, or any winged creature to be mentioned. And somehow, this man of the cloth pulled it off." By meeting with the minister and explaining their situation to him, Kevin and Gabi were able to come up with a ceremony they both could live with.

Before they were married, Roy wanted Amelia to convert to Judaism. It had nothing to do with his parents; the request came from him. Amelia thought about it, did some research and agreed to do it. Says Amelia, "I told him if I'm gonna do this, I want to be a Sephardic Jew, and I want to study the Cabala." She found a reform woman rabbi to study with, and she delved into the subject. Roy was a little taken aback by her fervor. Amelia says that's because it meant he had to work also. "I'm really serious about everything I do, and so Roy had to educate himself too." For Amelia, who is fascinated by religion in general, it was a year spent studying history with a great teacher. Toward the end, she began work on the marriage contract and ceremony. "It was a very traditional ceremony. I wore a crown, and I actually dredged up all kinds of historical references that the real Jews who attended had no idea about. I think it was a very good experience for Roy's family, who learned a lot about their own religion." Amelia's Irish-Catholic family didn't have a problem with it, except her mother, who was participating in the ceremony and was a nervous wreck about having to speak in front of people.

Will You Marry Us?

You really get in touch with the little kid inside you when you start talking to potential officiants. Generally speaking, these people are extreme authority figures, also known in some cases as scary monsters. Even if they're not larger-than-life composites of your grammar school principal, your parents and your local news anchor, they command a certain respect and can sometimes disappoint. Remember, these folks are just people.

One hard-sell minister told Joni, "I do great weddings. I leave 'em all crying. They're weepin' in their seats." Not a dry eye in the house, or your money back. Joni was a bit turned off by this guy's vaudevillian approach to the marriage ceremony. "I didn't want quite such a good show," she says. "I was looking for someone a bit more mystical—not too out there, but someone who was at least gentle and thoughtful."

That's what Victoria was expecting when she met with a very busy minister one morning at six thirty. "But he was brusque and cold," she says. Victoria was not particularly charmed, but she considered going with him anyway; he was available on their wedding date, and she didn't have any other referrals. The next morning, this minister's face was on the front page of the *San Francisco Chronicle*. Says Victoria, "According to the article, the guy had embezzled money from the vestry and threatened members with their lives if they told. It was unbelievable." Okay, that last part is probably not going to happen to you. But what a story, right? And "brusque and cold" is not so rare. Thanks to the allegations, Victoria was forced to look longer and harder for a minister, and she ended up with one she actually liked.

Marie wanted to get married at the church where her father was buried. She and Nick went one day to meet with the priest. Operating under the misconception that honesty is the best policy, Marie resolved to tell the priest (if he asked) that she and Nick were living together. "In the course of the conversation, he asked for my address and then he asked for Nick's, and they were the same," says Marie. The priest looked up and said, "You're living together now. You're fornicating. You have to get married immediately." Marie kept cool and said, "I'm sorry. We're not getting married now. We're getting married in October." Then the priest got very stern with them. All the soft, spiritual stuff went out the window. "He told us we had no choice and ordered us to come back and meet with him separately. I felt like I was nine years old and back in Catholic school," says Marie. She left in tears, partly due to frustration, partly in response to the scolding she'd received.

After that experience, Marie started rethinking the ceremony. "I definitely didn't want to be married by that priest. And I was totally turned off to the Catholic Church by what had happened." She thought they'd get married by a judge or in a Protestant church.

Her mother said no. "It's not like she even goes to church," says Marie, "but her friends are mostly Catholic, and I think she thought they'd 'all talk.'" So Marie and Nick found another church, Nick gave a friend's address as his own, and everybody was happy.

Someone Is Missing

*T*he universe of feelings that you experience when you're getting married is colored differently when you've lost someone close to you. Especially when it's your mother.

"I went to a favorite shop with my sister to try on dresses, and I went home sobbing," says Phoebe. "It was just so hard to do that with a sister, when I could remember my sister doing it with my mother only three years before." Phoebe says listening to friends complain about their mothers became almost intolerable for her. "At first it was so bad, I couldn't imagine how my wedding could ever become something I would look forward to." That changed, of course. Phoebe did look forward to her wedding, and ultimately she enjoyed it. But, she says, her experience was as much about missing her mother as about making a commitment to her boyfriend.

Wedding planning for Linda meant being on the verge of tears for six months. "I never knew when it would knock me down," she says. She went with her boyfriend, Dean, one day to try on tuxes and had one of those weird moments you sometimes get when, for a second, you see a person you know and love as a stranger. "And I realized that, to my mother, who had met Dean only once before she died, he *was* a stranger. I was marrying someone my mother didn't even know."

For some women, the situation is compounded by a strained relationship with a stepparent and the tension that arises out of a parent's loyalty to both new spouse and daughter. Samantha doesn't get along with her father's wife. "I came to the conclusion through therapy that I should have a talk with my father before too long about how I wanted my ceremony to be, because it was something I was making myself sick about," she says. "So I told him right away that I wanted him alone to walk me down the aisle, without his wife." Three months later, as though the conversation had never taken place, he said to Samantha, "So, have you thought about how you're going to have people walk down the aisle?" This man was in heavy denial because he was caught between what his wife wanted and what his daughter wanted. Samantha couldn't believe his wife would make an issue out of it. "Mixed with the obvious sadness of my mother's death, I had to deal with this." The subject was dropped for a long time. Finally, Samantha's father suggested that he first walk his wife down the aisle, then come back and walk Samantha. "That was okay with me," says Samantha, "because at least I wouldn't have to see it."

Abby lost her mother when she was sixteen. By age thirty-one, when she got married, she'd had a lot of practice missing her and trying to cope with that. "If you don't have a mother," advises Abby, "it's vital that you figure out who can create maternal energy for you around the wedding." For Abby that was her older sister, Kiki. "It's so helpful, because you do need a lot of nurturing when you're getting married, and a substitute is better than nothing." Figuring out how to handle all the discord of her extended family in terms of her wedding seemed impossible to Abby. "But Kiki was there for me every minute—to talk about that, or about my nervousness, or to look at the same two dresses three Saturdays in a row till I finally picked one."

Ways to Remember

How do you include someone you miss terribly in your big day? Through small gestures—Marie brought her bouquet to her father's grave after her reception—and bigger ones—Jenna sang a song at her reception dedicated to her deceased sister.

Elaine's mother's wedding dress had been missing for as long as Elaine could remember. But she was determined to find it and wear it to her own wedding. A series of phone calls led her to the attic of a great-aunt, about a hundred miles away. "Apparently right after her wedding, my mother had given it to a cousin, who ended up not wearing it. It was the mother of that cousin who'd had the dress for the last thirty-five years." Elaine didn't alter the dress at all, although the style was pretty dated. "I wanted to wear it exactly as she had."

"I was so close with my mother," says Phoebe. "I had to find a way to include her in my wedding ceremony." She and Todd met with the rabbi who was going to marry them to discuss it. "He asked if I had any ideas about how to do it and, of course, I didn't, but I knew that I *didn't* want what I'd seen rabbis do at some other weddings: 'So-and-so is missed today and is with us in spirit. Let us pray.'" It had to be more than that. So Phoebe looked through books she and her mother "loved together" for something the rabbi could read, but it felt so forced. "I was looking for a way to say something myself, and the task was just overwhelming—to pay tribute to my mother at my wedding in five minutes or less.

What I hadn't thought of was that this rabbi was a big fan of my mother's." Ultimately, Phoebe decided just to ask him to speak. "I didn't know what he was going to say, and of course, when he spoke I completely lost it. So did my sisters and Todd." But that's what Phoebe had wanted—to openly experience the sadness of her mother's absence. During the reception, her brother-in-law made a toast to her mother too. Guests told Phoebe it was the happiest wedding they'd ever been to, even though there were two points when most everyone was crying.

John lost his brother, Tony, two years before he got married. So instead of having a short church ceremony, he and Michelle opted for a full mass; that way they could pay tribute to both Tony and John's deceased father. The couple also included a poem Tony wrote as one of the readings.

As a tribute to her deceased father, Rosemary chose to get married in his church. "I'm not at all religious," says Rosemary, "so it really was kind of alienating for me. But it did make me very conscious of my father."

Some brides I spoke to who made private gestures (like Rosemary's or Elaine's) were nervous about paying tribute to a deceased family member openly during the ceremony or reception, even though they felt they wanted to. "You worry that you're going to make people feel uncomfortable," says Phoebe, "but that's okay. It's artificial to ignore the sad part of the day. Do whatever you feel you need to do to make it right."

A Bride by Any Other Name

There are three positions on the subject of taking your husband's last name: There's the conventional one ("I want us to have the same name. It makes us more like a family"); the separate-but-equal philosophy ("No way. Would he ever think of giving up the name *he's* had all his life?"); and the have-your-cake-and-eat-it-too stance ("I'll use his name sometimes and keep mine for work").

If you're of the first mind, you're probably not in for a lot of conflict here. Otherwise, read on. Among the men I interviewed, even the most forward-thinking seem to revert to a Neanderthal sense of territoriality when this topic arises. So even if it's a non-issue to you, there's a chance that to your future husband, it warrants hours of debate.

"I thought my husband was kidding when he brought it up," says Vivian. "He knew perfectly well that I wouldn't be taking his name." When he used the "having the same name makes us a family" argument, she made a suggestion: Let's make a new name out of both our names. Then we'll have the same name. "I would have done it too. But of course the issue for him wasn't really about having the *same* name; it was about having *his* name."

Leanne wasn't sure how she'd feel after she was married. "I thought maybe I'd want to take his name. So far [three years later], I've never used it, except on one occasion to throw a creditor off the trail." If you're undecided, after you're married switch back and forth, try out different variations. There's no law that dictates what you can ask to be called (witness Prince). The problem is it's a little hard to keep track when you vary too much.

The Woman with the Same Name as You

Are you familiar with the organization MILAYKYN (Mothers-In-Law Against You Keeping Your Name)? You'd think in the new millennium it would be suffering, but as its numbers dwindle, its die-hard members band ever tighter together.

Erika's mother-in-law paid for most of her wedding to George, so Erika made an effort to be agreeable and almost always was. She did not plan to change her name, and she knew George's mother would be surprised to hear that, so she consciously avoided the subject for as long as she could. Then it came time to order invitations and stationery. Says Erika, "George's mother wanted our thank-you cards to say 'Mr. and Mrs. George Gold.' I wanted it to be 'Erika and George,' because it's nobody's business what my name is. His mother said, 'They're not going to know who you are.' And I said, 'Listen, if they don't know who we are from "Erika and George," why are they buying us a gift?' Finally, I came right out and told her I didn't want to change my name. And she said,

'Well, why do you want to get married?'" Erika was as baffled by that logic as you probably are.

This is where the story gets frightening. George became convinced by his mother that Erika *should* change her name, and gave her a week in which to reconsider. "He was threatening to call the whole thing off if I didn't do it." George regained his sanity before the week was up, and when it came right down to it, he thought it was cool that Erika kept her name. But as far as George's mother was concerned, the issue was still unresolved. "I didn't want to bring it up again," says Erika, "because I didn't want to fight with her." Two years later, Erika still hadn't broken the news ("she never asked"). When George's mother called to tell the couple she was taking them to Europe and was about to buy plane tickets, Erika was forced to admit her real name; her passport would give it away.

Last-Minute Pressure

"My husband decided to go get our joint checking account going the morning of our wedding," says Clarice. Talk about an unusual sense of priorities. "While I was doing my makeup, he brought me a form to fill out and sign about how my name would appear on the checks." On the marriage license, Clarice had written her whole name with his last tacked on. "I wasn't sure what I was going to do about my last name, but I wasn't going to make that decision when I had to be at my wedding in three hours." Mitch wanted her to agree to use his last name on the checks. "We had a nice little wedding-morning fight over that." A good argument for not seeing each other the day of the wedding, eh?

Trouble Where You Least Expect It

You might not be surprised to encounter resistance from a mother-in-law or from a husband-to-be who fantasized that one day there would be a Mrs. Him. But when you're about to get married, the myriad people who have something to say about every decision you make is mind-boggling, and Pam, who never considered *not* taking her husband's name, was hit with a surprise attack.

"My friend Elsa sees me as living in the '50s, as a domestic throwback, especially now, because I have kids and stay home with them," says Pam. "Just before my wedding, she and my other bridesmaid said to me, 'Now don't tell us you're going to take his name!'" They tried to convince Pam how old-fashioned and inappropriate that was when in fact, it was perfectly appropriate for Pam and only inappropriate for the two of them.

A Practical Choice

Gail Gusemaneci spent twenty-six years trying to teach people how to pronounce her unusual last name. She was not so distraught over it that she ever considered legally changing it, but when the opportunity arose to have a new name, she took it. Her husband's last name—Flugelsterner—is hard to spell, yes, but it's rarely mispronounced.

Jealousy, Resentment and Other Forms of Ill Will

Generally speaking, sisters and friends are positive entities, right? But one of the scary things that can happen when this new identity "bride" is thrust upon you is that a usually positive entity won't feel happy about it and will turn into a repository of negativity. You've been through a lot of ups and downs with these people, and with sisters especially, many of the downs have likely been petty situations that are forgotten the next day. But this is bigger, and if someone you love and count on turns really nasty when you're getting married, unfortunately, you're going to remember it for a long time.

A friend or sister or cousin who is jealous of the attention you're getting or who is simply competitive about getting married will make you more self-conscious than you already are. And if you let her get to you, you'll also probably feel guilty and angry. You have to do a quiet analysis of the situation, then talk with her about it if that makes sense, or find a way to rise above it.

With Sisters Like These . . .

"My sister, Eve, was the most difficult person you could ever imagine," says Kayla. "Anytime the subject of my wedding came up, it was like, huff, huff, huff, and she'd leave the room." This started at the beginning of a year-and-a-half engagement. They were both living at home at the time. "I remember hearing her bad-mouth me to her friend over the phone. She said I wasn't helping around the house and that I was taking advantage of everyone." Meanwhile, Eve started to plan a wedding of her own. "It was kind of sad, really. She was hardly crazy about this guy. She just couldn't stand the fact that I was getting married." Eve dropped her own wedding plans as quickly as she began them, and the hostility continued. Their mother, sympathetic to her younger daughter, discouraged Kayla from confronting Eve about her behavior. "But it got to the point where I had to. I said, 'Look, either you shape up, or I don't want you to be my maid of honor. What is your problem?'" Eve wrote to Kayla, apologizing and explaining that the whole thing was hard on her. She pulled it together and suddenly became very solicitous. "I think forcing Eve to verbalize what she was feeling made her realize she was being unfair and that I didn't deserve the kind of treatment she was giving me," says Kayla.

"My sister Anne was pretty angry that I was getting married first," says Kathleen. Anne had been with her boyfriend for five years and Kathleen and Jonathan had been together for less than a year. "I felt so guilty, I gave her a surprise birthday party a month before my wedding. I thought that might make her be nice to me about the whole thing. It worked for a couple of days, but then she went back to being nasty." It wasn't that Anne was consistently mean. She helped out in a workmanlike way. She even made Kathleen's headpiece. "But considering how close we were, she was very cold. And she kept openly doubting my relationship with my boyfriend. She asked me a couple of times—once on the night before the wedding—'Are you sure you want to marry Jonathan?' Not in a nice way, but in a way like she couldn't believe I was actually going to do it." Kathleen didn't have the nerve to tell Anne to cut the crap. She was afraid that if she did, her sister would come back with, "What are you talking about? Didn't I make your headpiece?"

Tough Love

If discussing the problem is not an option, there's only one thing to do: eliminate the situation (no, I don't mean you should have your sister rubbed out). But in a very quiet way, stop including or depending on her. That's hard when she's always been a big part of your life, but often resentful sisters will rationalize their crabbiness as a reaction to being asked to do wedding-related stuff for you. So don't ask her to do anything. Don't involve her any more than she asks to be involved. I know it's difficult to cut out someone you love from one of the biggest events of your life. Plus, there are factors that complicate things even further (you have a mother in common, for example). But if you don't want to take her abuse, don't leave yourself wide open to it. Obviously "forgive and forget" is not working out here, because she keeps coming up with new stuff to disapprove of. So pull back. Let your sister come to you. Assume she's not part of it, not there for you, and then maybe she'll discover she wants to be.

Jocelyn's sisters were less than enthused about her wedding. "They're sort of too progressive for marriage, and they thought it was weird that I was doing it," says Jocelyn. She didn't care too much. "I wasn't surprised, but my mother really wanted them to participate," which they did begrudgingly for a while. Finally Jocelyn explained to her mother that dragging her sisters around to look at wedding dresses was for her a very personalized version of hell. The planning became much more pleasant when Jocelyn's mother let her sisters off the hook.

Greta was really close with her sister, Meg. "I knew she could be very judgmental, but it was never directed at me before," says Greta. When Greta started to plan her wedding, things began to change. Meg, who is gay, started to really resent the fact that she felt she couldn't come out to her parents, especially when Greta's relationship with Stuart was being celebrated so publicly. "It became a big issue that Meg couldn't bring her girlfriend to the wedding, but she was the only one stopping herself. *I* wanted her girlfriend to be there and so did Stuart." Meg began to mock or criticize every aspect of the plans. "I was embarrassed in front of her because I know she thinks that the only good wedding is a wedding where you go to a justice of the peace and a few people go out for dinner afterward," says Greta. It was as if Meg was perpetually rolling her eyes and saying with her expression, "Quit being so tacky." For a few weeks, Meg actually refused to go to the wedding. Even after she flew to Atlanta, where it was being held, she wasn't sure she would show up (she did). The one upside is that Meg's behavior eliminated Greta's conflict about who to choose as her sole attendant; she chose a friend.

A Friend in Need (of Attention)

Arielle's childhood friend Sally threw a hysterical fit at Arielle's shower. "It would have been funny if it wasn't so terrible," says

Arielle. Motivated seemingly by nothing, Sally burst out crying, ran to the bathroom and locked herself in. She emerged only after six women at the party, including Arielle's mother, had a turn consoling her through the door. "She did the same thing at her own twelfth birthday party," recalls Arielle, "because we were paying too much attention to someone else."

When Carol saw her longtime bud Claudia gliding from courtship to engagement to marriage like a storybook princess, she grew bitter. "Carol had a really tough time when she got married last year and she was having a difficult first year of marriage," says Claudia. "I think that's where it came from." Carol's husband, the youngest child of six, had never done the breaking-away thing. His parents were completely dependent upon him. They never learned to drive because he or one of the other kids took them everywhere. He even wanted to invite his parents to meet up with Carol and him on their honeymoon. Real daytime talk-show stuff. So Claudia was the recipient of a few zingers from Carol: cracks about the diamonds on her ring ("Well, I think that little one is *sort of* clear"), intimations that she was rushing into things. Traumatized by her own wedding experience and still fighting for her husband's independence, Carol couldn't handle Claudia's good fortune.

When Molly first started planning her wedding, she came home one night to an angry voicemail from her friend Sarah. "She said I had turned selfish," says Molly, "that all I had talked about for the past month was the wedding, that I never even asked about how *she* was anymore." If this happens to you, try to take a hard look at the situation before you attribute it to jealousy and dismiss it. Is she right? Is it true? Step back and take a look at yourself. Molly thought maybe Sarah had a point. They talked about it, and Molly apologized and made a concerted effort to change her behavior. But a few weeks later, she was greeted at home by another angry voicemail. This time Sarah was mad that she hadn't been consulted about the date of Molly's shower. Her tone was very dramatic, as if this was the last petty indignity she could tolerate. "I realized then that with Sarah if it wasn't one thing, it would be another, and there was very little I could do about it."

"A Sister-in-Law Is Neither a Sister Nor an In-law. Discuss."

I should say here that not a lot of people complained to me about their new sisters-in-law. It seems s-i-ls are not nearly as common a source of tension as sisters or friends can be, but when there is trouble there, it can suck in a big way. Your husband's sister has known him forever. If she's jealous or disapproving, she can (and probably will) make you feel the significance of that history, try to exclude you, and create a general sense that she is closer to your husband than you are. Of course, she needs his cooperation to be really effective. But men can be doofuses, and they are sometimes oblivious to the fact that they are being manipulated, especially if the manipulator in question is as practiced as a sister or mother can be. Anyway, to those of you who have a troublemaking sister-in-law, I'll say the same thing your mother said about that nasty girl in sixth grade who teased you about your boobs (or your lack thereof): She's just jealous—ignore her. Does that help? No? Okay, how about this: Lie awake all night thinking about how she hates you and how she can, in fact, ruin your marriage and will probably kidnap your child, if you were to have a child, and might be on the phone with your boss at that very moment trying to get you fired. Feel better?

Between Rick's possessive mother and his two possessive sisters, Alice was getting a triple whammy of negativity. When friends threw a shower for the couple and Alice called to invite Rick's younger sister, Amy (the only member of either family who lived in the same town as Alice and Rick), Amy said she was "really busy" that weekend. "I told his older sister, Judith, that Amy didn't even want to come to our shower," says Alice, "and she said, 'Well, for Amy, it's like a death [that Rick's getting married].' And I said, 'Is it for you?' And she said, 'Well, if I wasn't married, yes. Now I have my own life.'"

Yikes! This anecdote truly defies commentary. I've got to say, not a lot of people, even in this age of therapy and meds, have the nerve to articulate such a hurtful and inappropriate sentiment. This is one occasion in which communication was not the answer, or if it was, Alice should have gotten her thoughts out in the open too ("May you rot in hell, evil wench"). She didn't. Actually, she was glad Judith said what she did. "I would rather deal with honest hostility than hostility masked as something else," she says. That's what you call a highly evolved bride.

Stepping on Toes

By now you know that, as much as you'd like to keep your wedding focused exclusively on the two important people, you simply cannot; there are too many players involved. But emotions are so intensified during major family events that there's no way you can make everyone happy. People are going to bitch about you behind your back, and you can't let it make you crazy; for every choice you make, there are six you ruled out and two injured parties associated with each. And I'm not even talking about the people you're not going to invite. I'm referring to people who are included but are not included enough—or in the right way—for their taste. Close friends and family members consider their role in your wedding significant, and they want to know that you do too.

By the Book

Grace's and Herb's families planned a lot of extra activities surrounding their wedding. The night before the rehearsal dinner
there was a party at the bride's mother's house. To both, they invited all the out-of-town guests and everyone in the wedding
party, with a guest. "We ended up with our whole group of college friends there, except one couple—because they weren't in the
wedding party and they weren't from out of town. We didn't leave
them out on purpose. It just worked out that way. They were really
hurt." The same thing happened with the brunch that was held
the day after the wedding. "At the end of the reception, there was
this awkward moment when the college group left together. And
we said, 'See you tomorrow' to everyone but these two friends,
who we hadn't invited to the brunch either." Grace was strict
about sticking to her self-imposed guest list rules for the auxiliary
events. She enjoyed saying things like, "I had to draw the line
somewhere," even when Herb tried to persuade her otherwise. But
when the fun of being in charge was over, she wished she'd given
the matter a little more thought and bent the rules. "I thought I
was being practical, but I went a little overboard."

A good rule of thumb is to do what will ultimately make you
the least uncomfortable. When you're looking at things on paper
or planning the practical aspects of an event in your mind, it's
difficult to conjure the sickening feeling of confronting someone
you've unintentionally hurt. It can be considerably worse than you
might think because it's the kind of stuff that lingers. Of course,
I'm not advocating catering to everybody's whims. You just don't
want to walk away from the whole experience with regrets. And if
it's not a matter of spending more money, or generating a whole

new batch of hurt feelings from other slighted friends, you might want to *in*clude rather than automatically exclude.

Only a Bridesmaid

Joni was trying to be pragmatic when she selected a maid-of-honor. She planned to do a tremendous amount of work for her wedding and knew she'd need lots of help. "My sister, Jane, lives in Brussels and she has three kids, so I didn't even think about asking her. I wasn't even sure she was going to make it to the wedding," says Joni. So Joni asked her boyfriend's sister instead. "Looking back, I see it was weird that I didn't even talk to Jane about it. That's very typical of my family. I never explained why I made that choice, and she never told me that she was upset."

The day before the wedding, Jane, one of six bridesmaids, spoke up. Joni, stupefied by her sister's sense of timing, tried to address the situation by asking her maid-of-honor to step down to the role of bridesmaid and let Jane take her place. But this maid-of-honor had done much more than your typical maid-of-honor. She had worked hard on the wedding for almost a year. And her brother, the groom, was not happy with Joni's suggestion that she be dethroned. "So that didn't work out," says Joni. "The day of the wedding, Jane told me she wouldn't be in it. I think there was more to it than she said." Sounds like Jane's a little psychotic, but we can learn something from this little tale anyway. Say it with me—"communication."

Overreact, Why Don'tcha?

Michelle and John had been good friends with Paco and Shoshana for years. Then they had a fight. About a year before Michelle and John got married, the couples made up, but they weren't friends like they used to be. "It was the type of situation where you could go either way, but we decided to invite them," says Michelle. At the reception, just before dinner, Michelle caught sight of Paco's and Shoshana's backs as they scooted out the door. "They got up and left because they weren't seated with some of our closer friends." Hey, guys, Emily Post says it's customary to stay through dinner, then leave early and complain about your seat for the next fifty years.

Evil Stepmother

Mari had Sheila, a demanding new stepmother, to handle, and her mother's recent death was already making the wedding-planning process more bitter than sweet. "For a month I felt like it was Sheila's wedding, because all the issues were about her, and she was the one who needed most of the attention." Sheila wanted to be under the chupa (that's the canopy under which the bride and groom stand during the ceremony). Mari wouldn't have it. Even Mari's sisters' husbands were not going to be under the chupa (Mari's original measure to keep Sheila out without being too hurtful). Tension was mounting, and Mari felt she had to do something. "I invented a bone to throw her. I told my father, 'It would mean so much to me if Sheila would do the blessing of the bread.'" That did the trick. Sheila felt special; Mari got her way.

Bestowing Small Honors

There are lots of opportunities to make people feel special, and the best are the ones by which you benefit. I don't mean for that to sound so Machiavellian. Obviously, if you ask someone to do a reading, for example, she's helping you out by becoming part of the performance and you're honoring her through the gesture. It's a symbiotic thing.

Don't feel bound by tradition here. "I wish I'd thought of having my friend Renata do a toast. It just didn't occur to me that there could be more than one, and I knew the best man would do one," says Lynn. "But because we didn't have a wedding party, this really close friend, who actually introduced me to my husband, wasn't part of the whole show, and she definitely should have been."

Maybe there's a friend or relative you'd like to somehow include who wouldn't be comfortable with any of the more public tasks. Lisa asked her godmother to hold the money-filled envelopes. "I gave her a bag she could keep under the table. She loved the responsibility." At the end of Cathy's reception, she gave her bouquet to her favorite aunt.

Motivated by good intentions, Alex and Rosa got themselves into a jam. "I wanted to include my father somehow," says Alex. "Since our invitations involved a drawing, and he's an artist, I asked him to do it." The problem was, Rosa's sister was designing the invitation. And Rosa and Alex had a vague idea of what they wanted. That gives you four cooks where there should have been one. When Alex's father gave him the drawing he'd done, Alex took it to Rosa's sister, and it didn't work with the design she had already come up with. So Alex went back to his father and said, "Could you do it over more like this?" not realizing that his father had spent a good amount of time on it. No, revisions were not a possibility. Heavy awkwardness followed. Eventually Alex had to deal with telling his father, "Thanks, but no thanks."

You have to honor the people who are helping you too, especially where there's creativity involved. You can't tell your friend that she's in charge of arranging the flowers but she has to work with your cousin and three of your aunts. No fair. And even people who are handling less artistic tasks won't want to share the responsibility with someone they hardly know. Offer the name and cell number of a potential assistant to each helper. Then, if your brother thinks he could use a hand with his bus-monitor duties, he'll have someone to call.

Best Friends and BFFs

I recently overheard a conversation (on speaker) between my upstairs neighbor, Christina, and a friend of hers. (Don't start with me about the ethics of this situation. I heard the conversation while we were both in the hallway, one floor apart.) It seemed like Christina was not so nuts about this friend. Maybe they were old friends who outgrew each other. Maybe she never liked her. I don't know. But the friend called to tell Christina that she and her boyfriend were getting married. Then the friend said, "Are you up for being a bridesmaid?" There was a pause and Christina said, "What do you mean?" I winced. It was a nauseating moment. Another pause. "Are you asking me to be in your wedding party?" Now, I don't know Christina too well, but I'm pretty sure she's not a total monster. What I gathered from my eavesdropping was that it seemed to Christina that she was in no way a good enough friend to this person to be in her wedding party.

Wouldn't it be a bummer to get a reaction like that? I know

what you're thinking: "That would never happen to me. I know who my friends are." You're right, it probably wouldn't. In fact, you're much more likely to experience the other extreme—people left out who want to be in. But you might be surprised by a luke-warm reaction from a close friend.

Matthew and Gregg were roommates through most of college. When Matthew announced his engagement, marriage wasn't even a remote possibility for Gregg, who had recently been dumped by his girlfriend of three years. In fact, Gregg was a little shocked. They were only twenty-two, after all. What was the rush? "I think he felt like I abandoned him when I met Susan," says Matthew. If that was so, the wedding symbolized to Gregg the final sayonara. When a glowing Matthew asked Gregg to be his best man, Gregg said he "would have to think about it."

People who say mean stuff like this are either not listening to themselves, or are seriously needy. Gregg wanted a little attention. He wanted Matthew to become acquainted with his resistance to a wedding he deemed premature (i.e., it was too soon for Gregg to give up Matthew). Matthew, who expected nothing less than a hug and a silly grin from his buddy, was hurt and deflated.

Hey, Gregg, what's there to think about? Nobody is asking for your commentary here. The question wasn't, "Do you think now would be a good time for me to get married?" It was, "Will you be my best man?" Gregg came around with a little coaxing.

But you don't have time to coax right now. If someone has to think about whether or not she wants to be in your wedding party, cut her loose. Bridesmaids who require emotional baby-sitting are not worth the trouble, and you do not need negativity swirling about you at such close range. If that means having a smaller wedding party, so be it.

Often there's just plain jealousy at play here too. Some women who meet with resistance attribute it to the fact that the bitchy party wants to be a bride and feels like she's lost some sort of race. Michelle asked her cousin Donna to be in her party. Says Michelle, "She called me back and said she couldn't afford the dress, because she was in another wedding the same month. But I had heard her at Christmas going on about the big raise she got. It wasn't the money." I can't believe any bride would bother to be hurt by such an obvious display of jealousy. Really, these people are doing you a favor by refusing to participate.

Oh, Monty! Pick Me!

Maybe you're lucky enough to have six sisters, a ready-made wedding party, and no one else expects to be asked. But probably not. So what do you do? When you think of your closest friends, you realize they don't know one another. Two are from college, one is from work and one's from elementary school. Adrienne teaches feminist theory, and Rosanna loves Howard Stern. You fixed Millie and Maryann up with the same guy at separate times, and later he dated them simultaneously (that wasn't your fault). In any case, this is not something to worry about. You're not asking these people to move in together. They'll get along fine at the wedding and the auxiliary events, and those are the only occasions on which they'll see one another. They don't have to bond heavily or even exchange e-mail addresses. *You* have to chill out though, if you're the type who can't have fun if somebody within a five-mile radius has a hangnail.

If you don't have an obvious wedding party, choosing one is kind of a mini version of making up a guest list for your whole wedding. And the same principle applies: The size helps you eliminate possibilities and determine your choices. I read in some magazine that you should have *x* number of ushers for *y* number of guests. No, thank you, we'll just pick our good friends. The size of the wedding party is up to you and your boyfriend. But if there's a discrepancy between what you each want, one of you will be put in an awkward situation.

"There were four friends I wanted as bridesmaids. They were the only people I would have even considered," says Samantha. "Chad wanted his whole fraternity." Okay, she's exaggerating. But he did want seven groomsmen. "He claimed there was no way he could cut that number down." Samantha was put in a position to try to match that, so she had to do something she felt was artificial: move into her next layer of friends. "I felt funny asking these people to be in my party. It was really hard to pick among them." Samantha struggled with this for a while then came to the conclusion that she felt too strongly to choose three more bridesmaids just to match her husband's groomsmen. She kept her four and he kept his seven. They walked down the aisle in threes (boy-girl-boy), except for the best man and maid of honor.

Kelly and Matt were not the least bit concerned with symmetry. Their five groomsmen walked down the aisle one by one, and Kelly's sister (her only attendant) followed solo. (If you're planning a rule-breaking processional, watch out for a raid by the Etiquette Police.)

Eva says to be prepared before you start announcing your engagement. "When I told a pretty good friend I was getting married," says Eva, "she said, 'I can't wait. When are we getting the dresses?' I was stupid and never told her I didn't want her to be in the wedding party. Every time I think about her at the altar with us, I get mad at myself for being such a wimp." But how do you handle this situation even if you're prepared for it? I guess you have to be ready to make your intentions clear immediately. When you sit down to tell the potential assumer you're getting married, follow immediately with, "I wish I could have you in my wedding party, but . . ." That sounds awful, but it would be worse to end up like Eva, unable to bear the sight of her own wedding pictures.

And what about people you "owe" because you were in their weddings? Forget that. You could get stuck with a totally hideous party of cousins and sisters-in-law if you were strict about that policy. But if you think it's necessary, sit down and have a talk with each person who might feel slighted. Cover all the bases.

Party of One

Julia thought one of the benefits of not having a wedding party would be eliminating the possibility of slighting potential brides-maids. But, surprise, surprise, she was the recipient of plenty of negative vibes by people who disapproved of her decision; they wanted her to have a wedding party just so they could be in it. "It's like getting mad at a couple who eloped because you didn't get invited to their wedding," she says. "I wanted the ceremony to be very simple—just the two of us. But all I heard from my boyfriend's mother was, 'Who are the bridesmaids? Who are the bridesmaids?' She kept saying she was personally hurt that I wasn't having brides-maids, because her daughters should be in our wedding."

Julia didn't get along with Barry's sisters, and they had been really difficult about the wedding from the beginning. "I had been a bridesmaid in one of their weddings, but that was a wedding of three hundred people and a train of ten bridesmaids." So Julia told Barry he should have his sisters be his best women. She said, "*You* feel a connection to them. I don't. And you're asking me to do something I'm really uncomfortable with." But his mother and sisters kept kept pushing Julia, by way of Barry. "We were having these terrible fights. Really bad. He said, 'For me, please do it.' So finally I did."

Julia realizes now that since she felt so strongly about not having a wedding party, she should have talked about it right from the beginning. "I wish I had just gotten the four of us [bride, groom and mothers] together and said what I wanted to do before any of this had a chance to happen." Early on, things are relatively trouble-free, because nobody has had an opportunity to disagree. That's the time to announce major departures from tradition. Then resistant parties have months during which to get used to your ideas, and maybe by the time the wedding rolls around, they'll have lost their momentum for being angry.

Mitch would have liked to have had groomsmen, but he ended up asking just his brother. "I've got so many really close friends who fall into three or four distinct groups," says Mitch, "that I never could have picked a wedding party. It would have been the King family."

Erika wasn't into having a wedding party. "But I thought I had to. I just kept looking through magazines at the bridesmaids' dresses, thinking, What's plain? What's plainer?" Her boyfriend's mother suggested that she have just one attendant. "And I thought, Oh, you're right. I can do it nice and classy and simple. This is what I really wanted, I just didn't realize it was an option."

Everything's an option. Whatever makes the most sense for you is right. Ginnie and Chris had the same best friend, so they made him their "best person" instead of choosing a best man and a maid of honor.

Some Things Are Decided for You

Andy struggled for a couple of months about which of his two closest friends should be his best man. He had more of a history with Phil, but he and Frank had actually been closer for the past two years. He talked about it with his girlfriend, considered having two best men and even discussed it with Frank. When he came to a decision, he mentioned it to his mother and she said, "Your brother is going to be your best man." Case closed.

Light Work

Bridal magazines and wedding blogs talk incessantly about the duties of the best man and maid of honor. I think if you expect your wedding party to do much more than pay for some overpriced attire and provide emotional support, you're out of line. If someone wants to give you a shower, she will. But don't be gross and *make* your friends do it. Being in a bridal party should be a treat, not a burden. I'm not saying you shouldn't ask for help with little tasks. Bridesmaids and groomsmen are behind the scenes, like you and your hubby-to-be, so they can help you make the magic work.

Tina was maid of honor at her sister's wedding. "Denise was the most organized bride I've ever seen," says Tina. "She had a spreadsheet of tasks that everyone—including my father—had to follow. When we were taking pictures at our mother's house before the wedding, she looked at her chart, turned to our brother and shouted, 'It's two thirty! You're not supposed to be here!'" One of Tina's tasks was to keep an eye on Denise's train as she walked down the aisle. "I was a nervous wreck about it. In the church during the ceremony, she was signaling to me with her eyebrows and I went over and fixed the train, even though it looked okay to me. She kept signaling, and I went back and straightened the train a little more." Denise was still signaling. It turned out that her headpiece was falling off because her father had accidentally tugged on it after he'd walked her down the aisle and kissed her.

If you want your best man to make a toast, you might remind him about this. Not everybody knows the traditions or whether you want to comply with them. My mother was at a wedding recently where the best man didn't know he was expected to make a toast, and the groom was sort of waiting around for it to happen. Near the end of the wedding, when no toast had happened, the groom opted to do one himself.

A bold yet diplomatic bridesmaid (or groomsman) might not mind keeping an eye on the microphone during the reception for you. If she notices your cousin Selma preparing the band to accompany her in a rendition of "Unchained Melody," she can run interference till you're able to find someone to talk Selma down. Choose a bridesmaid who's not too shy to escort a drunken rambling guest away from the mike in the middle of his unscheduled toast, and who's cool enough to get away with bossing people around a bit.

Childish Thoughts

Choosing which kids to have in your wedding party can sometimes be more politically risky than choosing among the adults in your life. If you think friends are touchy about not being asked themselves, wait till you see a mother react when someone else's kid is picked over hers. If there are only a couple of kids in your life you'd even consider, you're okay in terms of politics. But you'd also better have a pretty good sense of humor. Because when you have kids involved in any type of performance, the number of things that can go wrong increases exponentially. Even your very special, brilliant, beautiful nieces and nephews can be prone to fits of shyness or temper.

Rita, Andrew and their wedding party were standing at the

back of the church waiting to start the processional. Everyone was lining up and getting ready. At the front of the line was Maisy, Rita's eight-year-old niece and flower girl. "Suddenly Maisy walked over toward the wall," says Rita. "She refused to go down the aisle first. She wanted her mother to walk with her." With only seconds to go, everyone tried to convince Maisy to go first, telling her all at once that the flower girl had the most important job, that her aunt and uncle would be very disappointed if she didn't go first, blah, blah, blah. Maisy could hear through their sing-songy talking-to-a-child tones and detect the urgency of the situation. The pressure was too much. The little girl burst out crying, drawing all eyes toward the back of the church. In a minute, the wedding party had reordered itself and started down the aisle. Maisy came out when she was ready—just before the bride and groom.

When you invite a child to be in your wedding party, you also invite the parents of that child to participate, maybe a little more than you had intended. "One of my bridesmaids was my husband's ten-year-old niece," says Gail. "Her mother decided she didn't like the dress we had chosen for the attendants and asked whether she could have a different dress made for her daughter. Actually, she didn't ask. She just told me flat-out she was going to do it."

Gail may have been a little insulted, but she took this opportunity *not* to have a fight—probably a smart move. The high-voltage current that runs through your wedding can turn every difference of opinion into an indelible confrontation. Sometimes it's just not worth it.

Jekyll and Bride

—A Word of Caution—

*T*his book is all about standing up for yourself and becoming empowered. But there are some dangerous interpretations of this type of advice. Some perfectly rational, thoughtful, considerate women get caught up in the "this is my day" thing and behave in ways they would have found abominable before.

Olga, usually a very easygoing person, got a little out of hand about two months before her wedding to Blake. It started one night when Blake's mother, Edie, called him with some devastating news: Her husband of twelve years was leaving her. Says Olga, "My first thought was that she should have waited till after the wedding to tell us."

But Edie couldn't wait. For one thing, she needed quick legal advice, and her son was also her lawyer. She was also looking for emotional support. Blake's relationship with his mother had always struck Olga as too dependent, but because the couple lived so far away from Edie, it had never become an issue.

A few days later, when a distraught Edie concluded a voicemail to both of them with "Of course, the wedding will go on . . . I guess," Olga became enraged. She saw Edie's behavior as typically manipulative. "I thought it was sick of her to push Blake's buttons at a time like that. It never occurred to me that she was truly feeling desperate." Blake was a wreck, worrying about his mother's situation. So he took off from work and flew across the country to North Carolina to see her. He also hoped to talk to her husband and find out what was going on. The last thing on his mind was the wedding, and Olga resented that.

This would have been a good topic for Olga to bring up with her therapist, but unfortunately, she didn't have one. Instead, a few days later, she let her anger explode at Blake. "Your mother would do anything to ruin our wedding," she blurted out. Blake was shocked. The confrontation led to a huge fight, unlike any the couple had ever had. Even while Blake was slamming the door behind him, cursing about this hideous new aspect of Olga's personality, Olga realized how selfish she was being.

Under normal circumstances, Olga never would have dreamed of embracing the resentment she felt, but her status as a bride-to-be distorted her perception. And at the moment she thought it was reasonable to be most concerned about her big day, even when her boyfriend's mother was experiencing a legitimate crisis. "I can't bear to think about it," she says now. It's easy to lose your perspective when everyone around you is encouraging you to do just that by treating you like royalty. "Not that it's anyone else's fault," says Olga, "but I still wonder why my mother or my sister didn't give me a good slap when I was in the midst of all my complaining."

Often the prima donna syndrome manifests itself in less damaging ways. Lindsay had very specific ideas about her wedding. When I asked her advice about having things your way, she said,

"If anything, I think I was too assertive. I wanted what I wanted, and I think sometimes I got bossy with my mother." Lindsay found that because some people were so eager to please her, she quickly became frustrated when she met with anything less than perfection.

Your wedding is the most important thing to *you* right now, but other people, even those close to you, still have regular lives and everyday problems to deal with. Don't make unreasonable demands, because when you say, "Jump," they might say, "Go to hell."

"I was asked to be a bridesmaid by my friends Mindy and Oscar," says Clarice. She was really a friend of the groom's, so she was flattered that Mindy wanted to include her. Clarice lived in Manhattan, and the wedding was in upstate New York, about three hundred miles away. She was in college, teaching aerobics to support herself, and essentially penniless. She scraped together the money for her bridesmaid's dress. "But when it came time to have the dress shortened, Mindy insisted I come upstate and go to her tailor. I asked her to send me the dress and said I'd have it shortened in New York, or to tell her tailor that I'm 5'3" and to do the best she could." Mindy was outraged. No, she said, she would not send it via mail, UPS or FedEx. She was afraid something would happen to it. "After I saw it, I wished something *had* happened to it," says Clarice. Mindy refused to ship the dress. She said Clarice had to go upstate. "I couldn't. I couldn't take the time off from work. I couldn't afford to make the trip twice." In the end, Clarice shortened the dress with some safety pins the morning of the wedding. "We were never really friends after that."

Then there are some brides who want to exact revenge for all the wedding presents they've given, all the bridesmaids' dresses they've bought. "I want to make them pay," says Janet of her bridesmaids-to-be. She claims to have spent over $1,000 on bridesmaids' dresses for other people's weddings, and she is approaching her upcoming wedding with a wicked glee for evening the score. You don't need me to tell you that this is ugly, ugly, ugly. If you've got some kind of evil agenda, even if you think it's funny, trash it. There's plenty of real tension associated with weddings. Don't manufacture more.

PHASE

2

. . . .

Nuts and Bolts

*P*icture yourself in a swirling montage from a '50s movie. You at the dress shop in the perfect, simple gown. (Because you look so good in it, the store owner has decided to give it to you, even though it's $5,000!) You surrounded by the heady scent of freesia, flipping through pictures of bouquets while the florist sits patiently at your service. You tasting tiny forkfuls of salmon and truffles (clearing your palate with champagne), nodding approvingly to an anxious chef.

Hey, I've heard it's healthy to have a rich fantasy life.

But soon enough, the issue of money rears its ugly head and in many cases, puts a damper on your little daydream. Money. If you have a lot, you can make plans with freedom. If you don't, your choices are strongly determined by that fact. A prerequisite for doing a wedding your way is opening up your mind so that you're not restricted by traditional wedding options. Because if you are, you might end up "wanting" things that are outrageous and unreasonable and that you simply cannot afford. Stop thinking about it as a wedding for a minute and start thinking about it as a very special party. If you do that, all kinds of possibilities open themselves up to you.

Whether you're going offbeat or traditional, putting together a wedding reception is a massive job. And unless you have lots of free time, it can be utterly overwhelming. Even the most conscientious among us can become B-level employees while making wedding plans. When I was planning my wedding, making so many calls from work, my boss called over the wall partition one day, "How's that story about honeymooning in Maine coming?" Gulp.

Planning eats up a huge amount of time. I think that's why some people are not excited by it. "C'est moi!" some of you are saying. Well, maybe you have the option of being a guest at your own wedding. If your mother (or *his* mother) would be thrilled to set up the details, and you don't really care whether the bridesmaids' bouquets contain sweet peas or lily of the valley, leave it up to her. But Jan, who let her parents make a lot of the choices for her wedding, strongly suggests that you maintain veto power: "I nixed the crepe man and the flaming desserts."

If you *are* handling the plans, steel yourself; you're about to deal with some of the pushiest, most offensive people you'll ever encounter (no, I'm not including your mother-in-law). Florists, caterers, wedding photographers and their cohorts have a well-earned reputation for being rude and intimidating. They prey on the vulnerable. They push your buttons, and if that doesn't work, they push your parents' buttons. They are expert manipulators and you, caught up in the magic of the occasion, are like a hunk of Play-Doh.

They ply you with lines like, "You only get married once . . ." and "*This* is the way it's done." They try to convince you to spend more money than you have and to agree to arrangements you don't want. Their modus operandi is to act the expert and treat you like a know-nothing piece of dirt.

The thing is, these vendors are working for you. And the economy is not in such great shape; they need your business. Be prepared to bargain and, if necessary, to walk away. Don't be afraid to be tough. You might find some vendors considerably more accommodating than you expected. Lots of people I spoke with were very firm with vendors about their price limitations, and with a little compromising, they got what they wanted.

The best way to find vendors who do good work is through word of mouth. But be careful where you get your referrals. My grandfather loved every restaurant he ever went to. ("Steaks this thick, and all the bread and butter you can eat!") You might get better advice from a slightly tougher critic. And then there's the matter of taste. If a coworker who looks like she just walked off the set of *Dancing with the Stars* recommends a florist, well, think twice before pursuing it. There's a good chance you two don't have the same taste in flower arrangements either.

Of course, you could avoid the industry altogether. If you have certain priorities (you want to do something totally unique, you have no money to spend, you absolutely can't stand the thought of going the conventional route), there are lots of alternatives in these next chapters.

No matter who you're dealing with, get contracts. Odds and ends can add up, and then verbal estimates go out the window. Asking for a contract that includes the what, when, where and how much is not unreasonable. If a vendor acts like it's simply not done, say something equally patronizing, like, "Indulge me. I'm crazy. I need a contract."

Getting Organized

You'll need to create a spreadsheet and also get on Pinterest, where you can pin up ideas and looks you like. And for equal measure, you can go the old-fashioned way and get a binder, a three-hole punch (so you can add magazine pages, menus, the napkin that you doodled your dream dress on) and a shoebox for whatever you can't punch holes in and stick in the binder. There. That was easy. Now look at those To Do lists in bridal magazines and on websites and edit out all the ridiculousness ("Shop for Your Personal Trousseau . . . Consult a Men's Formalwear Specialist"). Take what's left, and you have the beginning of your earthbound To Do list.

Pay Up

The Better Business Bureau recommends that you use credit cards when you can, because they offer you protection in case something goes wrong. Also, credit cards buy you a little time in which to discover a problem. The BBB also says to try to pay as little as possible for deposits. Nice sentiment, but some vendors are not into negotiating about deposits. Go for it anyway. What have you got to lose? Their friendship?

When you call references (and you should call them), ask if they have any suggestions about doing business with that particular company. This is a good way to prompt people to remember any difficulties they might have encountered. Make sure you get a receipt whenever you leave a deposit. And, of course, check companies with your local Better Business Bureau.

Never Say "Wedding": Getting the Best Price

I know you're excited. I know you're blushing and bursting to tell. Well, I hope you find it really, really satisfying, because it's likely to cost you a bundle. If you can keep your mouth shut (and if you're going in person, take off any telling jewelry) you'll do much better financially. Don't say "wedding" anything when you're shopping. This is a signal that you are ready to spend too much. Simply don't tell them. They're not going to make the cake less tasty or the flowers less beautiful because they didn't know they were for a wedding. (Look for the "Never Say 'Wedding'" heading throughout this section for truly excellent money-saving advice.)

On Your Mark

Okay, prepare to start a second job as wedding planner (yes, it's also full-time, but at least it's temporary), and don't let the magnitude of the event make you too tense. "I'm a producer," says Alexa. "And I must say, my wedding was the most stressful job I ever produced, because I was the one who had something to lose if it didn't work out, not some client who I never had to see again."

This part—the planning—lasts way longer than the wedding, so I suggest you start having fun now. Really, you can't just be a bundle of stress for months and then expect to relax and glow because the calendar says to. It doesn't work that way. Now's the time to run those silly clichés through your head: "This is my wedding. It will only happen once. It's happening now." So, don't let the bastards wear you down. Be happy while you're being savvy and tough. Be light and full of joy as you haggle with an over-priced caterer. Be in the moment as you demand your deposit back from the sleazy photographer you just saw exposed on the local news. This is your day, as everyone is so fond of saying. Make it last for a few months.

Putting Together a Guest List

—And Other Forms of Medieval Torture—

*I*n the old days when a couple got married, the whole community came out to celebrate in the town square, bearing gifts (a mule, a shovel) for the happy seventeen-year-olds. Of course, the town square didn't charge by the head.

Coming up with a guest list can be one of the most trying activities you and your boyfriend will ever endure, and yes, you will endure it. It's truly every man for himself here. You against him against your parents against his parents. It throws you all into competition and brings out that ever-flattering trait, pettiness. Don't start with your Facebook friends. That's where you might begin if you were making a list of everyone you ever knew and sort of liked. No, you have to begin with some ground rules. Numbers, money, parents' needs. Deal with all that in advance. If making your fantasy guest list is fun for you, go for it. But then just delete it, or put a copy of it in the box where you keep letters from old boyfriends. Because whether you want a tiny group or a huge one, you're going to have to make compromises, and your Dream List will only make it harder for you to be flexible.

Early on, you'll have to sit down and say, "Okay, no camp friends. Nobody I haven't talked to in more than two years. Nobody I hate and have been pretending to like since college. No friends from the new job I started only five months ago." The more overarching rules you can make, the easier a first-draft list will be. (And as we all know, rules are made to be broken.)

If you and your boyfriend have been together for a long time and you have lots of friends in common, you'll probably have an easier time of it. But newer couples are coming from different places, so to speak, and each half has his or her own cast of characters. And then there are the relatives, at least your own times two, unless you're lucky enough to be marrying someone who was raised by wolves.

"My husband insisted that he simply had more friends than I did," says Jackie. "But I'd say his definition of the word *friends* is a little loose." Jackie also found that Cliff's parents were "quite insistent about inviting every couple from their town. I was trying to keep it small, and he just wasn't. Finally I decided I had to play by his rules or I would be miserable." They agreed to each invite exactly the same number of people, so Cliff's parents' list became part of his own, and Jackie could invite friends and relatives she wouldn't have included in her small dream wedding.

Your Folks' Folks

Touchy situation #432: dealing with your parents' guest list. To what degree your parents will dictate who's invited depends on a whole slew of personal factors—who they are, who you are, who you are in relation to who they are—and the not-so-personal matter of their financial contribution. The best advice is the same old advice: communicate. It won't always help, but it's the only thing that might. If you'd prefer to keep the wedding smaller than, say, the Democratic National Convention, talk about it early. Get your parents (and his parents) thinking along the lines of a limited guest list. I'm telling you now, though, even the coolest parents can be surprisingly inflexible about excluding friends and relatives from their kid's wedding.

"I never expected my mother to be that way," says Sarah. "She's usually not like other people's mothers." But when it came time to make the guest list for Sarah's wedding, her mother insisted on relatives Sarah would not have considered and friends Sarah had met maybe three times. "She said she'd pay for them, but that wasn't even the point." The point was, Sarah hoped to be surrounded by a medium-size group of people she knew and loved on her wedding day, not a throng peppered with almost-strangers.

This is one of the tougher issues you'll face. A lot of brides and grooms give in here, because fighting their parents would cast a perpetual pall over the event. Or because their parents are largely financing the wedding. If that's the case, you can't exactly get away with "I want, I want, I want." If they're throwing the wedding for you, your parents will probably have a lot to say about who's invited. If you and your boyfriend are paying for everything yourselves, it might be mostly up to you. And if there's a mix of financial sources, well, let the games begin!

Lindsay and Vinnie were completely dependent upon their parents for their wedding budget. Lindsay's parents offered to pay for 120 guests. Vinnie's said they would cover a hundred. That's how the guest-list split was supposed to be too. "But Vinnie reached a hundred and his parents kept adding people—a couple here, a family there," says Lindsay. "He didn't seem to understand that we had a limit. And we didn't have the money to cover it."

Lindsay almost had a nervous breakdown trying (and failing) to convince Vinnie to explain to his parents that more guests meant more money.

Great-Aunt Lavinia
(or, Who's Not Going to Make the Cut?)

Even if you're planning on having a biggish wedding, you won't be able to invite everyone. And among the people in your outer circle will be a few who will make the incorrect assumption that they're invited.

Marie feels like she was forced into her guest list by circumstances. She works at a magazine with a small, tightly knit staff. Everyone there expected to be invited. "People were actually coming up to me and asking if they were. They wouldn't have done that if they didn't think it was a given."

With the seventy relatives (on her side) that she "had to" invite ("that wasn't even worth discussing"), she had room for about twenty of her friends. "So most of them were from work, because I just had no choice," says Marie. "I didn't invite a couple of outside friends I really wanted to have, just because I thought they would be less offended than other people if they weren't invited." Marie lost one of those outside friends for good. "She blew me off every time I ran into her after that, and now we don't even speak."

To this day, my mother's aunt (by marriage) Lavinia says that "Fran's kids are very rude" for not inviting her to our weddings. She doesn't know our names because she hasn't seen us in twenty years, except at funerals, and her connection to the family—her husband, my mother's uncle—died long ago. I can live with Lavinia being mad at me, especially because she could never pick me out of a crowd and is just as likely to confuse me with one of my unmarried sisters at the next funeral we all attend.

"When I was best man for my friend Cal, I got a phone call from the mother of a guy we both went to high school with, Tom," says Mitch. Tom had not received an invitation to Cal's wedding, but was sure that was a mistake. His mother was afraid that Cal had sent Tom's invitation to her house and that she'd lost it. "I had to tell her, 'No, you didn't lose the invitation. Tom isn't invited.'" Cal's wedding was huge and completely financed by his wife's family. The only limitations on his guest list were his own. "He took his wedding as an opportunity to examine under a microscope every friendship he'd ever had," says Mitch. "He got a kick out of determining who 'deserved' to be invited. Tom, who once was a really close friend, didn't make the cut." Of course, Cal felt like a jerk when he heard about Tom, but it was much too late to do anything about it.

It's easy to lose perspective and forget who you are—a friend, a cousin, a coworker—and fall under the illusion that you are, in fact, someone else—a pragmatic party planner, an unfeeling automaton, a princess. I'm not talking about general rules that help you arrive at the number of guests you can accommodate. No, this is about that one friend you had to cut to stick to your number. When you hear yourself rationalizing about leaving out one person, take a minute and step back. It's natural and normal to get a little businesslike about this. You are, after all, the producer of a one-night-only extravaganza. And we all get some perverse pleasure out of making the rules and then trying to adhere to them ("I absolutely cannot invite more than twenty-two friends"). But if you take a minute to envision yourself not as a bride-to-be, but as the person you were the other twenty- or thirty-odd years of your life (and that you will be right after the cake is cut), you'll realize that maybe it's just not worth hurting someone's feelings. It sounds so corny, but when I asked people if they had any regrets about their weddings, the first thing many of them said was, "There's someone I wish I'd invited."

Kevin and Gabi worked hard to stick to a set number of guests, because they were paying for everything themselves and had very little money to begin with. "There were a couple of people I wanted to invite and who I knew in my heart would be hurt if they weren't invited," says Kevin. "And yes, they were hurt and no, they're not my friends anymore. My advice is, if there are two or three people who are on the fence, invite them."

Libby represents the other side of this coin: "You're going to offend *someone,* so you might as well just invite the friends you really like. Don't invite someone out of guilt; they're just thinking about themselves, not you, anyway." That may be true, but isn't there a chance that the offended person just feels close to you and wants to see you get married? Even if you're the type who doesn't take it personally when she's left out, remember that some people are more sensitive to being excluded. You know who they are. At least take the time to call or e-mail them and explain that the wedding is going to be very small (so you have to lie a little), and that's why you couldn't invite them. This is really difficult, but it's worthwhile if you don't want to spend the rest of your life ducking into doorways when you see these friends heading toward you on the street.

"You and a Guest ..."

Touchy situation #433: evaluating your friends' primary relationships and determining, in your infinite wisdom, which are "serious enough" to warrant an invitation for a companion. It is impossible to make this easy unless every one of your friends is either married (yes, you do have to invite their spouses) or extremely single. You are bound to find many somewhere in between. As usual, the easiest solution—to invite everyone with a guest—is also the most expensive. But Regina and Ted thought it was worth it. "We gave everyone the option, just because we thought our friends are old enough that they might feel uncomfortable alone," says Regina. "But a lot of people chose to come by themselves."

Bonnie and Martin made a request, then left it up to their guests to be courteous. Determined to keep their wedding small, they asked friends not to bring a date if they were not married or involved in a serious relationship. "Well, some people fought that," says Bonnie. "One relative said she had to bring a friend because it was too far for her to drive alone. A friend of my husband's said if she couldn't bring someone, she would need a ride and asked the groom to pick her up himself!" There was also a couple who wanted to bring their two grown children, who Bonnie and Martin had met once. "We said no, nicely, the first time they asked." But the persistent guests called three more times to see if, by some chance, the bride and groom had changed their minds. "So finally I caved in and said yes," says Bonnie, "and then ultimately they decided not to come."

Lindsay had sworn to herself long before that when she got married, she'd invite everyone with a guest, because she hates being invited to weddings alone. "But when it came right down to it," she says, "I couldn't afford it." So she used her judgment and tried not to step on any toes. When her cousin sent back his reply card with "will not attend" checked off, Lindsay's mother was upset to learn that it was because he couldn't bring a date. The cousin's whole immediate family would be there; he'd have plenty of people to hang out with. "Frankly, if that's the way he felt, I didn't want him to come," says Lindsay. "But my mother did, so she called him and told him he could bring his girlfriend." Lindsay let her mother handle most of the family guest list issues that cropped up. "She cared about it, so she dealt with it."

The Nerve!

As Rochelle and Danny sorted through their reply cards, they came across one from Rochelle's second cousin Gladys, who Rochelle had met exactly once. The card read, "We will be delighted to attend your wedding." (So far okay.) "By we, I mean me, my husband, Frank; my daughter, Sadie; and her boyfriend, Byron." Is this some new strain of dyslexia? Mistaking a singular (as in "you") for a plural (as in Frank, Sadie and Byron)? Or is the family such a tight, cohesive unit that Gladys simply thinks of them as one? Or perhaps it's simply what it seems to be: a case of record-breaking audacity. Someone call the *Guinness Book* people!

Reply Cards and the B-List

"Nick's friends had no clue that they had to RSVP, and that if they said they were coming, they had to come," says Marie. Even the people who do have a clue are terrible about getting those little cards back to you. Could it be any easier? It's stamped, addressed and practically filled out for you. But it's one of those things that goes into someone's bag only to be discovered a month later, crushed under the weight of sweaty sneakers and stuck to itself with a melted piece of Orbit gum.

Once the reply cards do find their way back to you, you're

faced with that dilemma: To B-list, or not to B-list? Not sure you know how to B-list? Here's how it goes. You send your invitations out good and early. Then, if you get enough refusals, you invite a small batch of satellite friends you didn't have room for on the original list. Can you see where this might lead to trouble? I think B-list people always know they're B-list. If you can live with that, okay. In a perfect world, we would be able to be honest about it. We could say to someone, "Listen, B-lister, I'd like to invite you to my wedding. I wanted to ask you in the first place, but I couldn't because of space limitations." And the B-lister would say, "That's cool. Love to."

The magazines and online experts will tell you that you can count on a 20 percent refusal rate if you invite more than 150 guests, but, as Ilene can attest, nothing is for sure. "We didn't get one negative RSVP," says Ilene. "Not one. That's the way my family is. We're a bunch of nuts. There's a faction that lives in Michigan, and they all came [to New Jersey]. If anybody hadn't come, it would have been a big scandal. That's all everyone would have been talking about all day long. I mean, my grandmother's cousin had to be invited to this wedding." So don't take a chance on over-inviting based on the statistical promises of some random wedding blog. You too might be "blessed" with such a devoted group of family and friends.

What's the Matter with Kids?

My future husband and I watched as our friend's young nieces and nephews took over her wedding. We are major kid lovers, but we were in total agreement about not inviting kids to our upcoming nuptials. "The last thing I wanted was to play ring-around-the-rosie with a little boy and girl at my reception," he says. Then my friend's four-year-old daughter became intrigued with the occasion. She asked about it every time I saw her, and absolutely lit up at the mention. One day she started to describe what she was going to wear, and her mother interrupted to tell her she wouldn't be going. Before she had a chance to explain, I changed my mind; I decided that she had to be invited. Suddenly it didn't make sense to exclude people I loved from the celebration just because they were little.

But there's no denying that kids change the dynamics of a wedding. And certain locations where breakable objects are part of the decor are just not child-friendly. If you decide against having kids (at your wedding, I mean), make it very clear to anyone who might misunderstand. Some people don't go anywhere without their kids. And a nursing mother might assume you know that where she goes, the baby goes. It might be worthwhile to call parents. Keep in mind you may be tempted to e-mail, but a call might be better since tone isn't always clear via e-mail.

Jennifer invited her cousin with his wife. The reply card came back saying that he, his wife and their six-year-old daughter would be glad to attend. Jennifer couldn't let it go because there were at least seven other little kids she had pointedly not invited. "I called to explain, and luckily he was very nice about it. But it took me three days to work up the nerve."

Karl has a cosmic attitude about children at a wedding. "I'm all for it. I mean, if they're part of the family, absolutely. Having three or four generations at your wedding puts a lot of stuff in perspective." Kids keep you from taking yourself too seriously, which can be nice on such an intense day. They force a little bit of real life into even the most magical situation. Maybe that's not what you have in mind—infusing the day with a sense of reality. That might be your perfectly valid reason for keeping kids out.

If they're going to be there, though, you'll be best off if you do a little extra planning. Eva wanted to make sure the five little kids at her wedding were occupied and having fun, so she made goodie bags for each of them. "They got bubbles, a little car and a slinky. It gave them something to do at the reception before the dancing began." Lois prepared little baskets full of flower petals for the kids to throw (when cued) at the bride and groom. She enlisted the help of a calm parent, who handed out the baskets and explained to the kids what to do. "I remember doing that at a wedding when I was nine years old," says Lois. "I think kids never forget being included."

Some brides and grooms hire a baby-sitter to occupy the kids; that seems excessive to me unless you're really trying to keep them away from the party. Otherwise, parents should be okay to take care of them. One child-loving guest told me he got more than he bargained for at a recent family wedding. Jeff was having fun doing magic tricks for his six-year-old nephew. Then people started bringing kids over to him, dropping them off while they went to dance or get a drink. "I became the house baby-sitter," he says. "For a while I didn't mind, but I don't understand why people brought their kids to the wedding if they didn't want to hang out with them."

If it's not a major hassle, you might want to think about feeding the kids their dessert a little early. In my extensive wedding-going experience, immediately precake is when some four- to eight-year-olds simply lose it. They're cranky, they're tired, they want their cake. They don't want to *look* at their cake for a number of hours, *hear* that it's time for cake, *see* the lady in the big white dress cut the cake, and watch as their cake disappears into the abyss to be sliced. Dessert right after dinner might make sense. A nice boxed cake from the supermarket would do you fine.

Occasionally children (a.k.a. "practiced germ and infection transmitters") can be a last-minute hazard. Charlotte got a call at seven A.M. the morning of her wedding. "Polly, my husband's nine-year-old sister, our flower girl, had chicken pox." So she called all the people who were bringing babies to the wedding, along with the two pregnant women (that she knew of) to warn them. "Polly couldn't be kept home. It wouldn't have been fair." The little girl fought hard not to scratch as she headed down the aisle, and spent the rest of the wedding being escorted from empty corner to empty corner like a leper.

Location, Location, Location

*H*ave you had the dream yet where you're at your wedding and it's in this big old stone castle, and it's freezing cold and there are no tables or chairs, just musty ledges that people have to lean on and, oddly enough, an indoor pool half full of fetid water? And you're huddling for warmth with your third-grade teacher (it's a dream), shooing away the bats, and you think to yourself, I should have just gone with that reception hall. Have you had that one yet?

It's scary to try to do something different. Booking a place for your wedding that's not specifically built for weddings means more work for you. But don't be pressured into thinking that halls or restaurants where weddings take place every weekend are inherently better than other spaces. What they are mostly is more convenient. Reception halls are well-oiled wedding machines, places where a staff can iron out all the details for you. But you can take a different route if you want to; all you have to be is smart, resourceful and determined.

Start with your dream (not the one about the castle, your fantasy). What do you envision? Some people see a lush green meadow with picnic tables, baskets of fried chicken and guests who look like they stepped out of an F. Scott Fitzgerald novel. Some picture a gazebo outside a quaint Victorian inn or a secluded beach house at sunset. Some imagine a chandelier-lit ballroom.

Don't fight it. Just know that you'll have to compromise. When you start looking around, you'll discover that finding a location is the toughest practical wedding-arranging task. Dream locations can easily consume your whole budget. So try to find something that *resembles* what you had in mind, and go from there.

The Great Outdoors

The reason outdoor weddings are so cool is the same reason they can be a disaster. There's an element of danger to the weather. It's exciting. And when you wake up on your wedding day and the sun is shining brightly, you really do feel like the gods are smiling down upon your union. But once you've attended a rainy or unseasonably cold outdoor affair, you start to think it's not worth the risk.

Kelly says to check the *Farmer's Almanac* before scheduling an outdoor wedding. It was accurate once, and that was enough for her. (Maybe you should look into your crystal ball or flip a coin. Or hang rosary beads on the door. I hear that works too.) And even though hers worked out well, she doesn't recommend an outdoor wedding. "It's just too much to worry about." The very real possibility of bad weather means being prepared for wet or muddy ground (do you want to put down a floor?). And a tent, much as its name conjures an image of something you can roll up and carry on your back, is not cheap.

Decide What's Important

Okay, let's get a little more real now. In terms of location, what matters most to you? Ambience? Views? Glamour? Are you looking for the absolute best price and willing to make all the arrangements yourself? Or would you rather spend more and do less? When Brian and Melanie first started planning, they didn't take into account their schedules and personalities. They both work twelve-hour days and six-day weeks. "We looked at a few empty loft spaces where you had to hire everyone yourself," says Melanie. "I wondered when we would possibly have time to hunt for a caterer, a florist, a band. We don't even have time to make dinner." The job just seemed too big, and suddenly Melanie wasn't looking forward to it. "We realized that we're the types who would rather go to a place where they make all the arrangements for you." They ended up at a more conventional wedding location that was affiliated with all the necessary vendors, and were able to relax because they didn't have to do any footwork.

Priority: A Place That "Calls Your Name"

When they first started shopping for a location, Joanne and Evan tried to go the traditional route. "We looked at country clubs and reception halls, and they just didn't seem like us," says Joanne. At a hotel they visited, on Joanne's mother's suggestion, the "wedding pimp" took them outside, where the pool was, and said, "Lots of people like a Hawaiian theme out here." Yikes! They gave up on conventional locales, and actually stopped looking altogether for a little while. "We wanted to find a place that called our names." And they did—a restaurant in an old renovated barn. "It was so down-to-earth and normal, it felt like it was ours." The place had never been used for a wedding before, but Joanne wasn't worried about that. "In fact, it made the whole thing very cheap, because I think the owners didn't realize what other places charge for weddings."

"I wanted to have my wedding someplace different," says Regina, "so I called every interesting place in Philadelphia that I could think of—the zoo, the academy of music, all the museums." She discovered that you can have a wedding almost anywhere. "I think these places are always desperate for money. That's why they're available for parties." She and Ted chose the Franklin Institute, a science museum. The reception was held in a huge rotunda. "A couple of exhibits were left open for our guests, like a heart you could walk through, and some interactive electricity exhibits." The band was set up just to the left of a giant statue of Ben Franklin. The museum had only one caterer it would allow through the door, so that was easily settled. The Franklin Institute was just what Regina had wanted—a place that was specifically hers and Ted's, where they'd never been to a wedding before, and probably never would be again. "And we can go visit it anytime we want."

Margaret was waiting for some kind of "sign" that she had found her wedding locale. When she and her boyfriend, Jake, traveled from their home in Chicago to Montana to visit Jake's daughter, they stumbled upon an inn built in the 1920s. As soon as they walked in, Margaret said, "This is where we're going to have our wedding." An agreeable Jake said, "Okay," in spite of the fact that it was a plane ride from where they or any of their friends lived. This inn, which Margaret had never visited before, was something she had pictured almost exactly in her head—the dark wood, the firelight, the snow drifts up to the windows. (Hey, didn't I see this story on *Unsolved Mysteries*?) "I knew my sister and her family wouldn't have been able to make the wedding if we had it in Chicago," says Margaret, "so I had pretty much given up on their being there, till I found the inn." It was about a half-day's drive from where her sister lived, and most of the other thirty guests were excited about the trip. Margaret was so utterly satisfied with her wedding, I don't think she had one regret to contribute to this book. Her advice is, take your time when you're searching for the perfect place. You'll find what you're looking for eventually.

Priority: A Grand Setting

Scott and Lia weren't sticklers about the food or the flowers or even what they wore. But they wanted a really nice location for their evening wedding. Just before they signed a contract with a space they weren't thrilled with (but was within their budget), they went to check out a lavish hotel, just for the hell of it. They knew the price-per-head range because a friend had had her wedding there two years earlier. It was much more than they could afford. "We were laughing when we went in, because we knew they'd think we were out of our minds," says Lia. But before the wedding coordinator could start his spiel, she told him, "This is what we can spend. Can you do anything for us?" The wedding coordinator didn't miss a beat. "We can work with that," he said. Scott and Lia made a couple of compromises—only cold hors d'oeuvres, and a limited choice of entrée (chicken or chicken), but they got the fabulousness of the space.

Celia and Peter wanted a magnificent setting for their wedding. Because they chose to have a cocktail reception and not serve dinner, they were able to afford a more expensive location with great views. "It was about half per head what the place charges for a full meal," says Celia. "If you care a lot about the atmosphere, think of where you can cut back so you can put more of your budget toward location," she suggests. She and Peter went for recorded music, and they also brought their own cake.

If you're paying for a great space, you should certainly take full advantage of its best features. But some plans require a test run. Erin and Ken's wedding was in a daylight photo studio known for its view. The ceremony was scheduled so that its backdrop would be a magnificent, unobstructed sunset. The problem was, the sunset on that clear day was extremely bright, and looking into it, the guests were practically blinded. Another thing, when people are backlit, they become silhouettes. That was the effect on this particular bride and groom. "Nobody could see our faces," says Erin. "The photographer did the best she could, but none of her pictures of the ceremony came out."

Priority: Scrumptious Food

Molly and Jeff chose the restaurant they did for the food. "We've had some pretty awful meals at weddings," says Jeff, "and we wanted the food at ours to be great." They ended up at a hundred-year-old steak house where there are lots of parties, but not a lot of weddings. The price per head was lower than more wedding-y places, and the feel was very Old New York. "The atmosphere couldn't have been better. We didn't want the mood to be like every reception-hall wedding we'd ever attended." And guests raved about the food.

Priority: Cheap-osity

Location is probably the toughest element to take care of for next to nothing, especially in cities, where space is at a premium. You're not going to find what you need by doing a general Google search. The key is networking and persistence—ask anyone and everyone for leads. Be resourceful and creative about what's available. Don't be put off by a space that's unadorned. A great iTunes playlist, some strong speakers and a hundred votive candles can make anyplace seem ambient. And full of people, it could be great. As my mother says, "as long as it's clean." There are a couple of other necessities, though: a kitchen, or at the very least a refrigerator and a sink; bathrooms; easy access for older people or people who are physically challenged; and sufficient power for the sound system you plan to use.

I was sure we couldn't have a wedding at all, because there was just no location we could come close to affording. We'd been to an outdoor wedding that was on the grounds of this old estate about thirty minutes from where we lived. When my husband called to ask the couple about it, we discovered that the place cost them $360. It was actually a public park, owned by the town. We had to do a little truth-exaggerating to book it for our wedding (it was supposed to be used only by residents of that town). But one phone call, and it was ours. During the reception, a town resident was having a game of catch with his daughter nearby, and a few little kids (including our tiniest wedding guests) were enjoying the monkey bars and sandbox. It was, after all, public property. But the trees were outrageous—a hundred years old and gigantic. It was the perfect place for a wedding. We really lucked out. I never would have even asked about the place; it seemed like it must be expensive because it was so beautiful.

Charlotte and Billy had their reception at the firehouse in Billy's hometown, a big, plain space they could use for free. (If you get a free space, you have a karmic obligation to do volunteer work for about three years.) They decorated with painted tablecloths, wildflowers and dozens of helium balloons (they rented a tank), which streamed ribbons from ceiling to floor. "I was worried about the low ceilings and the fact that it was kind of dark," says Charlotte, "but I couldn't believe how great it turned out with just a few hours of work."

Alexa and Joel weren't sure where to begin looking for a space. They had just moved to California and had no network to tap into. "And we'd decided that we'd rather spend our money on a good party than on a special place," says Alexa, so they didn't have a big location budget. She called to order a book that listed local wedding sites. While chatting with the sales rep who answered the phone, Alexa mentioned how much she was planning to spend and asked if the book listed spaces in that price range. Says Alexa, "After he stopped laughing, he said, 'Well, there are only four or five places, so let me just read them to you.' He probably figured I couldn't afford the book." None of the places he recommended were big enough. With very few local contacts, Alexa decided to try working backward. "My friend referred me to this very reasonable caterer, who I immediately hit it off with. And the caterer told me about a couple of places in our price range." It makes sense. Local wedding-industry people have dealt with lots of different locations. So if you're at a loss for referrals, tap into that resource.

Ugly Details

When you throw a big party and you're the "magic maker" for a slew of guests, you have to consider every element. Ensuring that things don't go wrong is so much more important than adding a lot of right things. If your reception is at a wedding-type joint that's used to making a large number of people comfortable, don't worry. You've paid away this particular brand of anxiety.

We had 122 people at a place with exactly two bathrooms. Not two restaurant-type bathrooms with lots of stalls and mirrors and a couch. Two *toilets*. Sounds like that would have been a bit of a problem, right? Well, it was. Especially because the bathrooms were right off the very tight area where the tables were set up. So the line for the women's room kind of wound through the seated guests. It was lovely. The obvious solution would have been a couple of Portosans, because the wedding was largely outside and the weather was warm. We didn't think of it. (The three times we'd visited the space, there were *plenty* of bathrooms for the two of us.) If you end up with a place that has two ordinary homestyle bathrooms and Portosans are not an option (i.e., it's wintertime, there's no place to hide them outside), there's one thing you can do to alleviate the problem a little. Cover the signs that say "Women" and "Men" with something that simply says "Bathroom," or if you're feeling genteel, "Lounge." This will at least siphon some women into what would otherwise be the underutilized men's room. Beyond that, I can only recommend a cash bar.

Then there's parking, the bane of every city dweller's existence. If there's a parking lot, you're all set. But if your wedding is at, say, a private home, you need to figure something out. (Did you ever see the remake of *Father of the Bride?*)

John's wedding was at his mother's house. "You can't find parking in that neighborhood even if you live there," he says. So he made a deal with a hardware store owner about a block away. "I basically rented his parking lot for the day." It was big enough for forty cars, so it could easily accommodate the seventy-five guests who were expected. Ideally, you make these kinds of arrangements so far in advance that you're able to include a little note detailing them with the invitation. If you don't think of it till later, that just means you need to enlist someone to stand outside and keep an eye out for well-dressed people who are cursing and circling the block slowly.

One more thing. Make sure there will be someone at your reception site who can accept deliveries the day before or the morning of your wedding. Karl's mother tried to deliver her homemade wedding cake the morning of Karl and Crystal's wedding. "It was early September, and she was worried about the heat later in the day. She wanted to get that cake in the refrigerator," says Karl. She arrived at the restaurant at ten A.M., and at ten thirty she was still outside, trying to shade the buttercream frosting with her body. "We were told that someone would be there at ten, but I never confirmed that." When an assistant manager moseyed up to the door at ten forty-five, he was surprised to find someone waiting for him, almost in tears. "I guess the opening time is a little casual," says Karl. "I should have called to firm up the plan."

Joni had a similar, but more expensive, experience. It never occurred to her to call and confirm that someone would be at her reception site. "The groundskeeper was there every weekday. But the day before my wedding, he was someplace else." A truck from the party rental company showed up to drop off the tables, chairs, silverware and glasses, but nobody was home, and all the doors were locked. Joni had to pay a hefty fee for inconveniencing the delivery people, who had to leave and come back early the next day.

So Far Away

—Long-Distance Planning—

*Y*ou are here. Your wedding is there. What do you do? Well, for starters, you loosen your grip on the reins. When you're planning from far away, you have to either know exactly what you want (and be able to convey that by phone, e-mail or text), have a reliable rep in town (in the form of a parent) or not care too much about the details.

Paul and Krista cared a lot. From Chicago, they arranged every single aspect of their Iowa wedding. "Our phone bill was astronomical," says Paul. But because he knew just about all the vendors in his small hometown where the wedding was to take place, he wanted to be involved in the process. "And if I had let my mother make decisions for us, it would have put me right between her and Krista. I would never do that to myself on purpose." The couple had a year-and-a-half engagement. Their wedding plans started immediately and continued right up to the day of their wedding. "It was exhausting, because we were so far away. We were sending drawings back and forth to the florist, renting all the

tuxes ourselves in Chicago so they would match exactly and becoming obsessed with all these ridiculous details, like napkin
rings." Paul says you really can't be that way when you're planning
long-distance. "It made us crazy. Maybe if we'd done it in five or
six months, it wouldn't have been so bad." But by the time the
actual wedding happened, both were wiped out and kind of dis-
enchanted (not with each other, with the event). If losing control
is something you have nightmares about, arranging your wedding
from a long distance is going to be tough for you.

George's mother planned and paid for his and Erika's wedding.
The couple lived in New York and the mother in Minneapolis. As
Erika watched, relatively passively, from a thousand miles away,
she began to notice similarities between their wedding and
George's sister's wedding two years before. "It occurred to me one
day," she says, "that I was having Jennifer's wedding." It was at the
same place with the same band and the same photographer. Says
Erika, "But then I was like, Do *I* know a photographer? No. Do *I*
live in Minneapolis? No. Do *I* have time to haggle and never pay
retail? No. So who am I to say?" George's mother is a classy broad,
so it wasn't hard for Erika to trust her with the details. "She has
better taste than I do," says Erika, "and I had never thrown a party
before where there wasn't a keg."

Sometimes being out of town means there are tensions you're
too far away to buff. A blessing? Perhaps. Alice and Rick planned
their wedding from opposite coasts. She was in graduate school in
Boston; he was in law school in California. They chose to get married in North Carolina, where both their mothers lived. Basically,
Alice's mother was taking care of everything. "Rick's mother said
she wanted to be involved," says Alice, "but every time I asked her
to do something, she stabbed me in the back." One such incident
occurred when Alice suggested that Rick's mother join hers to
check out a possible location. "Instead, his mother went to see the

restaurant *without* my mother the day before they were scheduled to go." There was nothing Alice could do. "Confronting her over the phone felt stupid to me. So I let it go and just learned not to ask for her help again." But being away from the action was frustrating. "I wanted to be able to stick up for my mother. On the other hand, I know if I was in North Carolina there would have been a lot more screaming."

For Penny, a little distance was a positive thing. When she and Will were planning their Massachusetts wedding from Philadelphia, they found that the distance forced them to work efficiently. "We figured out everything from home—how much we could spend, what we wanted, what we could do if those options didn't work out—so when we went to Northampton for a weekend, we knew exactly what questions to ask," says Penny. And because having the couple in town was a special treat for Penny's mother, "there was relatively little tension. Everyone made an effort to be pleasant and work things out without letting them escalate into fights."

How Do I Look?

No matter how cool or shy or offbeat you are, what you wear to get married in is enormously important to you. It's the ultimate "what will I wear?" experience. And it's one thing you should definitely stamp your feet and flex your muscles about to have your way. Don't let anyone tell you what you *should* wear, or how you *should* look. This is your statement. You've seen it happen to your friends. They start by saying they want something simple—no beads, no appliqués, no lace. Then they go through the bridal shop wringer and come out all puffy-sleeved and glittery. "It was the plainest thing they had," they sigh. Or, "It would have been perfect without the fringe and the peplum and the sequins, but it only came this way." It's heartbreaking.

Don't let it happen to you. You don't want to be an object of pity on your big day. There are ways to find and afford what you want. First, don't be afraid to figure out what that is. A black cocktail dress? Go for it. Something long, but unusual and nonwedding-y? Great. A Cinderella ball gown? No? Are you sure?

Lots of cool women swear up and down that they don't want a conventional wedding dress, when really they sort of do. Or somewhere along the line they discover they do, and they feel a little embarrassed about it. Maybe they're afraid that going the traditional route in terms of a dress seems hypocritical when they want other parts of their weddings to be alternative. Or maybe because the symbolic element of wearing white is such a throwback, some brides get shy and think, Oh that's just not me.

But being a bride isn't "you" either. It's you for one day, or for the months it takes to plan your wedding. To some degree, you're playing a role, and for that reason, you should feel free to choose a costume, not just a dress. And anyway, it's *your* dress and *your* wedding, right?

Still, certain women feel the need to justify their choice. "At first I wanted to wear a minidress," says Marie, who was expected by her friends to show up at her wedding in something funky. But her mother convinced her to take a look at a couple of long traditional gowns. "The more I tried them on, the more I wanted one," says Marie. But she was self-conscious about what people might think. And for months she couldn't talk about her big white dress without apologizing for it.

Women look good in big white dresses. A flattering neckline, a drop waist and a huge puffy skirt can hide a multitude of sins. And since most of us haven't dressed up like a princess since childhood, we're entranced when we first see ourselves floating along in a gown, looking six inches taller and ten pounds thinner. So if your strongest urges are toward the traditional, don't fight them.

Something Borrowed

You will find, if you haven't already, that some people will offer to lend you their dresses. "Two women who weren't even close to me did," says Clarice. "One was the mother of a friend of mine—her daughter is already married and opted not to use the dress." The other was someone Clarice describes as a "friendly acquaintance," who took great pains to make clear that she wasn't presuming she'd be invited to the wedding; she was just offering her dress. "It's like these fairy godmothers come out of the woodwork."

"I think there are two types of brides," says Lia. "Those who keep their dress in a pristine state, who would never want anyone to even touch it, and those who are totally into having someone make use of it. Try to hook up with the second ones," she suggests, because some offers are just not for real. When Lia's friend Caroline said, "Wear my dress," there were too many strings attached. Says Lia, "She knew I was going to have to shorten the skirt—I'm 5'2" and she's 5'6"—and make the waist smaller, but when it came time to have the alterations done, she started saying stuff like, 'Oh, what if someday I have a daughter. I hope she grows up to be your size, so she can fit into my dress.'" No thanks. It's not worth it, no matter how pretty or pricey the dress is.

Sally borrowed a gown from her friend Lorraine. At first she was concerned about having one more person tugging at her dress sleeve with instructions and a personal agenda. But it turned out okay. "Lorraine just wanted to come with me for the alterations to make sure the dressmaker didn't do anything that she didn't agree with," says Sally. When you're dealing with someone else's property, you can't always get exactly, precisely what you want. "It was beautiful. It looked like it was made for me," says Sally. "The only thing is, if it were my dress, I would have made the neckline a little lower."

For Sentimental Reasons

If there's a dress in your family that was the height of fashion in 1962 (or, better yet, 1922), but doesn't quite cut it anymore, see if it's okay with the original or current owner (mother, aunt, cousin) if you make some changes. It's true what your grandmother always said—they don't make 'em like they used to. The workmanship and fabrics of older dresses are extraordinary compared to most of what's available today. If you're concerned about money, remodeling a dress is a very smart option. And it's kind of comforting to go into this wacky, surreal experience sporting a little piece of your personal history.

My grandmother was a seamstress, and she made my mother's wedding dress, a plain, straight silk-satin gown. After twenty-eight years rolled up in a paper bag, it had turned a sort of brownish color (other people said "champagne"), which I liked. I got a dressmaker to open up the jewel neckline to make it more flattering for me. She also made the elbow-length sleeves short and used the tiny bit of extra fabric to make the waist bigger. (My mother still had the corset, but I preferred to have the option of exhaling on my wedding day.) I never could have afforded a dress so beautiful. The alterations cost me $88.

If you're going to wear a dress that's in the family, you have to abandon your visions of the perfect, most flattering, made-for-me gown. Alterations will help make a dress more "you," but the basic shape will remain pretty much the same. Margo, dressmaker extraordinaire, says that older dresses usually have a little less fabric to play with, and it's unlikely that you can match the fabric, so major renovations are hard to do. She usually ends up adjusting the more flexible elements—neckline, length, fit—and respecting the line of the original dress.

"But if you like," Margo says, "within reason you can totally modernize a dress." Lulu brought her mother's dress to a dressmaker and asked that the skirt be split down the front, so it would open when she walked. Says Lulu, "Underneath, I wore tights that were covered with tiny pearls." She also wanted to lengthen the sleeves, but, since she couldn't match the fabric, her dressmaker took off the sleeves that were there and replaced them with sheer ivory bell sleeves. Lulu was thrilled with the results.

A Plain Gown Is Hard to Find

If everybody wants simple, unadorned wedding gowns, why don't designers make them? That might be a good topic for *The Today Show.* I don't know the answer, but I do have a suggestion. If you can't find what you want, have it made. Does that sound expensive? It's not. Some dressmakers can make your dream gown for less than you'd pay for an off-the-rack compromise.

Says Margo, "People go to dressmakers so they can get what they want. But what ends up happening is that it's also cheaper." Of course, you could spend a mint if you choose to have your dress made in an outrageously expensive fabric. But if you're up front about your budget, a dressmaker can tell you right away what your options are.

Many of the brides Margo meets are dismayed about not being able to find even one simple dress. "They come in weeping, because they've been shopping and everything's covered in sequins," she says. You can go to a dressmaker with a sketch of your own, or just a sense of what you want. But Margo doesn't recommend asking for an exact knockoff of a Carolina Herrera or a Vera Wang. "If you become obsessed with a specific dress, don't ask a dressmaker to copy it, because you're never going to be able to have it made exactly the same way." And a dressmaker won't (or shouldn't) do a dress that's completely someone else's design. "It's unethical, and it's borderline illegal."

What dressmakers are perfect for, though, is executing *your* idea. If your image is inspired by a $15,000 Christian Dior dress, that's fine, as long as you understand what you're asking for is the line, the shape, not a replica of that specific dress. The dressmaker will come up with a pattern and, with your help, choose fabric. You'll end up with a dress that is literally made for you, and of much higher quality than anything that comes out of a factory.

Stars in Your Eyes

If you choose to go the dressmaker route, you have more options than taking a neckline from this wedding dress, a sleeve from that one. You can do anything. So when you see a beautiful gown somewhere, take notes or do a sketch. Flip through fashion magazines, peruse websites and blogs, and watch lots of awards shows on TV (Jennifer Garner is always impeccably dressed). And watch some classic wedding movies. The magnificent styles of the '40s, '50s and '60s aren't available at Gowns Galore, but they could serve as inspiration for a skilled dressmaker.

As far as I'm concerned, the finest movie wedding dress of all time is Audrey Hepburn's tea-length Givenchy gown in *Funny Face*. Maybe only someone with the body of an undernourished ballerina could carry off a boatneck and cap sleeves, but the full tulle skirt would be gorgeous on anyone, and the veil is the most elegant I've ever seen—a very plain tulle hood, tacked to the dress in back near the neckline. Also great for a headpiece option is the LSD-induced wedding hallucination scene in the movie *Hair* (the 1979 film set in the '60s). For a more mainstream '60s look, watch *The Graduate,* and get a load of Katharine Ross. (If you're feeling vulnerable, I suggest you fast-forward to the wedding scene and press the mute button.)

The Un-Wedding Dress

If you're looking for a great dress that doesn't shout "Bride!" go where the princess dresses aren't. Shopping at "regular" stores introduces a bunch of new options. Visit your favorite boutique. Try that expensive dress shop you always peer longingly into on your way to work. And yes, go to department stores.

Major department stores offer personal shopper services. I always used to assume these were for rich people, but I was wrong. There's no charge, and the shoppers are happy to work within your price range. (What the store gets out of it is happy customers, and happy customers are repeat customers, *comprende?*)

Abby contacted personal shoppers at a couple of upscale department stores and described what she was looking for. She told them, "I don't want a dress that's at all traditional or formal, but it is what I'm going to get married in." The shoppers asked about color, length, size and price range. And they asked to meet her so they could see her body type and get a sense of her style. Then they started shopping for her. Are you getting this? They take *your* budget and all *your* specifications and, for no fee, they find you a handful of very "you" dresses (some of them were even on sale). Is there anything more perfect?

Abby ended up with an evening dress from Saks Fifth Avenue.

It was short and long at the same time. From the top—which was sleeveless with a scoop back—to above the knee, it was solid ivory, and beaded. Below that, all the way to the floor, it was chiffon—a little shorter in front than in the back—and some beads were scattered on the chiffon section. It was totally glamorous, just what she wanted. And it cost half what most people I spoke with spent on their wedding dresses.

Charlotte wanted something playful. "Our wedding was very casual," she says, "and we felt like we'd be more comfortable in casual clothes." She found a dress she liked at one of her favorite clothing stores. But it was black, not what she wanted. "I asked if it was made in white, and it turned out it was. They had it in white in California and Florida, but the New York stores only ordered it in black." Charlotte ordered a white one from the Florida store. It was a short party dress, with a full skirt and a crinoline covered in tiny white bows. She later dyed it pink and wore it to her brother's wedding.

Ann Marie, famed among friends for being wild and dramatic, found her dress in a local mall. She bought it for the gimmick. During the ceremony, it was strapless and pale lavender, with a shirred top and a full, long skirt. As soon as the reception officially began, Ann Marie requested a drumroll and tore away the long skirt to reveal the bottom of a strapless minidress, which she wore for the remainder of the party.

Yona sidestepped the industry but still ended up in a traditional wedding dress. "I didn't want to be one of those people who paid $5,000 for a dress," she says. So she got her bridesmaids together one day and went shopping at a factory outlet center. "We went to the Jessica McClintock outlet, and I tried on five gowns. We picked one and left." It was $75, and a size too large; the alterations ended up costing more than the dress.

Professional Discourtesy

By now you've dealt with a handful of wedding professionals, so you won't be surprised if bridal shop folk try to belittle you—or be-big you, as the case may be. Gail was told by the curt seamstress who measured her that she was a size 16, in wedding gown sizes (is that like dog years?). Now ordinarily, Gail was a 10, but how could she argue? The almighty measurement chart had spoken. "If it stopped there, it would have been just a little ego damage," Gail says. "But then she went on to add $30 to my bill for a 'large-size fee.' Not only was she blowing me up from a size 10 to a size 16, she was charging me extra for it! She made it sound like there would be fifty seamstresses slaving over this circus tent I'd have to wear."

Gail didn't walk out and tell the seamstress where she could put her "large-size fee." She didn't challenge the store's hidden-fee policy. She barely even argued. The seamstress had Gail's wedding dress *and* her deposit. When rude vendors have got you by the cojones, the only tiny revenge you can exact is in the form of bad-mouthing them to potential future customers. Nyeah.

But I don't have to tell you that if someone treats you this way *before* you've forked over any cash (the more practiced are careful to wait), you should simply leave. And don't forget to mention the fact that you'll be calling your aunt at the Better Business Bureau as soon as you get outside.

Close Call

For her alterations and her headpiece, Joanne went to a dressmaker who had been recommended by a neighborhood tailor.

But this dressmaker (who we'll call Ms. X) had what's known in elementary school as "poor work habits." Ms. X liked to live on the edge. Joanne was supposed to pick up her outfit a week before the wedding. Ms. X had had it for two months. When Joanne arrived, Ms. X said she had "a few more minutes' work to do" and would Joanne mind coming the next day. Okay, not so bad. But it happened four times. The day before she was getting married, Joanne got the dress, but not the headpiece. The morning of the wedding, Ms. X was still sewing seed pearls onto the headband.

In retrospect, Joanne wishes she'd lied to Ms. X about the date of the wedding. It all seems so obvious later, doesn't it? "I should have pushed it up a couple of weeks, just to be safe. It didn't occur to me at the time. I mean, I had been referred by someone reliable." Ah, but you need to talk to a *customer,* not just a colleague. The tailor who gave Joanne the referral never had to depend on Ms. X to have his wedding dress altered in time. Soon after her wedding, Joanne ran into Julie, a high school acquaintance, and in the course of chatting, discovered that Julie spent her wedding morning the same way Joanne did—pacing back and forth in Ms. X's shop.

Your Love-Hate Relationship With Your Dress

Okay, you bought a dress. But now you're wondering if you were hypnotized by something in the air at the store. How could you have been so hasty? You only went back to try it on eight times! Why didn't anyone stop you?

"There's a strong degree of anxiety surrounding that dress between the time you buy it and the time you put it on to walk down the aisle," says Celia. About two weeks before her wedding, she decided she hated her dress. "I never wanted to be a dowdy bride,

Never Say "Wedding"

Priscilla bought two potential wedding dresses at a sample sale, very different styles, and both a little dirty around the edges. She decided to see which dress "cleaned up better" before getting her heart set on either. "I'd heard over the years about a certain dry cleaner who was supposed to be the best in the area," she says. One night, she stopped at the renowned cleaner to find out about prices. "I've got two long gowns to be cleaned," she said. "One's strapless, one's beaded and full, and both are pale-colored silk. How much would you charge?" The answer came back quickly: "Seventy-five for the strapless, $150 for the beaded." Priscilla said thanks, and as she headed for the door, mentioned, "They're for my wedding, so I want them to be perfect." "Oh, they're wedding dresses," the manager exclaimed, practically drooling on his receipt book. "In that case, $200 for the strapless, $350 for the other."

I have to add a disclaimer here. Our friend and dressmaker expert, Margo, tells a scary story of a delicate wedding dress she made for someone and brought to a cleaner that had a sign, We Do Wedding Dresses, in the window. Well, they "did" the dress all right—when Margo went to pick it up, it was in shreds. I'm not saying you should pay three times the normal price to have your dress cleaned by some shyster, only that you should get a couple of very solid references before you hand your dress over to anyone. Priscilla's neighborhood cleaner took care of hers for $65 a pop, and all was well. (She wore the beaded.)

and for me the dress didn't feel sexy enough. My fear was that it was too boxy, or just too plain. I wanted to do something rebellious, and suddenly it didn't feel rebellious enough." So she went shopping again. She knew she couldn't return her dress; it had been altered. But as she frantically riffled through rack after rack, she resolved to sell the hated dress. It didn't cost her that much, she reasoned. She would post an ad on Craigslist the next day. Celia's plan lasted one afternoon. She called her sisters, who came over, took a fresh look at the dress and convinced Celia that it had plenty of sizzle.

Before she went shopping, Alexa imagined herself in anything but a traditional wedding gown. But she's one of those people who wandered into a bridal store, tried on a Cinderella dress on a lark, and loved what she saw. "I didn't want a big white dress. I was just looking," says Alexa. But she kept finding herself back in the store. And after she became the proud owner of the large shiny object, she grew terrified of it. "I couldn't believe I'd bought it. I was so scared to wear the thing. What was I thinking?" It became an ongoing prewedding joke for her, hating her dress. "I guess I was a little embarrassed about wanting to play princess at age thirty-five," she says.

There's a tremendous amount of pressure to find a dress that's perfect, but, as you know, nothing is perfect. So settle for close. It's a familiar progression: When you first saw the dress, you were infatuated, thinking about it when it wasn't around, mindlessly doodling its image. That lasted a while. And then when you two were separated for alterations, absence made your heart grow fonder. Now it's paid for, and you're married to it. Not as exciting as infatuation, but so much richer. Soon you'll even start to look alike.

Altered Perceptions

Molly's one regret about her wedding was the amount of money she spent on her dress, even though she supposedly "got a deal" through a friend. "You lose perspective when people start throwing these kinds of numbers at you. You think, Oh, well $1,000 is so much more reasonable than $3,000. But $1,000 was not reasonable for me." And after it was over, she had this big white reminder staring her in the face, mocking her indiscretion and on top of it all, needing to be preserved and stored at additional cost.

"If I could do it over, I would rent a gown," says Lindsay. "I really wanted a dress that was specifically my style, but it was crazy to spend all that money on something I wore for five hours." If you rent, you can find the look you want and pay a lot less to borrow it for a while. It can be perfectly you and way out of your price range, because you're only paying a fraction of the purchase price. Don't fall into the "why pay so much to rent something when for *x* amount I could have one forever" trap. It's not like a car. You'll never use it again. Never. It's a perfect renting situation. You need something expensive for one day, then you don't need it anymore. Okay, you want it for your daughter. Well what about *your* mother's wedding dress? Oh, you didn't want it? Out of date? Not your style? But you can't imagine that in the year 2045 or so, your daughter will feel the same way? Of the people I interviewed, only two wore their mother's wedding dress (that includes me). It's nice to be sentimental, but people want to wear what looks best on them.

Bride's Head Revisited

*I*f you're feeling blue, go to the most expensive bridal shop or millinery in your area and get a load of those headpiece prices! What could be funnier?

Lois spotted a perfect headpiece in the window of an expensive hat shop and went in to try it on. It was a flat bow on a headband with elbow-length tulle, unfinished at the ends. It was simple and perfect, especially with her short, full-skirted dress. It was also $750. She studied the overpriced item and left. The next day, Lois brought a small piece of extra fabric from her dress (she had requested the scraps, just in case) plus a drawing of the dream headpiece to a cheapo veil shop in Manhattan's garment district. She chose a headband and some tulle (basic white) off the rack and handed the guy the drawing. Lois's knockoff veil was virtually indistinguishable from its model, except in price—$85, thank you very much, and ready in three days.

Generally speaking the materials used for headpieces are very inexpensive—synthetic fabrics, plastic forms. Really, dollar-store-quality stuff. You're paying people a lot of money for knowing where to cut, and because, as a bride, you're wearing your wallet on your sleeve. If you're at all handy with scissors and a needle and you want to save yourself some dough, try to fashion your own headpiece. Get together with a friend and see what you can come up with. Supplies will cost you only a few bucks, and you'll have complete control over the design.

Veiled References

When someone asks if you prefer cathedral length or chapel length, is your answer, "I'm really not religious"? Let's review some terms so you don't feel like you have a "kick me" sign on your back when you go shopping for a headpiece. **Cathedral** is the longest veil length, with about five or six feet dragging on the floor behind you. **Chapel length** is the next longest, with about two-feet of fabric touching the ground. Next up, falling long, but not to tripping length, is **ballet length**, which hits at about the ankles. Shorter styles are **fingertip length** (measured with your arms hanging at your sides) and **elbow length**. **Merrowing** means finishing the edges with stitching. If you order a veil made of **tulle** (the stuff of tutus), the edges will be either **unfinished** (as in cut with scissors, just like you might do at home, for free), merrowed or **trimmed** (like with a narrow piece of satin). If you want a **headband** with some poufiness attached or tulle hanging from the back, the correct term would be "headband." Use similar logic if you're looking for a **barrette** headpiece. Those little yarmulke-like caps that go on the back of the head and have tulle or **illusion** trailing from the bottom are called **Juliet caps**. A crown of flowers is called a **wreath** (see—you knew that one, didn't you?). And a large or small piece of lace draped over your head is a **mantilla** (say it in Spanish). There are countless more choices, and there are also other terms for these same styles. So if a surly salesperson wants to pretend he doesn't know what you're talking about, he can, in spite of your preparation. That might be a good time to mention your tendency to throw up when you're nervous.

Going Topless

Kelly decided not to wear anything on her head. "I could go as far as the big white wedding dress but, for me, the veil would have been too much. I would have been, like, on the other side of the looking glass." Marie planned to do the same thing. "I wanted to go down the aisle with nothing on my head, so I would look like myself," she says. But her mother gave her a hard time. "You have *got* to wear a veil," she said. "That's how they can tell you're a bride!" Marie gave in, but just for the ceremony. When she walked into the reception, she handed her veil to her mother, who was

Fixing Your Face

Have you ever seen a bride head down the aisle—someone you know well—who is suddenly and inexplicably unrecognizable to you? You think at first it's the hairdo, but as she draws nearer, you realize it's her face. It's covered with unfamiliar shadings and contours. You're not sure they flatter her. *Boy,* you think, *her makeup certainly is ... abundant.* And then you remember that she said she spent almost $500 on her new wedding cosmetics.

"A friend told me not to do anything different from what

I usually do with my makeup, except to make sure I got some translucent powder so I wasn't shiny," says Halley. "She said, 'You want to look like yourself on your wedding day.'" Great advice. Especially because Halley wore her hair teased up in a big swirl. "That was plenty of new look for me, so I was glad to go with my usual face—just mascara and lipstick." One tiny change that might make sense: water-proof mascara, even if you're not "the crying type."

Says Charlotte, "I wanted to wear eyeliner on my top lid, but I've never been able to do that myself and get the line right. The week before, I bought makeup at a cosmetics store, and the woman there did my eyes perfectly." Charlotte tried to hire the saleswoman for the following Saturday, but she had to work. "She said I should just come into the store that morning and she'd do it then. Frankly, that was a little stressful—being at the store at nine forty-five, when I had to be at the wedding by noon. But it was worth it."

I wasn't used to wearing any kind of makeup on my cheeks, and when I bought some powder for my wedding, I didn't try it out in advance. Well, the morning of the wed-ding, I put in my contact lenses, after I'd done my makeup. The saline solution that dripped onto my cheeks left a wicked red trail. It was some kind of chemical reaction with the new powder. I was terrified, but it faded away within an hour. Anyway, keep your saline off your new makeup. Put your lenses in before you apply your makeup, and blot your eyes immediately to keep extra solution off your cheeks.

satisfied, and her nine-year-old niece made good use of it for the rest of the day.

Another alternative is decorating your hair. If you're wearing it up, you can surround a bun with fresh flowers. Just wrench them in there with some bobby pins. And remember Marie's story about the bride with a fine strand of ivy wound through her hair? But you might need some professional help with anything involving greens (a stylist, not a therapist).

The Shoe Must Go On

I've got three words for you here: comfort, comfort, comfort. Because if your feet hurt, it's hard to concentrate on anything else. (During the first dance, you'll be looking into your new husband's eyes, thinking, *Can we get this over with already?*) And, aesthetically speaking, if the shoes you have on are too narrow or too short, your gait is liable to resemble the Elephant Man's.

If you're wearing a long dress, do me a favor—don't spend a lot of money on your footwear. You will regret it. No one is looking at the two inches of shoe that peeks out in front when you walk. A brave comfort-oriented bride might opt for Birkenstocks or, for a little extra height, clogs or mules with a slight heel. Especially if she envisions the shoes spending most of the reception under her table.

Always comfortable are any version of a Mary Jane (give me a chance before you roll your eyes). All that means is a shoe with a strap. There are tons of cool styles out there. Think of Ginger

Rogers—she wore dancer's "character shoes," soft pumps with a medium-height heel and a strap. If you can't find white or off white, dance stores always carry a neutral beige. Ask your favorite local cobbler or shoe repair shop if shoe polish will turn them the color you need. They're pretty, flattering and great for dancing.

With a short dress, shoes are a third of your outfit, so you might have to sacrifice a little in the comfort department to get something exquisite. Still, remember who you are in terms of heel height and style. If the only time you've ever been more than an inch off the ground is when you were in other people's wedding parties, you're officially Not a High-Heel Person. Know this before you go shopping, and don't let any salesperson tell you otherwise. A small heel creates a very graceful line for your leg, and if you can't walk in high heels now, you won't be able to walk in high heels a couple of months from now. So unless you intend to be carried from spot to spot like a statue, find a shoe with a small heel that flatters your leg.

Stores that sell shoes to brides have higher prices than stores that sell shoes to regular humans (gasp!). What a shock. But having a vast selection of white or almost-white shoes all in one place might be worth the extra markup. Prepare to spend some time shoe shopping, because it takes a little while to assess the fit. In my days as a showroom shoe model, I discovered that you can make any shoe look like it fits, if that's what you're being paid to do. But you're not. So if you have to ask the salesperson, "Will that throbbing let up once I break them in?" you should probably pass.

Fit is key here. Take a nice long walk around the store. Major strides. Find a slick surface (like the uncarpeted portion of a department store floor), and see how you do. Not every place you walk on your wedding day will have shoe store–perfect slip-proof carpeting. Play Mother May I. Try a scissor step. Some giant steps. (By now your behavior has driven the salesperson away; take advantage of your time alone to examine the construction of the shoe and drop it a few times to test its durability.)

Taming of the Shoe

Once you've purchased a shoe with the right style, feel and price, do a little customizing if necessary. If the bottom is slick, try roughing it up with sandpaper. If that doesn't give you enough traction for all types of floors, go to a shoemaker and have some thin rubber treading put on the sole, just under the ball of your foot. "But my beautiful, delicate shoes!" you say. "They'll be ruined!" Do you want to dance or do you want to pose? Do you want to move freely, swanlike through the crowd, or do you want to inch tentatively, always keeping an eye out for the next available arm in the event of a wipeout?

Now comes the real time investment. Put Band-Aids on the backs of your ankles, where the shoe would otherwise burrow in and draw blood, don your shoes and go about your business. Do some stairs; this will bend the shoes and force them to conform to your foot a bit (*and* tone the quadriceps!). Wear them as much as you can around the house, so that on your wedding day, they're *your* shoes, not a new pair of shoes. And if in the course of the breaking-in process you discover that you have purchased two deceptively attractive instruments of torture, get rid of them.

Try to return them, if you haven't done any kind of major renovations. You know I am not one to waste money, but if the store won't take them back and they're simply killing you, put them in a box in the back of your closet, and make a mental note that when your next same-size friend gets married, you have some shoes she might want. Just because you bought them doesn't mean

Stocking Feats

You already know that you should have at least one extra pair of tights or panty hose handy, right? It's a hot bridal magazine and blog topic. Aside from that, apply the shoe policy to your tights or panty hose purchase. A short dress requires you to find something pretty, but with a long dress, go with what's most comfortable. Lisa decided to forgo tights or panty hose in favor of the ever-practical knee-highs. "I had a full-length gown, and I wasn't going to do the garter thing," she says. "I wore knee-highs because it was a hundred degrees out, but they also definitely facilitated going to the bathroom."

If wearing knee-highs will make you feel less than beautiful, how about thigh-highs? Très sexy and so much more liberating than having a tight band around your waist. There are some with seriously wide elastic tops, so they actually stay up. But try a pair out in advance. Dance around the house in them (with your shoes) for five hours or so. Experiment with a few brands. If the elastic is turning your leg blue, go up a size; you can always adjust the length by cuffing the top down.

Don't spend a fortune on your panty hose or tights. I did, as a stupid tiny indulgence. They cost an obscene amount. I never considered the fact that the dress I was wearing was lined with horsehair mesh around the bottom, to help hold its narrow tulip shape. As soon as I took a step, the horsehair caught the million-dollar stockings and began a shredding process that would continue for the duration of the wedding.

you have to wear them. Now go buy a nice, comfy pair, and chalk it up to experience. But if you were honest with yourself in the shoe store, if you really "listened to your feet" (and that's not easy for the less flexible among us), you should be able to make the shoes you purchased wearable enough so you spend only, say, half your wedding thinking about your aching feet.

Don't forget to share this advice with your darling husband-to-be. It's a wedding-related topic you can discuss without risk of fighting. (You: "Hey, honey, how are those shoes breaking in?" Him: "Great! Thanks for that tip. You're the best!")

Pretty Maids All in a Row

—Dressing Up the Bridal Party—

*R*emember the promise you made to yourself the last time you were in a bridal party encased in a puffy teal taffeta contraption? You swore you would never put your friends through anything comparable. You questioned the integrity of the bride. What kind of "friend" would take pleasure in humiliating you? And in front of a large group? And on video! And then, you became a bride-to-be. You started to think about shopping for outfits for your attendants. You spent too much time reading bridal magazines and wedding blogs. You flipped through catalogs. Your standards started to slip. You heard yourself remark, "Well this is much better than some of the stuff *I've* had to wear."

Is this you? If it is, I hope I can help deprogram you. Sit down in a comfortable chair, far from the bridal propaganda you have accumulated, and relax. It's time to open your mind again. Let the visions of uncomfortable, self-conscious women in vivid inflated pastels float away. Watch it go. Good-bye, image. Then see what floats in. Pretend you haven't made a decision about bridesmaids' dresses, and give each of the following options one full minute of consideration.

Option #1. Let the bridesmaids wear whatever they want.

Pros: Everybody's happy and feels comfortable and pretty; nobody has to spend money she doesn't have.

Cons: No uniformity.

Option #2. Ask them to get whatever they want in the (realistic) color of your choice.

Pros: Everybody's happy and feels comfortable and pretty; people can control the amount of money they spend; they can use their dresses again; there's some uniformity.

Cons: The variety makes you itchy; you like things that match.

Option #3. Shop with all your bridesmaids and select one dress everyone can live with.

Pros: You're happy; nobody's miserable.

Cons: Logistically difficult, especially because your college roommate lives one thousand miles away; nobody can agree, and you have to try to organize more than one shopping trip; tempers run high when style disagreements arise (your size-12 bridesmaid thinks the size-4 keeps intentionally suggesting dresses that work only on women who are built like a little boy, and you have to keep them in separate cars); money can be a problem.

Option #4. Shop with just your maid of honor for one dress that everyone will wear.

Pros: Easy, quick and painless for you; your maid of honor is happy.

Cons: The rest of the wedding party hates you both.

What's in Store

We've already discussed the possibility of shopping in a layperson store for *your* dress, but for your bridesmaids' dresses, that's an even more viable option. I don't just mean Ann Taylor. I mean Macy's and Zara and Banana Republic and the women's department at Bloomingdale's (not the evening gown section)—wherever you go when you haven't got a thing to wear and you want to look great. Typical bridesmaids' dresses are not even worth making fun of. I won't waste the energy. All the good jokes have been made, anyway. Why would you limit yourself to overpriced, stiff polyester gowns? You would never go near that stuff if you were shopping for yourself, right? Flip through fashion blogs and magazines instead of bridal ones. If you want full-length dresses, maxis are not hard to find. And "tea-length" is every dress that's not a mini or a maxi. Long, flowy, flowery dresses are easy to come by and look good on everyone. And even the nicest ones in department stores go for far less than what many bridesmaids' dresses cost. The hardest part is letting go of what you might have had in mind and what you've seen at other weddings. Even some bridesmaids themselves, when given the option of liberation, can't transcend the cliché they are expected to embody.

Tracy asked her two attendants (her roommates) to choose any dress they wanted. She went shopping with them, to department stores and dress shops. "We must have gone to a dozen places," says the amenable bride. "They didn't find one dress they liked. They actually told me they *wanted* to go to a bridal shop." The roommates wound up with something Tracy considered "kind of an awful bridesmaid's dress," with a ruffled bodice and an eggplant-purple polyester taffeta skirt. Tracy made a valiant effort, but her roommates were not satisfied that they looked like bridesmaids until they were wearing borderline ugly synthetic gowns.

At Least It Makes a Funny Story

Denise tried to be a considerate bride. "I chose a bridesmaid's dress that my friend Stacey had worn for another wedding," says Denise. "She was traveling three thousand miles to be in my wedding, and I didn't want to make her spend any more money." Four years later, it was time for Stacey to get married. The bridesmaids' outfits she chose included a pillbox hat with a big feather sticking up from it ("It looked like a goiter," according to Denise) and a long chiffon scarf. Okay, ugly's ugly, but that's not the end of the story. Denise had had a baby three months prior to fitting time and was still nursing. Stacey wanted Denise to stop nursing so she could fit into the tiny cocktail dress with spaghetti straps that went with the hat and goiter. ("Forget about that mother-child bonding stuff; *I'm getting married.*") After seconds of intense deliberation, Denise chose her baby over the dress. Since there was no way she could get her 44DDs into any size of that particular style dress, Denise told Stacey she'd wear the hat and scarf and would find a dress the same color as the others, but with more room up top. Stacey said that wouldn't do. She insisted Denise find a way to wear exactly what she had selected. So Denise went to a tailor, who took the dress apart, added panels to the bodice, and replaced the thin straps with more realistic ones. She spent $575 for the original ensemble, and another $225 for the alterations.

To Each Her Own

"I wish I'd just had each bridesmaid pick out her own style dress in a pastel color," says Eva. "It just turned out so silly. We bought a dress just because it didn't look bad on anyone. But it didn't really look good on anyone either. Big mistake."

Clarice told her bridesmaids to wear whatever they wanted to her outdoor wedding. Because they're all sisters (the bride too), they have a similar sense of style. Each independently decided to wear a short, solid-color trapeze dress. "It worked out better than I could have imagined," says Clarice. "Someone said they looked like beautiful little wood nymphs."

For her formal Saturday evening wedding, Lindsay asked her bridesmaids to wear something long, black and velvet. Those were the specifications. Then each went out and found what she liked. I'm so glad I did that," says Lindsay. "They all looked great and were happy." And a happy bridesmaid is a pleasant bridesmaid. Really, if you want your bridesmaids to look beautiful, let them choose their outfits. It's trite, but true: If you feel beautiful, you look beautiful. Lindsay also requested that the families wear black. Everyone was amenable except her boyfriend's grandmother, who believes it's bad luck to wear black to a wedding. But Lindsay was cool about it. So there was a roomful of people in black, a luminous bride in white, and one grandmother dressed in purple.

It Ain't Over Till It's Over

Once you've found what you want and dealt with the requisite egos, the hard part's over, right? Maybe. Things can come up. Alteration problems, strokes of fate.

Here's a little lesson in resourcefulness. Joanne didn't want her bridesmaids (a friend, her sister and her sister-in-law-to-be) to spend a lot on their outfits. She was also concerned that they be able to wear the clothes again. At a factory outlet center, they came across some nice, inexpensive suits. It was an easy shopping day; each bridesmaid found her size right away. Then Joanne's sister, June, learned she was pregnant. The wedding was five months away. "We had no idea what we were going to do," says Joanne. "She'd be huge by then." Wearing the jacket open and not zipping the skirt wouldn't quite cut it. So Joanne contacted the manufacturer (Chaus), explaining the problem and asking where she might find matching fabric so that a dress could be made for June. A couple of weeks later, she received a package in the mail from Chaus. Some generous soul at the company had sent her several yards of the fabric, free. A dressmaker fashioned a maternity version of the suit, stealing the buttons off the original, and they all lived happily ever after.

Change of a Dress

Don't forget to tell each attendant to have her own little "dress" rehearsal (ha ha). Kelly picked up her bridesmaid's dress for her friend Pam's wedding a few days in advance, but didn't try it on. "The day of the wedding, I started to put it on and it didn't fit," says Kelly. "I couldn't close the zipper. It was about a half inch too small. I had to take a seam ripper to it and tear it up so I could get into it." At the end of the wedding, Kelly heard Pam's sister [another bridesmaid] complaining about the fact that her dress was too big, "and I realized that I had her dress and she had mine."

What the Boys Wear

Greta and Stuart were running errands one day with Stuart's mother (who was pretty much the sole sponsor of their wedding), when the couple started talking about getting tuxes for Stuart and his best man. Stuart's mother said, "You're not wearing a tux!" He laughed, thinking her horrified tone was a joke, and said, "Yeah, I am." She said, "You can't do that to me." Greta and Stuart were baffled. "We were like, 'What? What did we do?'" says Greta, until Stuart's mother explained herself. "Her reason is that if you have a Sunday afternoon wedding, it's tacky to get too dressed up," says Greta. "But we didn't know. We figured, you get married, you wear a tux." Stuart persisted about wanting to wear a tux. His mother was mortified, and was certain that this was some kind of conspiracy to ruin her reputation. "She thought that behind her back we decided to unite about tuxes." The next day, she told Stuart if he was going to wear a tux, the whole thing was off. And Stuart, aware that a tuxedo wouldn't do him much good at an elopement either, backed down. The funny thing is, rule-followers beget rule-followers; now Stuart's snobby about anyone who would even think of wearing a tux to a Sunday afternoon wedding.

Luke and Victoria were in a similar position. Luke really wanted to wear a cutaway jacket to his daytime wedding. Victoria's mother was embarrassed and insisted he mustn't. But Luke and Victoria were paying for their wedding themselves, and so they both wore exactly what they wanted.

When Mitch went to rent a tux for his wedding, he was hoping, unrealistically, for something other than what he'd rented to be a groomsman in other weddings. "They dressed me up like a chauffeur, in tacky polyester plain black formalwear. I wanted something that would make *me* feel special," he says, half-joking, "so I got black tails with a white tie. I don't care what the custom is. Who's keeping track?" Well, certain of his guests would be, and the bride was worried about that. But that didn't matter to Mitch: "The only reason some people care is that *they're* following the rules, and they want company in their misery."

Tails, tuxes, double-breasted suits, khakis, scuba gear. Who really cares? If it's what he wants to wear, he should wear it. And to all those arbiters of etiquette who seek the wisdom of dusty old books to determine what's "inappropriate," I say, maybe it's time to get yourself a hobby.

Spreading the Word

*T*he invitation is your first chance to make a statement about your wedding (not to pressure you), and it might be the only memento friends and relatives have when it's all over. So think beyond engraved type and calligraphy (which is expensive anyway, and, let's face it, the envelope goes straight to the recycling bin; only the invitation makes it to the refrigerator door). Your invitation can set the mood for the whole occasion. It can be funny or sentimental or just visually your own.

The Basics

Okay, you know what information goes on an invitation, right? So does everybody, but I talked to more than one bride who had forgotten to include critical facts. Um, the time? The *date*? So if you're making your invitations yourself, or having them made by someone who's new to the process, use this handy checklist to ensure that you won't be banging your head against the wall seconds after you drop them in the mailbox.

- date and day of the week
- time
- your names (duh)
- exact location of ceremony and reception
- directions by car and by public transportation
- reply card, addressed to you
- return address on envelope

If you include a traditional reply card, you will discover an interesting sociological phenomenon. Some people forget to write their names on these before they send them back. Yes, even if there's a line preceded by "Mr./Ms." This seems rather obvious, and yet you will probably get at least a few that have "will attend" checked and no other marks anywhere. If you send a less traditional card—maybe a completely blank one—people are forced to think for a moment and write something that makes sense on it. In any case, there's a simple, widely employed system that will help prevent this minor inconvenience: Number each reply card (in a corner on the back) and keep a key. When you get the cards back, whether they're adequately identified or not, you can consult your list and see that reply card number 1 came from your brother and his wife, card number forty-seven came from your aunt Irma, and so on.

The Fun Part

You don't have to be an artist to do a really cool, inventive invitation. You just have to *know* an artist. No, I'm kidding. You can do your own invitation by utilizing design software and your brilliant wit. But if there's a graphic designer who wants to help you, take advantage.

Celia's father painted a dense watercolor border of hearts and flowers on a sheet of 8½-by-11 paper. He used a fine brush to paint all the crucial "where and when" information in the center. Celia had the original color-copied on better-quality off-white paper. The results were beautiful. "My friends thought each one was hand-painted," says Celia. Joni actually *did* hand-paint all 110 of her invitations. She claims to have enjoyed it, but then again, she was out of work at the time.

When you use color copies, you're a bit limited in terms of paper stock (you can't use anything too heavy) and size (it must be standard unless you want to cut the invitations down yourself). And it's a relatively expensive process. Silk-screening might be more economical if you're using only two colors.

Molly and Jeff wanted a friendly, colorful invitation, "something reminiscent of Miro." A designer friend had type printed in the center of oversize paper. Then he silk-screened (in purple and red) an illustration that squiggled around and through the type. Silk-screening requires that each piece be done separately, but it's pretty quick, and then each invitation is slightly different, a little work of art. The designer made postcards for replies, so Molly and Jeff wouldn't have to worry about including return envelopes.

Mitch and Clarice wanted to do something very specific for their invitations. There was a Greek myth that Mitch had read to Clarice when they were first together. The story was about a poor old couple who showed a stranger boundless hospitality, offering him everything they had, even though they were hungry themselves. The stranger was actually a god in disguise. When he revealed himself to the couple, he offered to grant them three wishes. The last wish they made was to be able to spend eternity together. So when they died, he put their spirits into two trees that stood side by side. The branches and leaves of the trees blended together, and the taller they grew, the more intertwined they became. Mitch and Clarice wanted an image on the invitation like the one at the end of the story. Clarice's sister, an artist, decided to make the invitations small and delicate. She had a rubber stamp made from an old etching of two trees. The type was printed in gold and color-copied, four to a standard letter-size page. She cut each sheet to make four small invitations. Then she stamped the image of the trees on by hand.

Eva and Mike, both artists, wanted to design their own invitations. "This totally flipped out my mom," says Eva. "It seems in her neighborhood, people look down on you if you don't have engraved invitations." So they compromised. The invitations were engraved, but Eva and Mike also engraved an illustration of a bride and groom—which Mike had done—on a notecard and enclosed it with the invitations. "The illustration became our logo," says Eva. "We used it on table cards, the church program and as inspiration for the design of our thank-you notes."

Make 'Em Laugh

Charlotte and Billy had designed a few wedding invitations for family members. When it came time to do their own, they went with an idea that they'd failed to convince their less pioneering siblings to use. The invitation was a 15-by-22-inch poster. Along the top in red type it said, "Please Join Us For Our Grand Union." Below was a huge photo of the couple with a shopping cart— Charlotte was in it and Billy was pushing—outside the aforementioned supermarket. (At their reception, the best man ended his toast with a wish that "every day will be a red-dot special in their

"I Just Need to Get the Zip Codes"

Gabi made a screw-up that stemmed from garden-variety disorganization. "When we wrote out our invitations, we had an incomplete list of addresses," she says. "We were missing maybe ten. So we mailed out the ones we could and made a mental note to contact our parents for the information we needed." (Did you catch that part about the "mental note"? That's what is known as foreshadowing.) Gabi's father and his brother, Neil, were not on great terms at the time, and six months earlier, Gabi's brother had opted not to invite Neil to his own wedding. Says Gabi, "We planned to invite Neil, but we didn't have his address." His invitation went into the pile that got mailed later. Two days before the wedding, Gabi called the flakes who hadn't sent back their reply cards; Neil was among them. When she contacted him, he said he never got the invitation. "He thought I was lying when I said I sent him one." Gabi remembered getting Neil's address and writing it on the envelope. She remembered mailing that last batch. "About a month after our wedding, we were packing up our apartment because we were moving," she says, "and guess what I found behind my dresser." The lesson: Don't touch your invitations until you have a complete list of addresses. When everything's ready, check the pile of invites against your guest list. And mail the invitations all at once.

Grand Union of love.") After these rather expensive invitations were printed, the couple realized that they forgot to include the time (see handy checklist on page 172). Luckily, Billy noticed the omission before they sent the posters out, each rolled up in its own tube, with $1.75 worth of postage; they made cards with the missing information and slipped one into each tube.

Michael designed a set of "nuptial cards" as an invitation for a friend. They featured little cartoon drawings that someone had done of the bride and groom years before. Michael reproduced and mounted each illustration on a small card; each invitee received ten cards and a stick of gum, wrapped together like a pack of baseball cards.

Florence, who's from New Jersey, and Hans, from Denmark, gave designers Nola and Morty free rein. The artists came up with an invitation that looked like the front page of a supermarket tabloid (remember *The Weekly World News?*). Underneath the headline "Woman Marries Great Dane!" were two separate photos—one of Florence, one of Hans—unauthentically fused together in tacky tabloid style. The details were on three separate sheets of 3-by-8½-inch card stock—just right to slip into an unassuming business-size envelope. The designers color-copied the "front page" and folded it to fit. And they printed names and addresses on the envelopes so guests would have no clue what might be inside.

It's How You Say It

If parents are paying for all or part of a wedding, they often get top billing on an invitation. But that doesn't mean you can't negotiate about how the rest of it reads. Just because it's in the book at the engraver's, doesn't mean it's the best way to say it. Compose your own. The wording can be as powerful or as understated as the visuals (a poem you wrote, or simply "Please come to our wedding"). But be prepared for family members with agendas of their own. Sometimes what you *don't* say is a bigger issue than what you do.

Long-Distance Orientation

Eva and Mike had a lot of relatives from the Midwest coming to New York City for the first time. "It was a very scary thing for some of them," says Eva. "Mike and I got tons of maps, tour books, museum guides, subway info and other touristy stuff and made packages to send to out-of-towners a few weeks before the wedding. It helped calm some of the more nervous people."

"When my mother-in-law saw the invitations, she had a fit," says Regina. Regina's parents were paying for her wedding. The invitation included only her parents' names and the names of the bride and groom. "But my mother-in-law insisted on having her name on there too. She wanted it to say, '. . . son of John and Jane Smith.'" Regina had casually discussed the content of the invitation with Ted's parents. "They said, 'Great, great,' but they weren't really listening, I guess." Ted's mother was relentless about this issue, so Regina had to trash her initial batch of invitations and have them reprinted.

If you sense the potential for this kind of mayhem, type up and print out what your invitation is going to say and have it initialed by all appropriate parties. Okay maybe the initials are unnecessary. But make sure to run it by everyone who should see it and get their approval.

Marla had her one and only wedding disagreement with her mother-in-law over her invitations. But Marla's stance was the opposite of Regina's. "I didn't want the invitations to have just my parents' names as the hosts, because it seemed to symbolize the idea of marrying off their daughter. So even though my parents paid for the wedding, I wanted Lee's parents' names to appear on the invitation too." But Lee's parents were divorced and Shirley, his mother, didn't want her name to appear anywhere with her ex-husband's because it would look like they were still married. Shirley told Marla she couldn't include her name. But this was important to Marla, and she pursued it. There was tension and arguing for a week, and then a compromise. The invitation read "Barbara and Marvin Hicks [Marla's parents] and Shirley Crane and Milton Crane . . ." Repeating "Crane" separated the names enough to sort of satisfy Shirley. She wasn't happy, but she could tolerate it.

Food Forethought

One of the great mysteries of wedding planning is how to feed 150 people (or even fifty people) without robbing a bank. Some couples have the budget to hire a caterer or book a restaurant; some don't. Either way, there are enough logistical hassles and surprise expenses to make you wish you were just serving beer and pretzels.

Discount Fare

The way to find cheap food for your wedding is to look at what's inexpensive in real life, then see if that can be adjusted to accommodate a crowd. Forget about caterers who do weddings; what you need is someone who does *food*. When you look outside the industry, you find prices that make much more sense.

The first wedding plan Linden and Wes made was hiring a Caribbean steel drum band to play at their reception. They de-

Nice Touch: A Cheese to Remember

Kelly put edible flowers over a huge wheel of brie, then covered the flowers with aspic, so when you cut a slice, there was a narrow layer of flowers on top, above the rind. "I can't take credit for it," says Kelly. "I got it out of a magazine. It made the buffet table beautiful."

cided they wanted island food too. So they asked the owner of a small local Jamaican restaurant if he would cater the wedding. They got big aluminum-foil roasters full of jerk chicken and rice, and paid four of the restaurant's employees to heat and serve the food.

Penny and Will had visions of big bowls of pasta and salad on each table, served family style. The owner of a local pasta specialty shop loved the idea when they brought it to her. She suggested a room-temperature pasta dish so they wouldn't have to worry about keeping the food hot if the weather turned cool (the wedding was outside). Because there was no serving involved—just setting up and clearing—the price was extremely low.

A potluck wedding is perhaps the least expensive alternative, but you need some serious organizational skills to plan it and pull it off. Lois and Michael had a version of a potluck wedding, but because only family members cooked, it meant a lot of work for a small number of people instead of a little work for everyone. "It turned out to be too hard on our families," Lois says two years later. "I didn't realize how difficult it would be until we were in the middle of it."

I considered serving a six-foot hero—half meat, half vegetarian—at my wedding. Super cheap, tasty and no need for servers. Unfortunately, my husband didn't want a six-foot hero at *his* wedding. Instead, we had lasagna and salad brought in from a deli. It was unbelievably inexpensive and it tasted great. Delis, even those that make great food, are reasonably priced by definition. And knowing that we had very little money to spend, the deli owner kept the number of servers down to a minimum.

Supplies Party

Some people have at their disposal all the supplies associated with feeding a crowd—dishes, glasses, flatware—because the space they're using for their reception is fully equipped. If you're not so blessed, you have two choices. One is to rent everything yourself, from cloth napkins to two kinds of spoons to three kind of forks to champagne flutes to coffee cups. Renting is pricey and complicated. You literally pay separately for each utensil. So ask yourself, is the price of salad tongs the kind of detail you want occupying your mind at this particular juncture?

Your other choice—one that is obvious if money is a very serious concern—is to embrace the paper plate, the plastic fork, the paper cup. They are your friends (even if they're often enemies of the environment). But these days you have a choice of more sustainable products, recyclable, biodegradable and/or compostable tableware (bamboo, for example) that also looks nice. If the budget is tight, why spend precious funds on knives and forks? People have those things at home. Why not buy more flowers, or serve champagne? Why not put the money toward something that means more to you?

If you're going extra-industry, make sure you confirm and confirm and confirm again. One thing wedding professionals have over other vendors is a strong awareness of the magnitude of their responsibility—that if they screw up, your majorly important event can be ruined. You might have to be the one to bring up the subject of contracts and foresee wedding-specific problems that could arise. In other words, if you're dealing with a vendor who's not used to working weddings, *you* have to be the wedding professional. As usual, saving money means doing more work yourself.

Is It Better to Be a Bride or an Artichoke?

Bride	Artichoke
Always the center of attention	Center always gets attention
Can't find a thing to wear	Looks great in a nice vinaigrette
Falls apart when steamed	Falls apart when steamed
Known for selfishness	Known for its big heart

Are You Being Served?

Even when you pay someone else to take care of most of your food worries, you still have to make decisions that will affect the mood of the party and your bill. In terms of money, the most important decision is about the type of service. A sit-down dinner requires more servers (and labor is gonna cost ya) and also more rentals, so that's the most expensive option. The more courses you have, the more plates, utensils and labor you have to pay for. Any setup where the guests are on their feet, moving toward the food on their own steam, means less work for the caterer—which translates into less money out of your pocket.

Marie wanted to have a buffet; her mother thought that a sit-down dinner was the only classy option. "I really wanted everybody to be able to eat what they wanted," says Marie, "and if I had a sit-down dinner, there were fewer menu choices. A lot of my friends are vegetarians, but my whole family wanted filet mignon. My mother thought a buffet was incredibly tacky. To this day, she's pissed about it." A lot of people agree with Marie's mother. I don't get it. Maybe it's because I'm on the side of the under-financed, but I think of sit-down dinners as kind of confining. Anyway, the expense rules out this option for a lot of couples.

Many choose to go with some kind of buffet, which allows guests to eat when they're hungry, have as much or as little as they want, and skip any dish with nutritional value, if that's their idea of a good time. Everybody has the same advice about having a successful buffet setup at your wedding: Make sure in advance that there will be adequate access to the food.

At Clarice's wedding, there was a long line of hungry people winding through the table area. "We had only two servers at the buffet. By the time people decide what they want and get served, it takes much longer than you think."

Charlotte's guests served themselves, but at first they had the same problem. "The table was up against a wall, but the line was moving really slowly. So we pulled it out and doubled the access." If you have lots of space, the best thing to do in a serve-yourself situation is spread things out so one person doesn't end up stalling the line for ten minutes while he fills up his plate. Also, put the same foods at opposite ends of the table. It takes a while for guests to catch on that what's at one end is exactly the same as what's at the other end, but once Uncle Louie gets wind of the disappointing news, it will spread like wildfire.

Regina thought she'd prevent traffic problems by having "food stations" set up around the room—basically a broken-apart buffet. But it didn't work out like she'd hoped. "The caterer set up the meat-carving station so close to the pasta station and the seafood bar, that it was just like a regular buffet," says Regina. "There was a line right through the dance floor, which annoyed me to no end."

Access to the food was a problem for Celia and Peter too, but not because of a line. They had an all–hors d'oeuvres wedding. "Through constant badgering of the restaurant in advance, we made sure there would be enough food for people to fill up on," Celia says. What they didn't consider was how difficult it might be to get at the food. The problem was, everything was passed on trays by waiters, so if there was no waiter near you at a given moment, there was also no food. "One fear you have with a cocktail party is that people are going to get smashed, because they're just drinking, drinking, drinking and then eating, like, a mini quiche."

Waste Not

Make arrangements in advance to have the extra food brought somewhere it's needed. Contact a local charity organization or church that will be able to accept the food or lead you to a group that will. Ask a friend or one of your attendants to take care of this. That means seeing that leftovers don't land in the garbage at the reception and also possibly loading up a car and dropping off the food.

If she had it to do again, Celia would restructure the service slightly. "Instead of having all the food passed on trays, I'd ask for a buffet of maybe crudités and finger sandwiches, something you can pick at while you're drinking, so you're not dependent upon a waiter who's not coming out often enough."

At most weddings, getting enough food is not really an issue. But Kimberly went to one where the guests became delirious with hunger. "They took us in a bus from Toronto an hour north to the country. We were there from eleven in the morning till six at night, and they didn't serve a meal—just hors d'oeuvres and alcohol, and cake and coffee," she says. "And we had an hour bus ride on either end. When we got back to the city, everybody rushed out to restaurants and had a big dinner." A cocktail reception can be a very cool option, but some conditions are simply not conducive to it. And guests who are unprepared (Surprise! We're not having dinner!) are likely to be disappointed.

Cash and Caterers

Heather was thrilled with her caterer. "The service was impeccable, the presentation was beautiful and the food was great." But the price, well, it was $1,200 more than she was told it would be. It wasn't the food or the liquor that cost more; it was the service and the rentals.

"We thought that we'd given the caterer the impression that we were trying to do this on somewhat of a budget," says Heather. She had met with the caterer to look at the website of the rental company and discuss how much of everything they needed. "But he took care of it—the chairs, linens, plates." Heather trusted that her caterer would not rent the most expensive chafing dishes possible. "Well he did. He rented the fancy ones instead of the cheap ones. And the good chairs and wineglasses too." On top of that, the estimate on the service was low. "He didn't tell me that the headwaiter, the bartenders and the house manager get more per hour." But Heather didn't want to make a big deal of it at that moment. "I'd just had a wedding. I was happy. And I wanted to go home happy." She didn't flip out; she just said, "This is $1,200 more than you told me it was going to be. I don't have enough money in my bank account to cover this."

Smart move. It takes some pretty quick thinking to figure out how to handle a money dispute without either getting taken advantage of or having your magic mood spoiled. A lot of people, caught up in the occasion, would have paid the bill saying, what the hell, it's my wedding, and then gotten mad at themselves the next day. Others would have confronted the caterer while he was trying to finish the job and probably would have ended up leaving angry. You have to watch out, because at the end of your wedding, you are not in shape to think rationally about business matters. Champagne aside, you have just undergone one of the most intense experiences of your life, and your perspective is all screwy. The same goes for your parents. Certain vendors take advantage of this, so talk in advance to parents who might be writing checks at the end of the affair, and steel yourself too. Make sure you or anyone who is shelling out cash knows exactly what is owed. Incidentally, when Heather talked to the caterer the next day, he did the honorable thing. He knocked money off his profit and split the difference with her.

The pricing structure caterers use is necessarily complicated; they're covering a lot of ground. When you first start talking to (I mean listening to) caterers, you'll be handed and e-mailed long lists of apparently reasonable prices. Dozens of tiny per-person fees (40 cents for a fork, $5 for salad, $4 per hour for the bar). You scan the column of numbers, thinking, "Uh-huh, okay, right, I see,

This Round's on Me

Find out from the caterer if you can purchase the liquor for the wedding yourself. You'll save a lot of money by going to a discount liquor store, and you won't have to worry about drinks being watered down. You can probably return any unopened bottles for a refund (ask about this). If your food people have a strict policy about supplying the liquor themselves, see if you can at least supply the champagne. At Olivia's wedding, the open bar was pretty cheap per head, but to include champagne all night doubled the price. So Olivia brought just enough champagne to give each guest one glassful for a toast. "I thought that would be a good way to conserve funds," she says. But when she walked into her reception, she saw three guests sipping the precious bubbly. "I was like a crazy person in my wedding gown screaming at the bartender, 'No! Stop! It's just for the toast!'" The caterer, embarrassed by Olivia's raving, took responsibility for the mistake and sent one of his waiters to buy more.

that seems fair." Then your eye makes it to the bottom of the screen and, Yoinks! Oh, obviously there's been an addition error. You feel bad for the caterer; he's been e-mailing this price list with a major typo for who knows how long. You're trying to figure out a nice way to tell him, as you do the math in your head. Then you realize that the total is correct. You feel faint. How can all these tiny numbers add up to *that*? They can and do. Now you know why weddings cost so much.

It may seem deceptive to have dozens of tiny figures on a price list, but it's to your advantage to have the fees broken down. That way, you can spot things to eliminate (one of the hot hors d'oeuvres) or replace (the expensive table linens). And connecting a specific price to each item or service makes it easier for you to negotiate. But find out how final the final per-head figure really is. See if a service charge and tax are included. And ask what extra expenses you should expect, like the price of the cake.

Mara was slapped with an unanticipated expense the week of her wedding. The rental company's policy was to pick up all its stuff the morning after a nighttime wedding. But the policy of the reception location was to have everything out right after the party ended. It would have been nice if these two establishments could have worked it out between themselves, wouldn't it? Didn't happen. Mara had to pay a fee of $550 to have the rental company pick everything up the night of the wedding at midnight.

And Now a Word From Our Expert

I asked Vera, who runs a very successful catering business, for some tips on dealing with members of her species. Here's what she said.

Don't choose a caterer solely on the basis of a tasting. "Brides learn that you're supposed to talk to eighteen caterers and taste their stuff before you hire one," says Vera. But at most weddings, caterers are more than merely the purveyors of the food. And just because the salmon is moist and flaky, doesn't mean the caterer will show up on time, have a pleasant waitstaff, and run a smooth show. Keep that in mind when you're doing your research. "The most valuable thing you can get is a really good recommendation," she says. "If you have a question about a specific unusual dish, ask to taste the dish." But when you're hunting for a caterer, spend your time collecting reliable referrals rather than going from tasting to tasting.

Look out for flat per-head fees. From a restaurant, this is probably okay—they own their own supplies. But from a caterer it can indicate padding on the cost of the rentals. A caterer should be willing to work with you on keeping the cost of rentals as low as you need them to be. "The chairs we rent range in price from $2.50 to $10 each," says Vera. With a hundred guests, that means the difference between $250 and $1,000, so pay attention.

Ask the right questions of references. When you call former clients, besides asking about the food, find out how the caterer treated guests and how well he or she managed the reception. Says Vera, "Two weeks before the wedding, I meet with the bandleader, the florist and whoever else is involved, and we talk through the setup and the event step by step, so no one gets in anyone else's way." If the caterer is supposed to be in charge, you don't want one whose first visit to your reception space is the day of the wedding.

If you're watching your budget, watch the rentals. You can save money by, for example, not serving another dessert in addition to the wedding cake. "It's not the cost of the strawberries and cream that will blow your budget out of the water," says Vera. "It's the rentals—a whole other set of plates and utensils."

Make all your wishes very clear in advance, and then get out of the way. "Confirm special requests the day before if you're worried," says Vera, "but it will work against you to become involved when the caterers begin doing their job." At a recent wedding Vera catered, the groom showed up in the morning and directed her staff to rearrange the tables. "We knew what he wanted because

Among Friends

When Diane and Marvin started planning their wedding, the first thing they did was call their friend Jean-Paul, a great caterer. Jean-Paul was very supportive when Diane talked to him on the phone. Then they got together to talk menu. "All of a sudden I realized, this is serious, this is a businessman," says Diane. Jean-Paul was throwing a lot of fast sales talk at her ("we can do *this* for you, or we can do *that* for you"), out of habit. "He was my college buddy until we were doing business." But Diane still considered Jean-Paul her friend first, and that's one reason she never asked for a contract. "He was giving us a deal, and I felt bad about asking for a contract. I was afraid I'd seem ungrateful or like I didn't trust him." But a contract is standard procedure. And if you're working with a friend, the momentary awkwardness you have to overcome to get things on paper is nothing compared to the nauseating sense of regret you might experience later. "I thought, I know this person, I trust him, he told me what it's going to cost, and that's that."

The wedding went smoothly. The next day, Diane went to Jean-Paul's office to thank him and bring him a check. Jean-Paul was surprised to see that Diane had already filled in the amount. "Oh, sweetie," he said, "it's more than this." In fact, it was almost $800 more. Diane was stunned. She protested meekly. Jean-Paul smiled and said, "That's why they call it an estimate, Di." Diane didn't have the nerve to take the issue any further. "I couldn't. He gave me a discount. I just wish I'd been comfortable enough to confirm the total price. Because even though it was less than Jean-Paul is used to charging, it was a lot of money for us to pay."

we'd discussed it in advance; he just didn't see it happening fast enough. He set us back an hour, and that affected the flow of the wedding."

Okay, so you voice your preferences. But what if you're dealing with a control-freak caterer who's afraid to do anything that deviates even slightly from what he does at every wedding? Brooke and Tony found themselves in such a position. "Our caterer insisted that the champagne be in the glasses when the guests took their seats," says Tony, who wanted to have open bottles of champagne on the table so people could serve themselves and one another. "I hate when the drink is sitting there before you are." When Tony overruled his decision, the caterer got all tense and huffy. He argued that "people get nervous. They don't want to do things!" Tony didn't care about appeasing the jittery caterer. He was much more concerned with keeping the feel of the wedding spontaneous and relaxed. And guess what—the guests knew just what to do with the open bottles of champagne.

Soothing the Savage Guests

*K*aitlin forgot to arrange for music for her wedding. Maybe it was because the wedding was in her parents' yard and there were only going to be fifty people there. Maybe it was because she was planning from a couple of states away. Or maybe it was because she was six months pregnant and she had other things on her mind. In any case, about twenty minutes into the reception, her teenage brother became painfully aware of the oversight. "It was like a funeral," he says. He addressed the silence by propping speakers in his bedroom window, pointed down toward the yard, and blasting R.E.M. (which he considered to be "cross-generational").

If you're concerned about the mood of your reception space, remember that the music can help transform it. More than lighting or decorations or a view, music can create an atmosphere. So give some thought to all the options.

By the way, if you've been handling a lot of the wedding decisions without the input of your betrothed, this is likely to change when it comes time to hire a DJ or a band. Generally speaking, boys like music (as opposed to, say, flowers, which, when asked, they're apt to characterize as either "nice" or "too smelly"). In fact, your boyfriend might have some very strong opinions about wedding music. A lot of people do.

Some firmly believe that live music is the only way to go. Come on. Is third-rate live music better than first-rate recorded music? To those who claim that a DJ at a wedding is tacky, I reply, compared to what? To a wedding band? Saying that DJs are inherently tacky is like saying that all men are pigs; you obviously haven't met the right one. The same is true of bands. It's all about who you hire and how you direct them.

Play-By-Play

"Ladies and gentlemen, appearing for the first time as husband and wife, Mr. and Mrs. I. M. Humiliated!" Aaaaah! Wake up, wake up. It's only a nightmare. But learn from it: Don't be lazy about who you hire to run the musical show. The DJ or bandleader is often also the emcee of your wedding. Think of your most obnoxious acquaintance (one who never gets your last name right) lording over a room full of your friends and family—with a *microphone*. Scary, huh? But you're the boss; you're doing the hiring. Start hunting for someone with the right skills and personality to be master of ceremonies. You don't want an emcee? Make it *not* happen.

"We saw a band at a friend's wedding and we really liked their music," says Carol. "But the bandleader was talking a lot, narrating the whole wedding." Carol and her boyfriend, Edward, wanted to hire the band for their wedding, but they wanted the bandleader to keep quiet, so they sat down with him and said so. "He was fine about it. He said the reason he was so vocal at our friend's wedding was that no one was running it, and then usually it's up to the band to move from one activity to the next." Eva and Mike were up front with their DJ too, and he respected their wishes for "no tacky announcements or big productions."

Well, what about *little* productions? Nancy's mother wanted to be introduced at her daughter's reception. In order for that to happen, the bride and groom would have to be introduced too, of course. The groom, Hal, was not into this. To him, a good bandleader is a mute bandleader. "He always laughs at a wedding when the couple makes an entrance as 'Mr. and Mrs.' That's what my mother wanted us to do," says Nancy, "and I wasn't changing my name, so it seemed especially silly." As a compromise, Nancy and Hal agreed to be introduced by their first names. So the parents got their little thrill, and the happy couple emerged unscathed.

Live or Shuffle?

Band versus DJ. There are two factors here: your budget and what you want the "sound" of your wedding to be. Money-wise, of course, a DJ is a better bet. It means one person to pay as opposed to a minimum of, say, four players in a band (yes, you pay by the head here too). And to really keep costs down, you can ask a friend to DJ. But make sure it's someone you can count on. This is a big job, especially if it involves transporting sound equipment. You or your designated DJ must check out the space in advance: Are there outlets in the right places? Three-prong where you need them? Bring lots of adapters and extension cords. In fact, you might want to pay a friend if he or she agrees to DJ. Sometimes people take tasks more seriously when they involve money. You can give a friend a fair price for a day's work and it still won't be half what "professional" DJs charge.

"I didn't miss having a band at my wedding," says Nick. "I'm in a band, so I don't consider live music a thrill. For people who aren't around bands all the time or who don't go to see music, maybe it's more special, but I'm used to it. And you can have the best bands in the world playing your wedding as long as you have records or an iPhone or iPod."

Truer words have never been spoken. Recorded music gives you tremendous flexibility. Yes, most wedding bands can play "I'll Be Seeing You" and a tarantella and "Stop in the Name of Love." But, let's face it, their renditions of all three can be eerily similar. Wouldn't it be nice to have Frank Sinatra and the Valtare Musetta and the Supremes instead?

Many people say no, it wouldn't. For Luke, "the excitement of live music is much better than a DJ." The band was his favorite aspect of his wedding. "Live music creates a real sense that it's a special occasion. I think it makes people want to dance more too."

No Money Down

If you've decided to forgo both band and DJ in the interest of saving some money, start making playlists: a couple of solid dance mixes, a few with a less driving beat, to play while people are eating (so they're not compelled to chew to the rhythm), and some slow-dance music, so couples can gaze into each other's eyes and reminisce about their wedding; single friends can have a chance to dance with the mysterious stranger of their choice; and your bitter cousin can mope dramatically at her table (like she does at all family functions).

Don't try to be a live DJ when you're making playlists; you can't predict whether the crowd will be ready to sit down after three up-tempo dance tunes or after six. So make whole playlists of each "music mood." When the crowd or the food dictates that it's time for something else, your iTunes-meister can just scroll to the next appropriate playlist, instead of leaving your guests hanging in a silent nether zone.

If your reception space has sound equipment, look at it way in advance. Then have the iTunes-meister go the day before (*avec* iPod or computer) to make sure he/she has no problem using the system (okay, maybe most people wouldn't, but *I'd* need a little time with a new system to feel like it understood me and I understood it). If you take the time to make decent quality playlists use iCloud or an external hard drive to back-up each one, in case something happens to your device. Give a backup iPod loaded with your playlists to a reliable party who can ensure that it will be brought to the reception. (I guess your mother has a lot going on that day, but you must have at least one friend you can trust.) When you're doing this kind of work yourself, your motto is "Delegate, delegate, delegate."

Mood Machine

Whether you go with a band, a DJ or an iTunes playlist, the type of music you choose will establish the mood of the event. The typical mixed wedding band playlist ("Old Time Rock and Roll" into "Endless Love" into "Hot Hot Hot") will create the mood of a typical wedding. No one will be offended, but maybe you want to aim a little higher.

Samantha and Chad wanted live music, but they knew they weren't interested in ordinary wedding bands. As Samantha puts it, "While they're meeting your great-aunt Edna's needs, your friends are laughing at you in the bathroom." So Chad asked the manager at a local bar if he knew a good R&B band. Samantha and Chad went to see the guys perform and loved them. And more important, the band had played a couple of other weddings, "so they knew what to do when someone requested a hora." The rest of the time, they stuck to R&B, and everyone danced, regardless of age. Even Samantha's snobbish music-industry friends remarked, "Hey, great band."

Darcy and Gus had their DJ play only old standards—George Gershwin, Cole Porter, Irving Berlin. "It created a very romantic old-fashioned atmosphere," says Darcy. "I didn't want to switch to rock, just so people could dance. That would have spoiled the mood. People who wanted to dance did."

The nine-piece Latin band at Jamie and Nicole's reception made the occasion incredibly festive. "It wasn't like any wedding I've ever been to," says one guest. "There was no downtime. It cooked for five hours."

Musically speaking, Bill and Debra had an all-sixties wedding. A lot of Beatles, Rolling Stones and Motown for dancing, and some mellower stuff (Joni Mitchell, Bread, Simon & Garfunkel) during dinner. It was the music Bill's parents had played when he was growing up, and he and Debra were attached to it.

Warning: Generation Gap Ahead

"Don't let your parents pick the band!" urges Luke. He and Victoria wanted a real rock 'n' roll band at their wedding. Victoria's mother insisted (in countless voicemails) that this would alienate the older guests and make them miserable. If it was up to her (it wasn't), she'd hire a painfully standard wedding band so, as she said over and over, "everybody would be happy." Except, of course, Luke and Victoria.

"Victoria's mother thought it was going to be a disaster and kept trying to get us to delete instruments: 'Do they *need* two guitars? Do they *need* a saxophone?' She thought it would be too loud and too much." But as long as you have another space where people can go for quiet, Luke argues, you should get a band that rocks, if that's what you want. The band Luke and Victoria hired was such a hit with the guests (many of whom can recall a time when a nickel could buy a roast beef sandwich, a side of potato salad and a Coca-Cola, with change left over), that the bride and groom ordered up an extra set on the spur of the moment.

Listen, Honey—They're Playing Our Song

Sometimes if you want something done right, you have to do it yourself. You'd think it would be pretty easy for a "professional" DJ to bring one specific recording to a wedding for your first dance together, but that is simply more than some of them can handle.

Marc and Lori wanted to dance to Al Green's recording of "Let's Stay Together." They didn't choose it just for their wedding; it was their song, for real. "The DJs told me they had it," says Marc. But at the reception, when Marc stepped over to remind them, they said something along the lines of "Duh . . . nope. We forgot." The record was in Marc and Lori's apartment less than a mile away, but of course it was too late. Forced into a quick decision they'd regret for the rest of their lives, they ended up dancing to the overplayed standard "What a Wonderful World."

Paul and Krista were warned by others who'd been burned. They thought they'd eliminate the margin for error by bringing

Dance Anxiety

Brandon was terrified to dance in front of people; he had an almost pathological case of stage fright. He expected Reba to be sympathetic and cool about doing without the traditional first dance, because the rest of their wedding was pretty unconventional. But she wasn't. Brandon was puzzled. Says Reba, "I was embarrassed to tell him that it was something I'd always dreamed of, because I thought that sounded so superficial." When she finally explained to Brandon that having a first dance together was important to her, he was surprised but understanding. They practiced at two weddings before their own. When their day came Brandon was able to get through his moment in the spotlight by firmly fixing his eyes on his blushing bride and keeping a cold compress nearby.

their own iPod with the song they wanted to dance to. But when it came time to play it, no one had any idea where the iPod was. (It was later found cooking in the August sun on the dashboard of their Honda.) The couple spent a good ten minutes rooting around the DJ area on their hands and knees, looking for it. Terribly dismayed and too flustered to make a snap decision, they deferred to the judgment of the bride's sister, who chose something off one of Mel Torme's albums of classics.

Jeff and Molly had a related problem, which might have been prevented if they'd spoken directly to their DJ instead of just with the guy who ran the DJ service. Says Jeff, "We wanted to dance to 'It Had to Be You,' but there was just this one caveat: It couldn't be the Harry Connick, Jr., version, because I can't stand that guy." Jeff called the DJ booker three separate times to confirm this. "And of course, that's the version the DJ showed up with." In retrospect, Jeff wishes he hadn't paid the DJ the full amount. "But," he says, "that wasn't on my mind at the time." Of course it wasn't. That's what certain sloppy wedding professionals bank on. You're having the biggest day of your life, and your business acumen is out the window.

When you do your confirmation calls or e-mails the week before your wedding, make sure the bandleader has prepared your song. And if you're dealing with recorded music, there's no reason to count on a DJ to bring a CD (especially after reading these tales of horror); buy it yourself and see that it gets to the reception. Assign someone the task of reconfirming with the band as they set up (yes, again), or of bringing the appropriate, well-marked CD to the DJ and verbally confirming what the song is. Your first dance together is a moment you'll want to make perfect, so take the trouble to ensure it will be.

Any Requests?

DJs or bands will either e-mail or hand you lists of songs they do or recordings they own and honor your requests. We had kind of a loose working relationship with our DJ, because he was sort of a friend of my husband's and because I brought all the songs myself (calling all control freaks!). As he was setting up, he said to me, "I thought I'd play something mellow as people arrive, maybe some Windham Hill." Tears welled up in my eyes. I tried to speak but couldn't. My sister jumped in, "No, please! No Windham Hill!" She put her arm around me and calmed her voice a bit. "Please just use the music we brought, okay?"

Definitely take the time to talk to your bandleader or DJ about your preferences. But don't forget that the bride and groom are not the only people at a wedding allowed to make requests. This is one of those "just let go" subjects. Your bandleader or DJ wants to be polite to your guests (they are the guests, after all). So even if you intend to devise a lengthy playlist, remember that you can't control the music completely.

Marie hired a band that played old standards, with a Billie Holliday–style singer. "They could also play rock, but I didn't want a lot of bad rock covers. But of course my cousins requested all these bad rock covers, and there was nothing I could do about it."

"My mother-in-law went up to the DJ and complained that the music was too loud during dinner," says Maris. "So he put on some kind of Muzak really low. I felt like I was at the dentist." On Maris's behalf, the maid of honor went over to the DJ station, picked out something she liked and told him to keep the volume as low as he deemed necessary while everyone was eating.

In addition to the list of 150 songs Regina and Ted wanted to hear, they gave the band a list of songs they absolutely did not want near their reception. Included in the "don't" list: "Shout" (as in "You Make Me Wanna"), "Celebration," "The Electric Slide" and "Hot, Hot, Hot." That sounds like a good start. You too might want to exercise your right to eliminate various aerobic hits from your band or DJ's playlist. But remember, an overzealous party animal speaks louder than a busy, distracted bride, so if you detect the melodic strains of Kool and the Gang while you're trapped behind Table #10, laugh it off; you'll live longer.

Hey, Mr. DJ

Some stuff to keep in mind.

- **If you bring your own iPod or records, mark them clearly and boldly.** "I didn't think of it," says Max. "I figured after the wedding, I'd just take back my stuff. But the DJ was out of there before I was, along with, accidentally, my iPod." Getting it back killed an entire Sunday afternoon."

- **Find out what's up with breaks.** At one point during my reception, I noticed a deadly silence. Now, I know a DJ has to take a break, but why should there be any silence when you're dealing with recorded music? Why didn't the DJ just use our playlist? He was nowhere to be found, so I fiddled with his computer myself. The DJ was not happy when he realized someone was touching his equipment. I guess I should have told him in advance that I would prefer to hear the same artist for thirty minutes than have a block of quiet.

- **Ask the DJ to send you samples of the music he/she plays at the reception.** Eva's DJ did it without being asked. "It's fun to have a dance mix of your wedding," she says.

- **If he's rude now, imagine how he'll be once he has your deposit.** Anita was being an efficient party planner when she asked "DJ Surly" if he had backup equipment. "No," said Surly. "My equipment is commercial quality. You could back a Mack truck over it." (Subtext: "You clueless bitch. Don't you take that tone with me.") But Anita was experiencing a healthy paranoia. This was her wedding here. "What about

accidents?" she asked. Surly replied, "That's never happened."
(Subtext: "Don't challenge me, woman. I could kick your
ass.") Then the subtext started leaking into Surly's actual dia-
logue. He became openly rude. "We had to ask him to leave,"
says Anita. "I should have known. The cat didn't like him."

Strike Up the Band

But read this first.

- **Beware profit-oriented logic.** Stephanie actually heard this
  from a bandleader: "For 120 guests, you'll need at least five
  pieces." What? I'd love to see the formula that helped him
  arrive at that figure. He didn't even have the nerve to direct
  his audacious advice to Stephanie. He said it to her mother,
  whose obvious insecurity tempted many a sleazeball wedding vendor to try his antics. Says Stephanie, "He made her
  feel like if she didn't follow his guidelines, she'd be humiliated in front of all her friends."

- **Watch out for the old switcheroo.** "When we first saw our
  band play, they had this one terrific singer who specialized
  in Motown songs," says Jessica. The singer cost an extra
  $500 (boi-oi-oing!), but Jessica and Bruce decided to go for
  it. "Two weeks before the wedding, the bandleader told us
  that Mr. Motown couldn't make it." He fast-talked them
  into a replacement—at the same price. The new guy was
  fine, but was no Mr. Motown, and was certainly not worth
  an extra $500. Regina and Ted found themselves in the
  same situation, but nobody had called to warn them. They
  booked a band far in advance of their wedding. By the time

Special Guest Stars

Some couples who used recorded music at their receptions worked a bit of live music into the proceedings with the help of guests. They scheduled a little performance in the middle of the party, to break up the eating, drinking and merrymaking. At Patti and Sam's wedding, the jazz quartet featured the groom. Lygia and Gavin both performed at their wedding. Lygia played classical cello as part of a trio; Gavin played jazz saxophone with a friend on piano. Tom asked his brother, who's the lead singer in a rock band, to do an acoustic set at his reception, right before dessert. If you really like the thrill of live music but can't afford to hire a band, this might be a nice way to go. For a short set, any type of up-tempo music would be fun, so talk to your musical friends or relatives and see what you can come up with.

the event rolled around, four of the seven band members—including the singer—had been replaced.

- **Can you divide?** Samantha and Chad, the couple who found their dream R&B band, also found themselves with a massive music bill. The band had thirteen members, and, no, they wouldn't divide themselves and have half the members play the wedding. That's one drawback to going outside the wedding industry; policies are not geared toward making life easier for a bride and groom.

- **Should the band play unplugged?** Tracy and Doug had a swing quintet at their wedding—a piano, drums, two horns and an upright bass, no vocals. "We'd just been to a wedding where the music was so loud, you couldn't have a conversation, so we asked our band to look at our reception space and see if they could play unamplified. I think it worked out great. The music was plenty loud on the dance floor and more exciting because it was coming straight from the instruments. But you could talk to people across the table from you without shouting."

Photographic Memories

*A*fter the party's over and the gifts have become just more stuff to dust, all you have are the photos and videos. Among the people I interviewed for this book, there were more who had regrets about this element than about any other (time helps block out most, but photographs are forever). So don't be cavalier about who you hire to take pictures, or you'll be whining about it to your grandchildren one day.

The consensus is that a good photographer is worth the money. But that certainly doesn't mean you have to go to Weddings-'R-Us and pay a flat rate of $5,000, "album included." In fact, quite the opposite. Many people told me they were happy they used non-wedding photographers. In finding the right person, the key is to know what your priorities are. Do you want mostly candids? Something a little artsy? Cool wide-angle shots? And what about personality? We've all experienced the patronizing smirk and "do as you're told" demeanor of an obnoxious, overbearing wedding photographer. You need someone you like, whose style is compatible with yours and who can be invisible and very aware at the same time (I'll spare you the marriage analogy here).

Spend some time talking to potential photographers to make sure they won't be offensive to your guests, or for that matter, to you. "The photographer was in my face constantly," says Michelle. "He would not quit. When we left the church and got in the car, all I wanted was to be alone with my husband for a minute. I asked the photographer to go away, and he just acted like he knew better. I hate the way I look in our wedding photos, because I was not in the mood to have my picture taken."

See, people have to like the photographer or you'll have an album full of scowls and phony smiles. So when you start looking, ask friends who have a similar sense of "nice personality" for referrals. Joanne was lucky. She knew the work and personality of a particular photographer well enough to be able to hire her without shopping around. "We tried hard not to spend much money on the rest of the wedding, but we were willing to pay for this woman. She had photographed my sisters' weddings, so I didn't even have to tell her who was who. It was her third time with us, and that really made a difference. I liked her and felt comfortable having her there."

Of course, what you want most is someone who takes great pictures. But people have different ideas about what a great photo is, just like they have different methods of assessing personality. A friend from work sent Clarice to her "wonderful" wedding photographer. "His photos were very conventional and not particularly flattering," says Clarice. So she found a photographer through an artist friend. "Our photos look different from all other wedding pictures I've seen. The light and composition are amazing."

There's an element of "The Emperor's New Clothes" to assessing photography; many people say someone is a "great" photographer because they've been told he is. Of course, everyone wants photos that are somewhat in focus, but beyond that it's pretty subjective. So don't feel pressured to hire a photographer your mother or friend or cousin swears is "the best in the business." Find someone whose work speaks to you. You don't have to explain why; you don't even have to *know* why. There are a lot of photographers out there; your mission is to find one who can take photos you'll love forever.

Posers

I was one of those brides who adamantly refused to spend any time away from the party taking posed shots. Who wants them? They look stiff and phony anyway. Lucky for me, I was pressured to do a few. "Candids only" *sounds* good, but many couples who stick to that plan regret it. Maybe you don't want a portrait-type picture of yourself in your dress. But you would probably love to have a picture of you and your best friend both looking at the camera with all four of your eyes open.

Posed shots don't have to mean bride and groom in the center with lines of stiff-limbed androids windmilling out from either side. They don't have to be head to toe either. That's one of the things that makes them look so unnatural. You can get your family together in a bunch and put your arms around each other. Or have close-ups done of you and your siblings, you and your husband, etc. My favorite wedding pictures are the ones the photographer took while our families were milling about getting ready for the posed shots.

"I regret having been casual with my photographer the day of the wedding," says Kelly. "There are so many pictures where I'm looking at someone else, and I'm not looking at Matt. Or where

I'm laughing and I have three chins. But there's not one picture of us together that people can remember us by."

Kimberly and Gene hired a photographer who does very good informal shots, "and we got what we paid for," says Kimberly. "But he didn't know how to organize the group for posed shots, and at the last minute, I decided I wanted a few." So she and Gene tried to orchestrate them, be in them and tell the photographer what to do, all at the same time. "People were distracted and looking in different directions. There's not one good shot among them."

If your instinct is to skip the posed shots completely, think some more. Right now the most important thing about your wedding is being able to enjoy the day—and that's the way it should be. But later the pictures are going to mean so much to you. I'm not saying disappear from your reception for an hour and shoot

Watch Out—Your Face Might Stay That Way

My beautiful little sister makes a goofy face every time a camera is pointed in her direction. We have dozens of pictures of her crossing her eyes, flaring her nostrils or twisting her mouth into an Elvis-type snarl. Does this ring a bell? I know you won't make funny faces at your wedding photographer, but if you're nervous in front of the camera, it will show. You have to find a way to relax or you might end up looking like a very well-dressed deer caught in the headlights. Your best defense is a photographer who can elicit a real smile and who's very quick on the draw. This is a majorly important thing to look for when you're checking out a photographer's book. Do the subjects look relaxed or like they're in pain? Are they laughing? Wincing? Of course, you can't depend totally on a photographer to make you appear comfortable ("I hate him! He made me look tense in every single photo!"), so employ a trick of the modeling trade: Ask the happy-to-please photographer to give you a count of three before he/she shoots. Look away till you hear three, then quickly turn your head toward the camera and smile. The result is the "someone I love just called my name" facial expression (a mainstay of the J. Crew catalog). You should also massage your jaw every now and then (watch that foundation!), stretch your mouth wide open and blow through closed lips, making an engine sound. (This is before the photo's taken, of course, not during.) If all else fails, a glass of champagne on an empty stomach is nearly foolproof.

every possible permutation. But a few shots will be a safety against regrets and will not steal a significant amount of fun time.

Regina and Ted thought it through and came up with their own solution: Two weeks before their wedding, when the leaves were changing, they went to a park with their photographer and had some shots taken. "We wore casual clothes, because all we really wanted was a nice relaxed portrait of us," says Regina. They didn't do any posed pictures at their wedding, just candids. "I never would have wanted those formal pictures in an album, so why bother?"

Eva and Mike decided to wait till the end of the reception to take the posed group shots, so they wouldn't waste prime party time. "Don't do this!" says Eva. It was a mistake. In their posed photos, everyone looks tired and messy. "My hair is starting to come undone, my mother has mascara under her eyes from crying, and everyone's clothes are rumpled."

Straight Shooting: Getting the Photos You Want

"I thought I'd be able to tell the photographer at the wedding the specific pictures I wanted her to take, which of course I wasn't able to do," says Regina. That's why you have to make a list of your "special people." But in order to be effective, the list has to be kind of short; otherwise the photographer will spend the reception peering at a piece of paper or scanning the list on his smartphone instead of catching the magic moments. "Try to look for somebody who seems to have a sense of what's going on around him," suggests Mitch, "because you won't have time to take him by the hand and show him the people you want photographed. He has to be intuitive and able to figure out to some degree who is close to you."

We told our photographer we wanted pictures of our friends and immediate families and not to bother photographing other relatives. And he did just what we asked. He was really sensitive to what was going on around him, and he got great candids. But, of course, he couldn't read my mind and distinguish between *my* friends and my husband's friends. There are no pictures of my closest friends, because they were not aggressive about getting in front of the camera, and there are many, many pictures of my husband's friends. I wish I'd told certain people to be a little bolder. Erika had the same kind of problem. "We're pretty wimpy in my family," she says. "To this day we all sort of resent and regret the fact that all the casual pictures were of George's family. We just didn't know you could tell the photographer what to do. We thought that *he* told *you* what to do. My family was too shy to say, 'Hey can you take a picture of us over here?'"

Of course you can tell him what to do. He works for you. Bark orders. Okay, maybe it's not necessary to bark. But make your wishes very clear, especially if you're dealing with a photographer who's not used to doing weddings.

Heather didn't make a list for her photographer or introduce him to her immediate family. "There are, like, four pictures of my friend's boyfriend, who I hardly know, and none of my brother," she says. It didn't occur to Heather to give instructions, because the wedding was not that large (ninety guests). "I just thought that over the course of five hours, there would be plenty of photos taken of everybody."

Human Pyramid

Josie says, "If you have a small reception, have a picture taken of everyone together." She did—all seventy guests plus the happy couple, surrounded by flowers in the churchyard. "It was a tight fit. My brothers were literally climbing the wall behind us to get into the frame. But I love the photo."

Photo Research

Stacia wishes she'd had some photos taken of just her alone. "My mother-in-law was upset to find out I hadn't—she has an empty silver frame on her mantel with my name on it—and ultimately, I know I should have. I spent so much time and money on the way I looked that day, I wish I had just one picture that shows off the whole thing."

To come out of this as regret-free as possible (that's what this book is all about, right?) really think about what you want in advance (meaning now). Just because you said long ago that you'd never take posed photos at your hypothetical future wedding doesn't mean you have to stick to it. Contradict yourself, and don't be shy about it. Do a little research to help figure out what you now want. Look at photos from friends' weddings. They'll give you ideas of what you like and hate. Are your favorite pictures the ones of people dancing? Or eating? Or staring off into space? Do you want a photograph of each table? How important to you is composition?

Then make sure you hire the right person. Kathleen, who wanted anything but typical wedding photos, was lucky enough to find an art photographer who had also shot a couple of weddings. That's ideal. If you hire someone who does beautiful portraits, but who has never shot candids at a party, or has never dealt with more than two subjects at a time, you're taking a chance. Jason and Sally wanted mostly black-and-white photos, but they didn't realize that would require a special photographer. As it turns out, the wedding photographer they hired wasn't used to working in black and white. "She never does, but she failed to tell us that," says Sally, "and most of the photos came out really dark."

A Picture's Worth

Be alert when you're finding out about prices. Some photographers break down fees (fee for a day's work, cost of film or digital images, cost of developing and cost of prints, if applicable); some don't.

Sometimes prints are included in the initial fee; sometimes they're not. "I got a price from one photographer that was much lower than others," says Mary. "It turned out that it was just his fee for the day and it didn't include anything else," most significantly, a hefty "service charge" tacked onto the film and lab charges. Be smart and ask lots of questions. Here's some more advice.

- If a photographer gives you just one figure, always ask for a detailed breakdown.

- Fees for black-and-white developing and prints might be higher than those on the price list, which are usually for color processing, so if you're interested, ask.

- Find out who owns the negatives or digital images and what it means if the photographer does. "About two years after my wedding, my mother finally got around to ordering some prints," says Pam. "I was actually going to order a couple more myself." But when Pam called the photographer, she discovered that he had thrown away her negatives. "He didn't even contact me to see if I wanted to buy them, which I would have."

- Shop around a little, even if you've found someone you want to hire. Before you agree to a price, you need to get a sense of what other people in your area are charging.

Cheap Shots

Some people who are looking to spend less money cut out the photographer first, thinking, Well, I could get anyone to take pictures. I'm not going to tell you that you *have* to hire a photographer, because if you don't have the money, you don't have the money. And besides, plenty of wedding photographers are lousy. But if you're going to arrange for something yourself, be really serious about it. As far as I'm concerned, you can serve Chips Ahoy! and Red Bull, skip the flowers and forgo the limousine, but don't be casual about documenting your wedding. As usual, it doesn't have to mean spending a lot of money; it can just be an expense of concentration and energy.

Disposable cameras, manned by guests, are cheap and fun. "Guests at our wedding did some creative things, besides taking nice close-ups of the people at their tables. They did pictures of food, the view, dancing feet. They're great," says Eva. She also discovered that you can get the cameras cheaper at some stores if you buy in bulk. A lot of people use disposables as a supplement to a hired photographer. I wouldn't count on them as my sole source of pictures; but you might want to use them in combination with a thoroughly prepared fantastic photographer friend. "Prepared" is the operative word here.

A friend of Charlotte's shot her wedding for free. Says Charlotte, "She had experience as an editorial photographer but had never shot a wedding before." That was a problem. "She didn't really think about getting pictures of all the different guests or photographing each table, and we didn't think of briefing her in advance." As it turned out, most of the pictures were of people the photographer knew.

If you're worried about this and reluctant to put too much pressure on a friend who's nice enough to help you out, cover yourself another way. Have a *staff* of photographers who each know different people at the wedding. Josie asked four friends and her sister to bring their digital cameras and smartphones. "They're all at least decent photographers, and two of them are great," she says. She gave them loose assignments—cover the family, cover the groom's friends—but told them also to take any pictures they wanted. "I think this is the best way to have a wedding photographed, even if you have the budget to hire a photographer," she says. "Nobody was hiding when they saw a camera coming, because the photographers were people they were comfortable with. And we got all kinds of perspectives."

Having people use their own digital cameras might make more sense than handing out disposable cameras. Aside from the obvious reason—that a better camera takes better shots (actually, I've seen some great photos taken with disposables)—friends might take the assignment more seriously if they're using their own equipment. Then they can just send you the images after the wedding.

Angela and Barry, who are art directors, had lots of professional photographer friends at their wedding. They rented a roll of white seamless paper (the solid backdrop used for fashion photography) and the apparatus to support it, and the photographers took turns shooting the couple and guests on the "set." Their wedding pictures look like a summer fashion story in *Harper's Bazaar*.

Will and Penny thought booking a photographer would be pretty easy, because they wanted someone for only about two hours—just during the ceremony and for a few posed shots of the family beforehand. They were going to leave the rest of the photography to family and friends to keep expenses down. But when Penny started making inquiries, she discovered that finding a wedding photographer who will work from four till six on a June Saturday is about as easy as running a marathon barefoot. During wedding season, it's a full day's work or nothing. When Penny went outside the industry, she was able to find someone: a local freelance photographer for a newspaper's website who was willing to charge by the hour, with no minimum.

Urban Legend

The brides I spoke to generally had only minor complaints about their photographers. But a couple of them said a friend of a friend of their aunt's pharmacist's cousin got screwed over by a photographer who didn't make it to the wedding. You'll eliminate that possibility, I know, because you're so committed to the Confirm Till They Hate Ya policy. But why not make sure there are backup people with fully charged digital cameras just in case?

Mo' Money, Mo' Money, Mo' Money

Like a lot of couples, Gabi and Kevin used their gift money to cover the checks they wrote at the end of the wedding. But they didn't budget anything for a major *post*wedding expense—prints. Now, three years later, they have beautiful contact sheets, but no pictures. "It was an additional several hundred dollars that just wasn't there," says Gabi. "We figured we'd take care of it when we had some money. But when do you ever have several hundred dollars of disposable income?"

Let's Go to the Video

*T*he traditional wording of wedding invitations is misleading. I think some should be more precise, and tell guests what they're in for. Like, this one would be a big seller if engravers offered it: "Please come to the digital documentation of our marriage. There will be a forty-five-minute intermission between ceremony and reception while the video crew relocates."

You know what I'm talking about. Stadium lights on 12-foot poles; assistants scurrying frantically about; the bride and groom perpetually blocked from view by equipment and camera operators; and the guests, just extras in a party scene. You sit at your eerily dark table. All you can see is a glow rising up from the center of the room. You figure the happy couple is dancing, so you close your eyes and try to picture them. Oh, they must look great. They probably have such sweet expressions on their faces. You're sure it must be very moving (for the crew—the only people who can see). At least you can hear the music. Maybe one day you'll watch the video.

No, not all digitally documented weddings are run entirely for the benefit of the camera. And some videographers can blend in as well as any guest who has an intensely bright light shining from his forehead. I just have a personal problem with digital video. For me it's spooky to reexperience such a momentous, emotional occasion on TV or the screen of your choice. Someone made an informal video at my wedding and when I saw it, I wanted to put it under the wheel of the nearest truck. It just freaked me out. I'll bet this was the same reaction people had to photography when it first came into being. My position is, of course, laughably outdated. But just as black-and-white photos have a certain romance to them compared to color pictures, all photography is romantic compared to any type of video. For me, video is just too real.

For Naomi, even still photos were too real. She intended to have no photographer at her wedding. "My in-laws insisted on one," she says. "They hired her. They paid her." Yes, ultimately Naomi was glad. "The photographer wasn't obtrusive, and because the whole thing went so fast, I was grateful to have some pictures." But when the in-laws started applying pressure about having the wedding captured on video, Naomi put her foot down. "They said, '*Are you sure* you don't want a video person?'" says Naomi. "In other words, 'Are you sure you're going to deny us the opportunity to have our son's wedding on video, Naomi? Are you sure you're going to do that to us?'" Yes, Naomi was sure. She didn't want her romantic memory of the event to be replaced by a harsher reality.

Almost Recording

Joni did not want her wedding on video. But a friend filmed the reception in black-and-white super-8. He added a soundtrack of classical and Dixieland music, and gave it to Joni and Fred as a gift. Joni loves this particular live-action record of her wedding. "It didn't demystify the day for me, which I was afraid a video would do."

"We wanted to remember our wedding as we felt it, not as it was seen through the lens," says Eva, so she and Mike never considered videotaping. But Eva's brother showed up at the rehearsal with his video camera, and Eva decided it might be fun to tape parts of the rehearsal at the church and the dinner that would follow. She's glad she did. "The video is very funny and touching, and it was great to preserve our vows on tape without having a video guy at the actual wedding."

To Record or Not to Record

You sacrifice some of the intimacy of your party when you open it up to lights and any kind of video camera. But is it worth it? And will you regret it if you don't do it?

"My mother wanted me to hire a videographer, and now I wish I had," says Michelle. "We had a really special folk mass that we worked so hard on, with all these great musicians and singers. All I have from that is the program. That music can't ever be duplicated, and I wish I could hear it again." (An audio recording also would have worked nicely in this situation, for a lot less money.)

One of Jeff's few wedding regrets is that he didn't capture the wedding on video. "I kind of figured my brother-in-law had it covered, because he always has a camera stuck to his eye," says Jeff. "But we have more footage of his three-year-old daughter than of the wedding." Like casual photography, casual video is bound to disappoint.

Paul and Krista were ambivalent about hiring a videographer, mostly because of the expense. Paul said, "If we're going to get this thing and spend the money, we'd better watch it." So they do, once a year on their anniversary. Whether they feel like it or not.

Libby feels no obligation to make use of her wedding video; she's glad she got it and recommends videos for all, but openly admits that seeing your wedding on video is a little bizarre. "I'm not going to watch it again till I have kids—or maybe grandkids— and they ask to see it," says Libby.

Robin also has a little trouble reconciling what she sees on the screen with her own wedding memories. "At one point in the reception we were seated in two chairs on the dance floor and all our friends were dancing around us. That was, for both of us, one of the most magical moments ever," she says. "We just felt like we'd been transported to another world. But watching it on video was a little odd. You're just observing yourself having fun. And it's on a different plane."

A Videographer Underfoot

Okay, after the fact, a video is something that makes a lot of people happy. But how about during the wedding? Did the cameras throw them off? Did the videographer bug the guests or over-illuminate any memorable moments? Hiring a videographer is like hiring a photographer—you have to factor in personality. This "wedding professional" is going to be interacting with your guests, so it would be nice if he or she were pleasant to be around.

Dan, our good friend in the wedding video business, stresses the importance of finding someone whose taste is similar to yours. "What *I* think is bad, some people like," says Dan. "One couple wanted me to shoot the whole bridal party at a park running in slow motion past the camera, and then intercut it with the wedding. I don't do that, so they went and found someone else."

Dan is a strong supporter of the independent videographer over the big video company. Talk to both, and see what you think. But Dan feels that "people who work for big companies don't really care about you or your wedding. They're gonna get paid whether you're happy or not. But someone who runs his own business has to answer to you. His name is on the line, so he has to make clients happy." As always, you should voice your preferences loudly. If you don't want the videographer to interview your guests, say so. If you do want interviews, "be sure to tell the videographer not to pressure people to talk if they don't want to," says Dan. "You'll end up with embarrassing, bad footage."

Tracy let her mother take care of hiring a video company, and she never confirmed her preferences with the two people the company sent. "I wanted the ceremony shot from far away, but there they were under the chupa as I approached," says Tracy. She got used to them and felt they were pretty unobtrusive, but you know what? They weren't, if you were outside the chupa trying to get a peek at the bride (like I was). They blocked the whole ceremony.

One reason brides and grooms come away believing their videographer was not in the way of the action is that, as the guests of honor, they are always on the correct side of the camera—they *are* the action. But as the subjects of their own documentary, couples often have one complaint: the relentless white light.

"Nobody wants the light. That's the first thing everybody asks about: the light, the light, the light," says Dan. "If you want a professional job, you're going to have to accept some light. And if you can't take the light, you might as well just have Uncle Harry do it."

Of course, if your wedding is outdoors in the daytime, light is not an issue. A videographer can be much less obtrusive under these conditions. Also, Dan says you should ask about the *specifics* of the lighting. "When you're in front of the camera and the light is on, you can't avoid knowing it, but a videographer doesn't have to light up the entire place." Find out what your options are.

Here's a suggestion that could save you some money: Don't ask the videographer to come to your house while you're getting ready. "It's a complete waste," says Dan, "because the photographer's setting up shots, the bride is getting ready and the videographer's just in the way." There are big companies that handle both the shooting and the photography, which eliminates any tension between the two elements (but don't let a package deal make you lazy about the details).

Also, be clear about exactly when the videographer's job ends. Some will hightail it out of there right after the cake is cut if you don't specifically request that they stay longer. And if you care how the videographer and assistant are dressed, say so.

Seven Questions to Ask a Videographer

- **What does the price include?** As in, what format, how many copies and what types of editing options?

- **Exactly who will be doing the shooting?** Will it be the boss, who you're dealing with over the phone? If not, arrange to talk to the person (or people) who will do the job, so you can explain what you want and what you don't want.

- **Is there an extra charge for more than one location?** Meaning the place where the ceremony is held, the place where the reception will be, and anywhere you want a video camera before or after.

- **How many people will be on the crew?** Dan recommends one camera operator and one assistant. "A camera operator working alone at a big event might be overwhelmed at times. But a crew of more than two impinges on your privacy."

- **Will you be wireless?** Or will you be dragging cables all over the dance floor, a lawsuit waiting to happen? This is a major factor in how obtrusive or inobtrusive a presence the videographer will be. (If there are cables involved, you'll probably be spared the "you won't even know we're there" pitch.)

- **What if the camera should, God forbid, break?** These people should have backup equipment. Ask about it.

- **How long will the editing process take? When can I have my video?** This might depend on which editing extras, if any, you opt for. Read on.

Postproduction

They say it's not just the director who makes a film great, it's the editor. And the same goes for your wedding video. Editing means the difference between uncluttered documentation and overproduced schmaltz. First, there are special effects, a matter of taste (not mine). Says Dan, "I think good coverage of the event is much more important than having the groom's head spin around." If you agree, you can just say no to special effects (and save yourself some cash). Then there's the more complex issue of music.

A couple of months after her wedding, Robin's parents went to the videographer's office and watched the video. "They noticed that as we walked down the aisle, something was wrong with the sound," says Robin. "It was all scratchy and shrieky. And they said, 'Fix this,' thinking, I guess, that the videographers could somehow restore the original sound." But of course, they couldn't, so instead they dubbed music over it. "The one thing I knew when I was planning my ceremony was that I didn't want to walk down the aisle to 'Pachelbel's Canon'," says Robin. So what music did the videographers replace the shrieking with? You guessed it. So much for the Bach concerto performed live by a string trio. "That was bad enough, but then the overdub switched to 'The Wedding March.' It was extremely stressful to watch." Later in the tape, some bad audio was covered with Lionel Richie's "Say You, Say Me." "They didn't even ask us!" says Robin.

Okay, this truly sucks. But you can prevent this kind of artistic license simply by vetoing it in advance. Tell your videographer that you want the real audio throughout. The murmur of voices, and the occasional snippet of conversation is plenty interesting. Or if you want music where the audio isn't good, choose some songs yourself. That might mean e-mailing a playlist to the videographer's office, but gee, talk about your worthwhile investments.

Amateur Hour

Sure, smartphones can be annoying, but after your wedding day, you may be extremely grateful that almost every single one of your guests owns one, brought it with them and shot video of your ceremony and/or reception from his/her perspective—all for free.

Flower to the People

Flowers are the wedding expense most likely to cause your boyfriend to burst out laughing and say, "But seriously, how much do they *really* cost?"

If you're going through the wedding industry, flowers are expensive. Just remember, though, that *all* flowers are beautiful, whether they're $50-a-stem hothouse orchids or dollar-a-bunch daisies (although daisies have kind of a weird scent that one minute seems outdoorsy and the next evokes a public bathroom).

If you have a florist manipulate every petal, you're going to spend some money. I can understand that impulse, because I know that certain floral designers are serious artists. Then again, do you need serious art at your wedding, or do you just need something really pretty and festive? We can debate this for hours.

The point is, if you want to save yourself a few thousand, you can handle the flowers yourself. Doing your own flowers is not like doing all the cooking for the wedding yourself. It's a hundred percent creative, zero percent practical; it can cost as little or as much as you want; and there's no chance that you'll leave anyone starving.

Even if you decide to go with a florist, the first step is to broaden your range of possibilities. Lose those images of stiff, spherical centerpieces. Sweep them away. Forget about words like "appropriate," "special" and "classy." Don't worry about what's right for a wedding. This is not *a* wedding, it's *your* wedding. The important question is what do you really like?

Honor Thy Space

Work *with* your reception site, not against it. Look at what you've got before you decide what you're going to do with the flowers. Even the plainest environment doesn't need as much decorating as you might think. The celebratory atmosphere and the guests will transform it themselves. People will be in beautiful clothes, and food is pretty—that's part of your decor. So don't make yourself crazy over the quantity and size of flower arrangements. More and bigger are not necessarily better.

In some settings cut flowers can get swallowed up by the grandeur of nature. So if your wedding is outside, maybe you want to forgo flowers or think on a different scale. Sheryl couldn't see the reason for big centerpieces when guests were surrounded by the flowers of her mother's yard. "But I love flowers, so we did something small that people could enjoy while they were sitting at the tables," she says. On each table she placed two or three little white creamers filled with pink sweet alyssum.

June and Dennis were married in a big loft space. Since it had floor-to-ceiling windows on three sides, with intricate molding, it sort of decorated itself. A florist made two large arrangements, using only one type of flower: big white French tulips (the ones with long, gnarly stems and fringed petals). The bouquets stood on pedestals framing the area where the ceremony took place. The only other decorations were clusters of votive candles on each table.

At Celia's stand-up reception, the view was the focus. She didn't want to bother with or spend the money on flowers for the tables, since no one would be sitting down. She and her two bridesmaids laid their large, streaming wildflower bouquets on the buffet table to decorate it. "At a lot of weddings, the bouquets go unnoticed after the ceremony," says Celia. "It was funny. We got so many compliments on the flowers at our wedding, and it was only three bunches." If you're having a big bridal party, consider having the bridesmaids' bouquets double as table decorations. This could cut your flower order in half.

Michaela says the plain basement room she was working with for her reception was completely devoid of charm—certainly more barren than elegant. The space needed something bigger than flower arrangements, at least bigger than the type Michaela could afford. So instead she rented trees—four ficus and three pear trees. Adding lots of green warmed up the room. On the day of the wedding, Michaela went to a discount rose store, got all the tea roses the place had and put a small bunch on each table.

Joanne and Evan set a mid-December wedding date because they both love Christmastime. When they found a restaurant in which to have their reception, they were happy to discover that it would be decked with boughs of holly throughout December. "I didn't even bother with flowers, except for myself," says Joanne. "The place was already so festive, I don't think anyone would even have noticed them."

Freeing the Flower Arranger Within

When you have cut flowers at home, they look beautiful, right? They make you smile every time you walk in the door. And that's without the help of a florist and with minimal fussing. I think the most striking flower arrangements are at either end of the design spectrum: extremely loose, or artfully crafted by a truly visionary individual. Ninety percent of what you see at weddings falls in the middle (arrangements that are "done," but without much inspiration). Trust the fact that relaxed bunches of flowers will be perfect for your wedding and that you are capable of executing this particular style of floral design. Without a lot of experience, this is the best way to go. You simply can't screw up if you just allow the natural perfection and randomness of a bunch of flowers to show itself off. Get a friend with a good eye to help (or better yet, to take over).

You might be able to purchase flowers for your wedding at the same place you occasionally buy a bunch to take home. If you know of a grocery store or an outdoor farmer's market where the flowers are decent and inexpensive, talk to the manager. Maybe you can place an order. If ordering is not a possibility, plan to do your flower shopping at seven A.M. on the appropriate day. Even buying flowers (that you'll arrange yourself) from a florist or online will be substantially less than paying for his or her services. And in that case, you can definitely order in advance. Then again, you could just wing it. No planning; just see what's available the day before or the day of the wedding. (Depending on your astrological sign, you may find this approach exciting or terrifying.)

If you're nervous about the flower arranging part of the job, rehearse the week before. Buy what you'd need to make two arrangements, and then fiddle with the stuff till you're happy. Take a photo (did I mention what an excellent wedding investment a good digital camera is?), and you're all set. This is also a great way to work out the math (i.e., how much of each flower you need). If you view flower arranging more as a chore than an opportunity for self-expression, why not go with just one type of flower? I actually think this is the most beautiful way to display flowers—a big bunch of tulips or a small bouquet of sweet peas. Then all you have to worry about is varying the lengths of the stems so you can fill the containers well. It also gives the reception space some uni-

A Martha Stewart Nightmare

One of Edie's bridesmaids, Ann, was almost eight months pregnant at Edie's wedding. Needless to say, the sheath dress the other bridesmaids wore was out. So Edie, a costume designer for a TV series, borrowed something from wardrobe for Ann to wear. "It was this fabulous silk overshirt—this million-dollar item—which she wore over a beautiful white silk maternity dress," says Edie. The outdoor wedding was serviced mostly by Portosans. In an effort to make the Portosans less rock concerty, part of the decorating staff (Edie and Marco's friends) spruced up the insides with votive candles and flowers. But it was kind of a tight fit for a big-bellied person, a flowy, diaphanous shirt and the element fire. Ann went inside, sat down and, poof, was instantly in flames. "She came running out," says Edie. "Her husband saw this flaming ball of white that resembled his wife and pulled her to the ground, rolled her around and put her out." Edie likes to end this story by assuring the horrified listener that Ann went on to have a beautiful, healthy baby girl.

formity, if you like that type of thing. And if you're getting your flowers through a florist, ordering a large quantity of only one type of flower puts you in a position to ask for a deal.

Wendy and Ben didn't even think about going to a florist. "Why spend the money?" says Wendy. It was the end of March, and daffodils were a dollar a bunch. "I got fifty bunches—two hundred and fifty daffodils. It took three of us to carry them all. We stuck them in bottles, vases, drinking glasses, everything we could find. It was like this tremendous burst of sunshine when you walked into the room."

Molly's sisters-in-law took care of the flowers for her reception. The restaurant where the wedding was held had a bunch of bud vases that normally each contained a carnation and some plasticy fern. The flower helpers replaced each "arrangement" with three or four yellow sweetheart roses and a sprig of baby's breath—to "weddingize" the dark, men's club–type interior. They made two larger arrangements of wildflowers, one for the restaurant's entrance, near the place cards, and one for the room where cocktails were served. The wildflowers came from a farmer's market; the roses were ordered from a florist in advance. Total flower bill: $450.

"So Where Do I Stick These Bloomin' Things?"

As far as plain old vases go, keep it simple and cheap. Guests are not scrutinizing them; they're enjoying the flowers. Shop online or at a discount store, and get the simplest designs you can find. The part that will most affect the arrangement is the width of the mouth.

Odd-shaped containers will give you ideas for specific types of arrangements. Try a flea market for antique bottles (old milk or medicine bottles are great). Anemones and poppies, which have well-shaped stems, might be nice in tall skinny vessels like these. Mason jars are good for a folksy look (maybe with black-eyed Susans or miniature narcissus). Small fishbowls full of cascading flowers, like lilacs, are beautiful and lush. (One bride I spoke with considered using actual goldfish centerpieces—the bowl, the water, the fish—but chickened out at the last minute.) Wide, shallow glass bowls with gardenias or camellias afloat are very elegant. Gardenias are expensive and fragile, so they make sense only if you have an extremely nurturing flower helper and a small party.

You can add a personal touch by using pitchers, vases and bottles of your own. (The only problem here is that all your stuff will end up at your aunts' houses when they bolt out of the reception with the arrangements.) The point is, don't limit yourself to what you've seen other people do.

Penny and Will managed to accumulate ten small decorative olive oil bottles between the time they started planning their wed-

I'm Not a Florist, but I Play One on TV

If you're doing anything ambitious with flowers or greens, like wrapping a bannister, make sure you ask the right questions when you buy materials. I got a bum steer on some fern. The florist knew what I needed it for, and he didn't say a word. It wasn't until the day of my brother's wedding that I discovered the stems were covered with fine, tiny thorns (a fascinating moment in my study of plant self-preservation, but poorly timed). Needless to say, working with the stuff was a little slice of hell. The job took three times as long as it should have, and my perpetual cursing did nothing for the mood.

ding and the time it happened. Since they were having family-style food service—big bowls of pasta and baskets of bread on each table—they knew there wouldn't be much room for flowers. The narrow-mouthed bottles worked as bud vases, and each held a single lush, white peony.

It's safest to put cut flowers together the day of the wedding; then you don't have to worry about staying power. But if you don't have a number of helpers, this might be impossible. If you arrange the flowers the day before, make sure you keep them in a cool, dark place (a refrigerator is best). Much as we humans enjoy a bouquet of flowers by a sunny window, heat means death to flowers without roots.

Save a Plant and Some Dough

If it offends your sensibilities that "fresh" flowers are really dead flowers, cut off from their life force, or if you just want to do a simple, beautiful, inexpensive centerpiece, think potted plants. Small terra-cotta pots of, for example, double begonias are gorgeous and cheap, cheap, cheap. Geraniums are nice too, though sometimes they're a little too tall to work as centerpieces (remember, people have to be able to see over these things).

With the help of a florist friend, Kimberly elaborated on this option and still kept the cost way low. Her centerpieces were six-inch terra-cotta pots of white cyclamen (the blooms look kind of like butterflies). Loosely wrapped around the base of each were a few strands of smilax, a green, twiny plant. And a few inches away was a circle of votives, "in the least expensive little glasses we could find," says Kimberly. Her florist buddy told her it was the cheapest way to decorate tables with flowers. Says Kimberly, "I couldn't believe how beautiful it was. It looked really . . . expensive."

Beyond Garden-Variety Florists

Okay, maybe doing your own flowers does not exactly float your boat, and you're prepared to pay someone to take on this responsibility. If you're shopping for a florist, don't approach it like you're looking for a dry cleaner. You know what I mean. ("Well this one is on my way to work, right next to that bakery where they make the good linzer tarts. It seems fine.") I'm serious about this because I love flowers so much. If you do too, take the time to look around. There are real artists out there, and they don't necessarily charge more than the workmanlike flower arranger who's affiliated with your catering hall. It might just be a matter of doing lots of online research, shopping in a funkier neighborhood or asking more people for referrals. Don't settle for someone who's "good enough" until you've checked out all the options. I think it's so worth the time investment. If you're going to spend the money, you should be thrilled with what you get, and the work should be way more artful than what you or a friend could do.

Our florist friend, Betsy, has some advice about dealing with the industry: "The first thing to remember is to be realistic about what you can get for your budget." Then you won't have all kinds of tension with your florist and frustration with your wallet. You don't know what you can get for your budget? Get some price quotes early on so you have a clue.

Cheap Thoughts

"People don't realize what a single rose costs," says Betsy. But once you know, you can work with a florist, stick to a budget and get something you love. And if you start with your head in the right place, you won't feel limited or disappointed. Here are some tips.

- **Be flexible as the weeping willow as it bends in the breeze.** "Some years market price for a flower is higher than others," says Betsy. So be willing to listen to suggestions for substitutions. If you go to a florist with a photo from a magazine and discover that the centerpieces you nave fallen in love with will cost twice what you can spend, ask if there's a cheaper way to achieve a similar effect. Keep in mind that you're not going to get exactly what you see in the photo. But you are an easygoing person. You can embrace the difference and become one with it, right?

- **Heed the cyclical wisdom of nature.** Find out what will be in season when you're getting married, and then utilize that framework. (Think "utilize" rather than "limit yourself to.") Working with what's available is easier, cheaper, more fun, more eco-friendly and, hey, it keeps you in touch with the earth. What could be better than a little grounding right now?

- **Stay loose.** Envision a free-and-flowy look right from the start. Wired flowers cost much more than bunches tied loosely with a ribbon.

- **Open your mind.** If you have a large bridal party, you could end up spending a lot of money for flowers that are enjoyed for about thirty minutes. Maybe the bridesmaids can carry single flowers wrapped with satin ribbons instead of bouquets.

- **It's easy being green.** Wrapping a chupa in greens is much less expensive than decorating the whole thing with flowers.

- **Let it be.** If you're being married in a church, don't feel compelled to decorate it. Says Betsy, "Most churches are so ornate already that flower arrangements get lost. Save the flowers for the reception."

More Dirt from a Florist

"If you're very concerned about getting exactly what you want, make sure you ask the florist to do a sample centerpiece in advance," says Betsy. You'll have to pay for it, but if you're a real stickler, it'll be worthwhile. Don't bother with the extra expense if you're going with a design right out of the florist's portfolio.

Your Precious Bouquet

In the business, this is known as your "personal flowers." (Doesn't that sound like something from a douche commercial?) Save money everywhere else, but if you're a flower lover, don't skimp on your bouquet. Pay special attention to what goes in it and, if you're putting it together yourself, allot plenty of time to work on it. Also, figure out how you're going to hold it together (you can crisscross ribbons to bind the stems tightly, but practice this in advance). Even if you're doing all the table flowers yourself, you might want to splurge for a brilliant florist on just your bouquet. I did, and I loved it so much, it was completely worth the extra expense.

Colette is a city dweller who loves to garden. She has a small plot of her own near her apartment, where she grows roses. Friends made Colette's wedding bouquet from roses they picked in her garden and some tinier flowers from a flower shop. Rita also had a homegrown bouquet. All the flowers in her aunt's sprawling

English garden were hers for the taking, and the morning of the wedding she and her aunt strolled through the backyard, scissors poised, and took the best of everything: peonies, sweet peas, lilacs, ranunculus. "If there's a garden in your life," says Rita, "use it for your own flowers. My bouquet was really personal. It meant so much to me."

Florist Knows Best

Allison wanted her chupa wrapped in viny greens. She was envisioning English ivy, or something like it. When she met with her florist in person, the florist informed Allison she'd be wrapping the chupa in what she always uses (what Allison describes as "Christmas tree branches"). Allison said, "But what about the ivy I mentioned?" "No. Not a good idea," responded the all-knowing florist, as she began bustling about her shop. She picked up the phone to make a call, then waved at Allison and her parents, as if to make them disappear. As far as she was concerned, this little meeting had gone on too long. She simply didn't have time for such stupid questions. Of course not; she already had Allison's hefty deposit. Allison's parents "didn't want to cause any trouble," so the three customers (you know, the people who pay, the ones who are always right) went home with their proverbial tails between their legs.

Then, after a pep talk from her boyfriend, Allison went back and demanded an estimate on the ivy. "Well, it's not just the price that's an issue. It's also that that amount of ivy is hard for me to get," said the florist. Okay. Why didn't you say that in the first place? Now we're getting somewhere. "The fir will be lovely," the florist insisted. "No it won't," said Allison, "because we're not using it." Allison demanded to know what her other options were.

"There really aren't any," said the very stubborn florist, her tone turning from patronizing to just plain belligerent. Allison, reminding herself how much money she was shelling out for this woman's services, worked up her nerve and said, "Well, I'll wait here until you think of some." It didn't take long for the florist to emerge from the back with three kinds of fern.

Never Say "Wedding"

When it was time to get wedding flowers, Abby called her favorite flower shop and said, "I need three handheld arrangements of wildflowers for a party." She specified no carnations, no baby's breath, no velvety wrap, and said she wanted them to be "all over the place," wild with twigs and bound with raffia, which is the style this particular shop specialized in. The florist asked how much Abby wanted to spend for each. After they agreed on the price and the approximate size, he said, "Can I ask what these are for?" Then and only then did Abby tell him that they were for her wedding. "A friend of mine had used the same florist for her wedding a couple of months earlier and had spent twice as much for bouquets half the size," says Abby. "I knew I should keep my mouth shut till the money was settled."

Say It Without Flowers

Joni and Fred skipped the flowers at their reception and had candle centerpieces instead. Each was different, composed of a cluster of candles of various shapes and sizes. One had as its base a vintage plate, another was set in a wide-mouth glass bowl, and another was on top of a swag of velvet. For some tables, they used antique candelabras. (Joni had intended to rent candelabras from the party rental place where most of her supplies came from, but it turned out to be cheaper to buy them.)

Nice Touch

Talk about using your resources. Paul designed little wooden trilevel platforms to hold votive candles, and called his high school wood shop teacher to ask if he could get some students to make them. (He paid them, of course.) Each platform held six votives. He had sixteen made, and they served as the centerpieces of each table.

It Is Balloon!

Penny and Will ordered a huge bunch of white, slightly iridescent balloons, and sandbagged them so they hovered about seven feet from the ground in one corner of their party tent. "It looked like a cluster of giant pearls," says Penny. "I guess people were drawn to them, because they ended up being an umbrella for the gifts."

Charlotte and Billy filled their wedding space with helium balloons, so the ceiling was covered with primary colors, and ribbons streamed down onto the dance floor. But they made one mistake. "We decorated the day before. When we walked in the next morning, the balloons had shrunk and were all over the floor," says Charlotte. "I think it was because we left the air conditioner on. That was to keep the cut flowers from dying." So don't try to do this in advance. Have someone inflate the balloons the day of the wedding to be safe.

Table Manners

Lois and Michael bought twelve plain white tablecloths to use at their wedding. But first they gave the tablecloths to friends to decorate. There was one covered with tropical fish, one with a cowboy theme, one stenciled with stars, squiggles and crescent moons, one with wide red stripes and one— painted by two little girls—with a bride and groom in the center. At the end of the wedding, the tablecloths were raffled off to guests.

Timing Is Everything

*W*hen should we send people over to the buffet? When does my sister sing the song she wrote for us? When can I make a toast to my family and the guests? Check other books and websites for solid answers to these burning questions. In this book, you're the director, so direct. The only advice that applies to every couple is to consider in advance how much structure you want. Once you've determined that, it's your responsibility to work out a schedule that feels good for you, or not to work anything out if that's what you prefer.

Here's where those fifty or so weddings you've attended might come in handy for reference. I know you love to complain about other people's weddings. So think about it. What was wrong with the timing at the last five weddings you attended? Or was the timing of each exactly the same, and *that's* what was wrong?

Regina crabbed about a wedding at which the dancing didn't start until dinner and dessert were over. But I think that might be kind of cool. Like a two-part party (three-part if you include the

ceremony). Or like going out to dinner with a hundred of your closest friends and then jumping in twenty taxis and going to a club.

It's all about your concept. Let's use the show-biz metaphor.
Do you want a free-form performance installation, or something
with an overture, three acts and a finale? It's up to you. Dennis
hoped his wedding would feel very loose and spontaneous. But as
the date grew closer, he and June realized that without some structure, there was too much to be nervous about. "I found myself
planning a lot more than I had meant to," says Dennis. "But it was
worth it for the peace of mind."

Gabi wishes she'd done the same. She and Kevin kept their
outdoor wedding very unstructured. "I realized it was a problem
right after the ceremony when I spotted the best man with a microphone," says Gabi. "He decided he was ready to do his toast."
The guests were all hanging out in the sunshine, having a drink
and winding down from the ceremony. It was just not the time.
"Besides, I was dreading what he might say. He can be pretty
foul." So the bride intervened and told him, "a little too force-
fully," to wait till later. Gabi says she wishes she'd scheduled a
couple of things—the toast, the cake—and left the rest to fate.
That way she wouldn't have been looking over her shoulder all day.
"Every few minutes I would check on the best man to make sure
he wasn't going to try anything. If I could have known in advance
exactly when the toast was coming, I would have been able to
prepare myself with copious amounts of wine."

Minor Adjustments

Crystal and Artie had a pretty conventional wedding, but felt that
the four-hour time period offered by the hall would be too short.
"We had 175 people, and I really wanted a chance to talk to

them," says Crystal. So she arranged in advance to have the party extended by an hour—fifteen minutes tacked onto the cocktails and the rest added to the reception.

Lindsay figured a little food, a little action, lots more food was the best plan. For her Saturday night wedding, she had cocktails at eight, the ceremony at nine, and the reception at nine thirty. "I don't like it when people are left to mill about in some hallway before the ceremony," says Lindsay. "They want to socialize." Personally, *I* want to eat. When I'm going to a nighttime wedding, I tend to eat very little that day in anticipation of stuffing my face and hating myself later. So I'm starving when I get there. I would love a little snack, and I know I'm not the only one. Consider this option if your ceremony and reception are in the same location. You don't want your guests fantasizing about endive and Roquefort during the most important moment of your life.

Let's Get This Over With

Kimberly says whatever your schedule is, try to stick to it. She and Gene had worked out the timing and discussed it with the caterer and the bandleader. But the house manager was really antsy to move the proceedings along. "We had these screens that separated the cocktail hour from where the tables were being set up," says Gene. "The house manager came up to me and said, 'The dining tables are ready. Let's open it up.' And I looked at my watch and said, 'No. We have ten more minutes in the cocktail hour. Everybody's still having fun and looking happy.'" At the stroke of seven, the band started playing and the screens were moved. "To me it worked really seamlessly," says Gene. "That wouldn't have happened if I'd listened to the house manager."

You've got to watch out for managers or caterers with too

strong a compulsion to "move it along." If there's an opportunity
to clear a plate, they'll jump at it. About ten minutes after dinner
was served at Herb and Grace's wedding, the groom was called up
by the bandleader (poor timing) to play drums. "Everyone got up
to watch," says Grace. "When they went back to their seats, half
the dishes had been taken away. Nobody got to eat their dinner."
To some caterers, the job is not to make the wedding go smoothly,
but to make the wedding end. When you're on the other side of
the buffet table, all these events look alike. You have to feed the
people and clean up, and then you get to go.

So look out for yourself here. Industry folk know that the only
people at a wedding who care about this stuff—the ones throwing
the party, footing the bills—are the ones who are too distracted
to pay attention to their work. And that's the way it should be. You
and your husband and your parents should be having a ball. You
shouldn't have to think about whether people have had time to
finish dinner before the dance music gets loud. But someone has
to. So ask your most assertive sibling, friend or attendant to keep
an eye on the way the party's being run. Give your helper license
to complain or even to storm into the kitchen on your behalf. It
will take some of the magic out of the celebration for him or her,
but it could make a huge difference for you. And the right person
will get a kick out of the assignment. Kimberly and Gene wish
they'd thought to ask someone else to watch the timing. "Doing
it ourselves made us even more anxious than we already were."

Keep the Customer Occupied

Timing the ceremony so it would segue comfortably into the reception was a problem for Joanne and Evan. "If you're getting
married in a Catholic church, you only have certain masses avail-

able to you. There was a ten thirty mass, and we'd be out by noon, but the reception halls would only book from two to six." I've heard this complaint from a few different brides. And boy, have I heard complaints from guests. "You're always in some town with, like, a drugstore and a bank, and it's invariably a hundred degrees," says Gregg. "The interim two hours feels like six. And *then* you have to go to a five-hour reception." Whether you feel responsible for somehow filling that gap for your guests depends, I guess, on how you were raised and if you've been in therapy.

Some brides leave their guests to fend for themselves and use the time to take pictures. Joanne and Evan ended up choosing a restaurant instead of a reception hall so they could eliminate the downtime and begin their party at twelve thirty. If you're willing to pay for it, you might be able to buy an extra hour at a hall. It might cost a fortune, but it doesn't hurt to ask. If the manager knows it could make the difference between you booking your reception there or having it somewhere else, he or she might find a way to make it happen.

Gimme, Gimme, Gimme

—Gifts and Registering—

*T*o some people, the concept of publishing a wish list is "a little '80s," to say the least. I was an antiregister bride-to-be. But I succumbed to the pressure, and in retrospect was glad I did. Here's the party line: People are going to get you gifts anyway, they don't know what you want, and they need help choosing. Got a problem with that? Agree wholeheartedly? Maybe you need more information before you make up your mind. Here are some pros and cons.

Advantages to Registering

- You get lots of stuff you want.
- You win valuable cooperation points with mother and/or mother-in-law.
- Returns are easy, in case you're strapped for cash.
- Free silver-plate frame from department or big-box store bridal registry.
- Socially approved acquisitiveness is fun!

Advantages to Not Registering

* You might get more cash gifts.
* You can hold your head up high and declare, "*I* didn't register."
* Hours not spent registering can he devoted to extra arguing.
* Surprises, surprises and more surprises!
* You can never really have too many chafing dishes/bud vases/ceramic hen centerpieces.

Here Comes That Greedy Feeling

If you're leaning toward not registering, be prepared for pressure from the grown-ups (the real ones—your parents, his parents), who worry that their friends and relatives won't know what to get you or that they prefer to shop online. To some parents, registering is simply "the thing to do." Phooey. Also, after years of buying other people's kids the wedding presents *they* want, parents might be keen on having the favor returned; your turn to register is also their turn.

Kelly thought that because she and Matt had been together for eight years, she would be exempt from some of the in-law wedding problems friends had. For one thing, she didn't think Matt's parents would try to tell her what to do. "They know me pretty well, and they know I can be headstrong," says Kelly. "I didn't want to register. I had decided a long time ago that that's just not the type of person I am." But this time Matt's parents wore her down. "They pushed and pushed me, and I ended up registering." There are good reasons to register, but pressure is not one of them.

You see, gift-getting is not a sentimental issue, and registering really doesn't affect your parents or your in-laws. So I vote you do what you want. The main reason to register is that then you get gifts you like and need. Yes, it feels a little false after having selected them yourself, and the gifts friends pick out for you or make themselves have a whole different meaning, but it's a nice efficient system that works. What I'm saying is, if you don't care either way, you'll probably be happier if you register.

Tiffany didn't. She ended up with an apartment full of *objets* and housewares she didn't like. Her advice: "Register. Getting gifts you don't want is much more trouble than getting nothing." A lot of the stuff was impossible to trace, and therefore impossible to return. Tiffany unloaded most of it at her parents' garage sale.

I Do Not Want What I Do Not Want

Okay, so you've decided to go for it. Where do you begin? The lists in bridal magazines or on store websites are a little too, um, thorough ("gravy boat—everyday; gravy boat—formal"). Those crystal cruets will really come in handy for your typical homecooked meal (baked potatoes and salad in front of a warm TV). You're you. Register for the person you are now, and don't try to register for the person you think you should be. Or the person someone else hopes you become.

Erika's boyfriend's mother talked dreamily about crystal, silver and "vision." "'Vision' meaning, to register for the china you'll still like thirty years from now," says Erika. This bride and her wealthy future mother-in-law were not on the same space-time continuum. "I would be absolutely freaking out listening to her. Whose life was she talking about?" Erika was a harried bride-to-be, working full-time and going to school every night. "We had no money, no furniture, laundry all over our apartment, and what—I'm gonna have a silver platter in my closet?" Registering for gifts that will be great sometime in the far distant future, when your priorities change, seemed ridiculous to Erika. "It got to the point where I was asking her, 'Can I just register for tuition?' She didn't think that was funny."

Clarice planned to do very limited registering. Her mother-in-law came back with this one: ". . . but people *want* to buy you silver place settings. That's the only present my relatives ever give. You *have* to register for silver." Was that a threat? Clarice feared it was: either silver or nothing. So she and Mitch did as they were told. "We went and registered for a pattern we didn't hate, the plainest thing we could find," says Clarice. And really they were hoping hard for the stainless-steel flatware, which was expensive compared with the random utensils they had stolen from their respective college dining halls years earlier. "No one bought us either."

The Road Less Traveled

Sometimes the variety online or in department stores can be overwhelming and the designs a little underwhelming. "We just didn't like anything we saw in Macy's," says Michael. "Most of it was okay, but nothing really grabbed us." He and Lois had always bought gifts for friends at a little Italian ceramics store, and they found out they could register there. They picked out dishes, bowls, mugs, platters, cannisters and planters for their garden. "I'm so glad we thought of it," says Michael. "We got the best gifts."

The digital age has made it too easy for small stores *not* to offer a registry service. And if a store you like doesn't, talk to the owners. They'll probably be very happy to oblige. You're essentially saying, "I want to bring you a lot of business. Please help me." Retailers respond to this type of thing. The only necessities are that the store accept major credit cards and have a website and phone. Ingrid found a potter through a local shop and registered with him for dishes and bowls. She gave his number to out-of-town relatives who preferred to shop by phone.

But what if you don't need dishes? What if you're pretty well set up already? Some couples are. They have flatware and a pepper mill and (gasp!) even place mats. "I didn't wait until I got married to get a ladle," says Adrienne. She wanted to register but had no desire to replace everything in her home, so she took a different

Keeping Track of Booty

Jeff and Molly thought a friend of theirs might have given them a card with a check enclosed at the wedding, but they weren't sure. "I vaguely remembered seeing one," says Molly, "but it never turned up again." And they never asked. Tracy isn't sure if her boss gave her a gift. She thinks he didn't, but what if he did? That means he never received a thank-you card. Tracy lives in terror of this possibility, and has decided that she has no choice but to quit her job. Let's get it together here, folks. Remember that spreadsheet and binder I told you to create? Well, you need a section devoted to the gifts you receive, and there will be many. Start a page for each ancillary gift-getting occasion (showers, engagement parties) and reserve a few pages for the wedding proper. The rest is obvious: Name, Gift, Thank-You Note Sent; instead of just checking off this last one, put a date—this will pressure you to take care of it sooner (for more pressure, read on). And thanks to Tracy's tale of horror, you will no doubt remember to include an additional column for money gifts: Date Deposited.

tack. "We were about to move to a new house that needed a lot of work. All we had was a hammer and a screwdriver, so we registered for some tools." If you're in a comparable situation, transcend housewares and appliances. What do you want or need? Sporting goods? Musical equipment? Camping gear? You can even register at L.L. Bean. (Maybe Erika should have talked to NYU about starting a by-the-credit tuition registry.)

Wrap It Up, I'll Take It

The only "should" in registering applies to registering for what you want. If that's an easel and some oil paints, great. If it's a juicer and a coffeemaker, fine. If you have a linen fetish, go for that. Of course, money can be an object. If everything you register for is in the $5,000-cake-stand range, you're only screwing yourself and putting your guests in an awkward position. Be real. You can include a couple of fantasy items if you like, but make sure you register for lower-priced stuff too. Keep in mind that some guests feel obligated to buy gifts through a registry, and make sure there are items on there that are affordable for everybody.

Just Do It

This is a sad story about a couple I'm very close to. In fact, you might almost say I'm a part of this couple. Okay, it's me. To protect his identity, I will call my husband the Great Procrastinator. We were married one May. During our honeymoon, I wrote thank-you postcards to a group of friends who had composed a song for us and performed it at our wedding. When we got home, I did a handful more, although I felt bad about the fact that it took me three months to finish my half of the guest list.

Over the course of these months, I periodically reminded the Procrastinator of our obligation. We would make plans, block out whole weekends for the writing of thank-you cards. Then, instead, he would decide to rewire a room in our rented apartment. (The task was *that* distasteful.) Eventually, concerned about our reputation, I offered to cover for him and write to his friends and family from both of us, although this certainly was not part of our original agreement. He refused: "I hate thank-you cards that are all written by the bride." He had lofty ideas. "I'm going to write long, personal notes to everyone." This from a man whose last completed letter was part of a sixth-grade homework assignment.

Christmastime came and went. I would wake up in a cold sweat after dreaming of slighted in-laws wielding sharp objects. By this point, I felt it was too late for me to write to the Procrastinator's relatives: They would blame me for the delay, call me inconsiderate and hate me forever. The notes had to come from him. I begged the Procrastinator to get on it. Sometime in February, he sat down and wrote four cards. It took him three hours. I'm sure they were brilliant, but at this point, quality was simply not a priority.

I'll spare you the rest of the gory details: the fights, the nightmares, the perpetual angst of not having handed in your term paper. It ended two years later when, just before a major Procrastinator family gathering, he sat down and cranked out the rest of his cards. Most of his relatives received them the day before the party. That was really nice for me, hearing cracks from people I don't even know about "our" thank-you cards coming two years after the wedding. All I can do now is tell friends not to send us thank-you cards (not one has had a problem accepting that offer), and pass my story on to brides- and grooms-to-be. I can consider my suffering worthwhile if I can help even one couple avoid a similar fate.

Curtain Up

—The Ceremony—

*Y*ou almost forgot about this part, right? Maybe that's because the prospect of all the most important people in your life sitting there—quiet, attentive, eyes transfixed on you—is a tad terrifying. But this show-within-the-show is supposed to be what the whole wedding is about, and there are so many ways to make it your own. The funny thing is, a lot of couples who work very hard to make their reception just what they want don't give much time at all to customizing the ceremony.

The Creative Process

Kimberly and Gene found themselves falling into that trap. "We'd been planning this party—the great-food, great-dancing, what-are-you-gonna-wear party—and all of a sudden it was like, wow, we're having people together so we can express all this stuff. How are we going to do it? And what do we really feel?" says Kimberly.

She and Gene were lucky enough to find inspiration in the minister they hired to perform the ceremony. They spent three intense
sessions with her. "She gave us questions to go over on our own,
like 'What do you love about the other person? What has changed
since you met the other person about what you love? What are five
values you have in common?'" Kimberly and Gene don't sit around
gabbing about this kind of stuff much. "To talk on that level was
very difficult. And the minister really helped us with that."

Ilana and Dan were not sure they would ever get married, not
because they were less than committed to each other, but because
they had problems with marriage as an institution. "On the other
hand, we knew it would bring so much joy to our families if we
got married," says Ilana, "and we did want to celebrate our commitment." So they decided to do it, but instead of calling it a
wedding, they termed their event a "commitment ceremony." One
thing that helped motivate them was meeting a new friend, a progressive feminist woman rabbi. Says Ilana, "Before I knew her, I
could never imagine anyone I would want to have marry us." For
Dan and Ilana, creating a ceremony meant starting largely from
scratch, although not completely. "Judaism is a part of our lives,
so that was our starting point. But a lot of the traditional aspects
of the religion are gender discriminatory." So Ilana and Dan wrote
their own ketubah (marriage contract), which focused on love,
mutual respect and equality. "It also talked about the fact that our
commitment should give us strength to confront some of society's
wrongs." They incorporated traditional Jewish songs and blessings
into the ceremony, made a point of including as many friends and
family members as possible, and kept the structure very informal—
no aisle, no white dress, no flowers.

"Creating a wedding ceremony is a great opportunity," says
Nat, "because it's a chance to make a work of art. You have to
communicate with people on multiple levels. Art is beautiful and

art means something, and that's what your ceremony's like; it's a vast mosaic of allegories and metaphors and superficial beauty." After Nat and Maureen tried for weeks to come up with an overall concept for their ceremony, agonizing every step of the way, Nat had a little epiphany. "I realized, well, wait a minute, the whole spirit of the event is love, and you shouldn't have to agonize. As long as it's from the heart, it will be meaningful."

There's a fine line between caring a lot and agonizing. The latter, though, is unpleasant. Although this show requires a lot of behind-the-scenes planning, you shouldn't work *too* hard on it, because you'll wreck the magic for yourself; when the curtain goes up, you really want to be able to get into your part. So don't put too much pressure on yourself to reinvent the wedding ceremony. This is a creative act, and it should be more fun than it is demanding.

The House

Where do you want your friends and relatives to be? Sasha and Finney had people gather around them in the park where they were married; their aisle was marked with posts (made by Finney) connected by draping ribbon. Rebecca and Ian made a very wide semicircle of chairs that was only four rows deep. And Sheryl and David had a full circle of chairs surrounding their chupa, so that at least some guests could see their faces. At certain sites, the structure of the house is not so flexible. If you can control it, though, think in advance about what you want, and make your wishes very clear to whoever is setting up.

When Kathleen arrived at her wedding, she was very bummed to see that the chairs were about a mile from the giant tree under which she and Jonathan were to be married. "The front row was at least twenty feet from the spot, and the aisle was fifteen feet wide," she says. "I never thought to explain in advance. It seemed obvious to me that if the ceremony was under that tree, the chairs would be set up near the tree, right?" No, no, no. "Obvious" is so subjective. Explain, confirm, e-mail it, e-mail it again and confirm again. That's the only way to get things exactly as you want them to be.

Making an Entrance

In traditional Jewish ceremonies, the bride and the groom walk down the aisle with their respective parents. Sarah decided to do it alone. "My father had died, and my mother didn't like the guy I was marrying," she says. "I was going into this marriage alone, and walking down the aisle on my own symbolized that for me."

Clarice and Mitch walked down the aisle together. "I never considered walking with my father and being handed over to my new owner," Clarice says. "I suggested we each walk with our parents, but my husband didn't want to do that, so we walked together."

The Script

Kimberly and Gene were so blown away by their cool minister that they told her they didn't want to know in advance what she was going to say in their ceremony. "Spontaneity was really important to Gene," says Kimberly. "We gave the minister the readings, and we gave her our vows separately. She wrote her part based on that." The couple had only one stipulation: "We didn't want her to say 'God' too much." In fact, the minister ended up not saying 'God' at all. (Later, Kimberly's aunt remarked to Gene, "I noticed God wasn't invited to your wedding.")

Some couples are uncomfortable asking a religious officiant to perform a secular ceremony. But if that's what you want, you have to be able to say so. And if you're afraid your officiant will consider your request audacious, well, maybe you're dealing with the wrong person.

Ad Libs

Tracy and Doug met with a rabbi who was a friend of a friend a few weeks before their wedding. "He was warm, friendly and thirtyish," says Tracy. "Not an authority figure at all." Part of the service he performed was about the short time he'd spent with the couple, and the impressions he had of them. Tracy and Doug loved what he said because it was thoughtful and sincere. "He didn't pretend that he knew us a for a long time or make generalizations that could just as well have been about any couple."

If only it could always be that way. For Jeff and Molly, the officiant's freestyle routine scored about a 1.5. This minister came to them through three degrees of separation (he was an acquaintance of Jeff's cousin's minister). "We met with him once, just for a few minutes, and he seemed okay," says Jeff. The bride and groom were planning to write the vows portion of the ceremony themselves, so they figured, what could go wrong? "He had sort of a ready spiel," says Jeff. "He told us he talks about everlasting love and marriage, and all that. But he didn't mention that he likes to talk about terminally ill cancer patients. He left that part out." You see, during Jeff and Molly's ceremony, seemingly out of nowhere, the minister launched into a story about a dying woman (his point being the power of the "everlasting love" she shared with her dying husband). Yikes! The morbid tale lasted only about a minute, "but it seemed like hours," says Jeff. "By the time I emerged from my stupor and realized I should interrupt him, he was winding it up."

The lesson is, "He seemed okay" is not a thorough enough assessment of the person you're counting on to perform your one and only magical, memorable wedding ceremony. So if you don't know this person, you might ask for a more specific description of what he plans to speak about, and while you're at it, maybe e-mail him or her a list of a few caveats (i.e., no cancer stories, no animal-testing anecdotes, nothing about human trafficking).

Your Lines: The Vows

"I'm a very vocal person," says Naomi, "so I didn't want anybody to put words in my mouth." Naomi and Ron's decision to write their own vows grew partly out of the fact that they'd lived together for many years. "It was sort of like a declaration of something that had been private for a long time, a chance to say out loud, 'Yes, we really want to be together.'" Naomi and Ron wrote their vows separately. "We read each other's way before the wedding, but it really was different when we said them out loud."

Rebecca and Ian also wrote their own vows, but in an effort to make the ceremony even more powerful for themselves, they didn't look at each other's vows in advance. "The first time we heard them was at the actual ceremony," says Rebecca. They both wrote very different things. "Mine was more of a poem, a list of promises. Ian's vows were not just about promises; they were more how he felt about me and about our relationship."

Ilana and Dan (of the commitment ceremony) did not want the vows portion of their ceremony to be the focus. For them, the heart of their statement was the marriage contract, and so they did the traditional oath only in Hebrew. "We wanted to speak the words," says Ilana, "but not draw too much attention to their meaning."

Some people believe that composing your own vows is the only way to go. If you feel uncomfortably pressured in that direction, remember that it's okay not to. Using traditional vows doesn't make you less committed, or mean you're less creative. There's a certain resonance to the simple and familiar words used for millenia to signify a union between two people. And there are very sound arguments against some types of self-composed vows.

When vows are so revealing that they make the people watching feel uncomfortable, or so personal that they don't have any meaning at all to onlookers, the point of being married in front of a group is lost. "The sense you get sometimes is, 'We're wiser and more special than people who came before,'" says Mitch. "Ultimately it's a contradiction to do something so intimate in front of other people."

I read that at Frank and Kathie Lee Gifford's long-ago wedding, the celebrity bride and groom whispered their vows into each other's ears. That's the most extreme version of excluding the congregation I've ever heard of. The whole idea behind having a public ceremony is expressing these things out loud in front of a group of significant people. A wedding is not just for the bride and the groom; to some degree, it's for everybody in attendance.

So don't be shy about going more conventional with your ceremony than seems appropriate to your personality. A good ceremony can place the specialness of you in a historic context. There are things that are part of the emotional public domain—poems, songs, biblical passages—that are moving largely *because* they're familiar. When you use one, everyone thinks, "Ah, yes." Millions of people have related to it; bringing it into your ceremony helps people relate to one another and bonds you to the universal experience. That's part of the purpose of ceremony. And thus ends our little sermon for today.

The Element of Surprise

Kelly and Matt had a heavy-duty year-long "debate" (that's a nice word for it) over who would marry them. Matt's parents were set on a rabbi or a cantor. Kelly was set on a judge. Matt was floating, jellyfish-like, between them. "Ultimately, what we ended up deciding to do was have a judge marry us and have the cantor sing at the ceremony," says Kelly. "And Matt wanted to break a glass, so we did. So Matt was very happy, and I was very happy. And his parents were not *un*happy." Kelly enjoyed seeing the reactions of unprepared guests when, after a few words by the judge, "this woman appeared and just started singing in Hebrew. It was a very eclectic affair."

The minister Alexa and Joel found was completely open to having couples edit her ceremonies to their liking. "She was very cool," says Alexa. "She sent us eight different ceremonies and told us to use whatever we wanted out of each, or write our own." There was a piece in one that Alexa and Joel particularly liked: The minister would hand the bride and groom each a rose and say she hopes they'll give each other a rose every year on their anniversary. "One day I realized we should make that a little more personal," says Alexa. So at the right moment in the ceremony, instead of presenting a rose, the minister offered her and Joel each a shot of tequila ("that's sort of our drink") and the wish that every year they'll remember their wedding day with love and a celebratory shot.

Comic Relief

Before the heavy part of the ceremony, but after a couple of straight readings, Clarice's brother read a poem by Ogden Nash. "People laughed, and we felt such a sense of relief," she says. "It lightened things up a bit and snapped us both out of our hypnotic state. Then we were much more able to be 'in the moment' for the vows."

I was at a wedding where the best man pulled a sudden "gag." He interrupted the proceedings right before the vows and announced that the groom had instructed him to flip a coin to help determine whether he should "go through with it." He flipped it, and it turned out to be a double-headed quarter and ha, ha, ha, what a knee-slapper. Maybe I'm old-fashioned, but I didn't think it was funny. Neither did the bride. But the groom's buddies were doubled over with laughter, so who am I to say?

Audience Participation

Gabi's favorite moment in her wedding ceremony was when she and Kevin had a chance to turn around and look at their friends and family. "The minister asked the group to bless us and to always help keep us together and happy, and to signify this by saying, 'We will.'" It made Gabi conscious of the crowd as a friendly force. "It wasn't until that point that I really realized how much love we were surrounded by," she says.

Long before they finally got around to throwing a wedding, June and Dennis talked about having a ceremony in which their friends would somehow marry them. Legally they would still have to be married first at city hall, which wasn't appealing to them. So they trashed that idea. But when they *did* get married, they wanted to include something in the ceremony that involved all their guests. So they came up with a plan. As the wedding guests entered, each was given an envelope with his or her name on it. Each envelope contained a copy of the same poem, with different lines highlighted. Says June, "We wanted to add an element of levity to the ceremony, so the poem we chose was light and whimsical." A friend of the bride's gave instructions to the crowd of one hundred: Read aloud the lines that are highlighted on your own copy and just follow along the rest of the time. Dennis's brother, who knew in advance about the poem, recited the first few lines, then June's closest friend had a couple of lines, then other family members, and so on. "All my British aunts read a line together," says June, "and all Dennis's coworkers read at once, and so on, until everyone had read a line." Toward the end of the poem, Dennis had a line, June had a line, and the whole congregation read the last four lines together. Says June, "Everybody was smiling by the end."

Timing

"The minister who married my husband and me gave us good advice," says Sophie. "He said that through the number and length of the readings we chose, we should try to make the ceremony last at least twenty minutes. He said it takes a few minutes to realize what's going on, and if the whole thing took only five minutes, we would have no memory of it." It's true. Ask around. It really is very dreamlike for the first few minutes. So you might want to make the ceremony a bit longer than your instincts tell you to. Don't worry about your guests; many of them will be really into it. And a ceremony that's twenty or thirty minutes is not going to be difficult for anyone over the age of eight to sit through.

Nice Touch: Hanky Panky

"I hand-painted on the invitations our names intertwined," says Joni. "And I silk-screened the same design onto hand-kerchiefs that were handed out before the ceremony. It was sort of a joke—you know, for people who might cry. But at the same time it was nice."

The Score

I was at a wedding where a violinist, a cellist and a bassist were playing a lovely Vivaldi concerto as the bride walked down the aisle. At least I think they were. Their arms were moving, and they were swaying, the way rapt musicians do, but there was no music. It was like a silent movie. I think the wind was blowing the wrong way or something. Actually, the trio was simply too far from the chupa. If you want the guests to be able to hear the music, whether it's live or recorded, you need to do a quick sound check. It can make an enormous difference.

Joni and Fred found themselves short one ceremony musician. A friend had written something for two violins and an accordion. "The cousin who promised to play the accordion got cold feet and backed out at the last minute," says Joni, "so I had to audition accordion players over the phone for two days."

Emma and Gary asked the keyboardist and the guitarist from their reception band to play during the ceremony, but only the keyboardist showed up in time. "The guitarist walked in ten minutes into the ceremony," says Emma. "I had already written a check to the band, which included extra money for these two guys.

So my advice is, wait till the end of the wedding to hand out checks or send electronic payments."

Jim's attitude about music for the ceremony was, Why bother? There was no wedding party; the processional would be over before you knew it. Who needs it? Well, apparently everybody. One guest describes the silent processional as "excruciating." There was no rhythm for people to walk with, so the bride was out of step with her parents. "You could hear her scolding her mother because there was nothing to drown out her heated whispering." And can you guess why the couple didn't opt for the obvious alternative (i.e., iTunes playlists)? You got it. The misguided music snob of a groom thought it was tacky.

Now, I ask you again—is recorded music tackier than utter silence is awkward? You know where I stand on this. But I'll admit, recorded music is not without its difficulties. When the iTunes or computer is inside and the ceremony and speakers are outside, coordination can be an issue. Wendy and Ben instructed their DJ to fade slowly up on a cheerful Dixieland rendition of "The Wedding March" right after their big "I now pronounce you" kiss. But the guy was not expecting the ceremony to be so short, and he was off somewhere having a cigarette when he heard the applause. By the time he made it back to his equipment, the couple had already walked back down the aisle. "We stalled before we headed back, hoping he was just a few seconds off in timing or something. I was so pissed off," says Wendy. "In those photos, I'm making an awful face because I was waiting and waiting for the music to come on." It didn't occur to Wendy or Ben beforehand that the DJ would walk away from his station. Because the ceremony was short, they should have told him (at least three hundred times) to stay put.

Don't be afraid to make a statement with your ceremony music. Yona and Miles considered walking down the aisle to

"Rock 'n' Roll Part II," by Gary Glitter, but opted for an Alicia Keyes tune instead. Ann Marie and Vincent used a live instrumental version of the Beatles' song "Something." And Penny and Will walked to a recording of James Taylor's "The Secret of Life."

If you're using recorded music at your reception and you want to introduce a little live music into the proceedings, the ceremony might be a good opportunity to do it. Ask a friend who plays any musical instrument (with the possible exception of the banjo) to help you out, and open up your mind to the kind of music he or she is comfortable performing.

Rehearsal

As unromantic as it sounds, some kind of rehearsal makes sense. That doesn't mean you have to speak your vows more than once or even hear what the officiant is going to say during the ceremony if you don't want to. It's mostly for marking paths. If you and the groom are the only two ceremony participants, you can probably skip the rehearsal. But if you have people reading, or walking with you, or playing music, you need to show them where they should be and teach them their cues. A quick rehearsal will make a big difference the next day; once all the performers (including you) are comfortable with where they're going, how they get there, when they speak and when they listen, they'll be able to be relaxed and focused for the real thing.

With This Ring

*W*hen I went to a discount jewelry store to purchase a pair of plain gold wedding bands—the exact rings I'd seen at Tiffany for more than twice the price—I asked the salesman why he thought anyone would go to Tiffany. He said, "To shop." That's probably one of his favorite lines, but it sure worked on me. In fact, until I heard it, I was seriously considering making the purchase at Tiffany, even though the saleswoman there treated me like I was a vagrant who'd wandered in by mistake. The thing is, even at twice the price, the rings were affordable, and it almost seemed disrespectful of their significance to pay so little for them. And maybe if you spend more money on them, they work better. Like, they really bind you together, and all those fears and worries you have about the ability of two people to stay together forever, they fly out the window once you walk out of the store with that little turquoise bag.

I'll never know that peace of mind; I went with the inexpensive ones.

No matter how little it costs, though, when you hold that precious little object in your hand, you have a moment of lucidity. You say to yourself, "Oh, I get it now . . ." Maybe that's why a lot of untraditional folk opt for the gold band; the symbolism of it is so powerful that it sort of unites you with the common experience *marriage.* Or maybe it's because they're just not into jewelry, and a gold band is as simple as it gets.

But getting rings that no one else has can be really special. Charlotte and Billy had silver rings made by a friend: flat bands with "Charli & Billy" stamped through the metal in tiny type. *Très* funky. You don't have any jewelry-artist friends? Make some.

E-mail or go to the jewelry-making department of your favorite local art college. Ask for someone who has a clue. Tell this helpful person that you'd like to pay a student to design and craft some wedding bands (two would be a good number to order), and ask if you could post something to that effect online or on the department bulletin board. Find out from your helper if a post in the school's online paper or on its Facebook page might be a more efficient route to brilliant as yet untapped craftspeople. Kids will e-mail and call you and bring you sketches, we hope. And the price will be reasonable because you can just make an offer. See, this is good for the art kid and good for you. The kid needs pictures for his/her portfolio, plus some good word of mouth (which you will start). You need rings. Exploit each other.

You should also visit craft fairs if you're looking for something unusual. Maybe you'll find a couple of rings that are calling your names (how embarrassing!). If you don't see what you want, but you find a jewelry artist whose work you like, you can commission some rings. And take a look around museum shops that carry reproductions. Maybe you'll get some ideas. If commissioning seems viable, you can have a version of an ancient design made in a precious metal so it will last.

Erika has something to say about precious metals. "We were talked into platinum on the engagement ring, but we got white gold on the wedding bands. The platinum cost much more money, but you can't tell the difference. Maybe if we live to be a thousand, we'll see how much more durable the platinum is and we'll say to ourselves, 'Good thing we went with the platinum. This white gold is crap.'"

Secret Code Rings

One of the fun parts of buying rings is deciding what to inscribe on the inside. Get whatever you want: your nicknames, a private joke (it had better be a short one, unless you have very big fingers), the date you first said, "I love you." Don't be bound by tradition here. And don't ask the jeweler, "What do most people do?" Jessica and Bruce inscribed the number of the subway line on which they met, and the date of that fateful meeting. Maybe you want to engrave something you say to each other all the time. Or if your endearment is too long, use just its initials. (If Rick and Ilsa had made it to the altar in *Casablanca*, their rings might have said HLAYK.) Don't be too shy to inscribe something personal. So what if the engraver has a little laugh at your expense?

Something Old

Antique rings are always unique, and they're often not expensive. But be careful if you shop at a flea market for merchandise of this ilk (i.e.; anything worth more than a Bobby Sherman 45). You don't know what kind of metal they're selling you until you bring it somewhere else and have it checked out. Shop only at "respectable" flea markets, where you see the same vendors week after week in case you have to go back and deck someone for ripping you off. Or, of course, at a nice, well-rooted store. And shop around a lot, so you're prepared to haggle. These people make up prices based on the vibes they get from you. And when they hook into that wedding vibe, dollar signs clink into the place where their eyeballs should be, à la Daffy Duck.

Penny felt the improvised price on the diamond band she wanted was high because the owner of the antiques store knew it was to be her wedding ring. "So I got my friend Lisa to go in without me and admire the same ring, just to see what price the guy would give her," says Penny. The plan backfired. The store owner tried to use Penny's interest in the ring to persuade Lisa to make an impulse purchase. ("It probably won't be here tomorrow. I have a bride who has her eye on it.") Then when Penny went back, the owner stuck to his price, because if Penny didn't want it, there was another woman who did. Hey, didn't Lucy and Ethel have the same problem with a mink stole?

It's Only Fitting

"When my husband and I purchased our wedding bands, I started wearing mine around the house, just for fun," says Gabi. "I was trying to get used to having a ring on my hand. It cracked me up. He made me stop though. He said it was bad magic to wear the rings before the ceremony." That's what happens to you when you're getting married. You're so spooked, you start making up your own superstitions. But Gabi made a discovery while she was experimenting. "The ring was too big. I could easily slide it off my finger, even in the bathtub [where the heat makes your finger expand]." She had it made smaller in time for the wedding. Whew!

Rich's ring has always been too small. The first word that comes to mind when he thinks of it is "tourniquet." "I had it made bigger right after I got it. Then, later that summer, it felt too tight again." It's a very wide band, which can be really uncomfortable in warm weather, when the size of your hand expands. Lots of men have never worn a ring when they pick out a wedding band. So you might want to pass on the advice that the wider (and more "manly") a ring is, the less comfortable it's likely to be.

Even though it was made specifically for him, Michael also finds his ring less than easy to wear. "I just can't get used to it," he says, after two years of trying. His proposed solution is to have one tattooed around his finger. Now *that's* commitment.

Don't Ring Me; I'll Ring You

At Kelly and Matt's wedding, when the moment came to exchange the rings, there was only one, from Kelly to Matt. "Matt loves wearing a ring," says Kelly. "I think he feels like it proves that he's married, and that's partly why he wanted to get married in the first place, to sort of change his status. But for me, changing my status wasn't so important. And not wearing a ring wasn't really a political decision. It was more practical—I don't wear jewelry. And I wouldn't start now just to announce myself as married."

Dan and Ilana were anti-ring too, but their reasons *were* political. (They're the ones in the previous chapter who had a "commitment ceremony," pointedly not a wedding.) They liked the idea of exchanging a gift that symbolized their commitment to each other, but rings were too closely associated with an institution they didn't want to support. So instead they went for small sapphire earrings. They bought a pair and split it.

Making a Clean Getaway

*G*oing on your honeymoon immediately after your wedding is like taking a six-month steam bath and then diving into an icy lake. Under the right conditions, both would be pleasant. But back to back, they're slightly cruel and very bracing.

This is no ordinary trip you're taking. It comes on the heels of one of the most momentous, exciting, stressful experiences of your life, so plan accordingly. Words of wisdom from your bride and groom friends in this book: If you can, wait a day before you leave. Have your wedding night, then return to (sort of) normal for a day, open your gifts, see your family or friends (whoever best represents normalcy for you without causing you lots of grief), then go.

You need some time to get together with people and gossip about your wedding so it can become part of your personal mythology (pardon the psychobabble) and you can own it (more psychobabble). It's all about putting things in perspective. I don't mean you should spoil the magic of the event and come back down to earth. But it's hard to maintain the magic by yourselves, and to avoid crashing, you should come down a little with the help of people who were at the wedding and who are dying to talk about it too.

"The morning after our wedding, we left for Italy," says Pam. Being suddenly alone and in a foreign environment was kind of traumatic. "I was dying to talk to my mother. Rich and I both felt kind of lonely and homesick." They even considered cutting their trip in half so they could go home after a week.

Amanda was glad she and Troy gave themselves a day to recuperate. They used the time to sleep, see their families, and take care of last-minute travel chores, like packing and lining up someone to water the plants. "I didn't want to have to worry about whether or not I remembered to pack my bathing suit the day of my wedding," says Amanda. Jeff could have used a rest day before his honeymoon. "It might have been nicer not to fly to Hawaii with a hangover," he says.

And if you've done a lot of work yourself for your wedding, I demand you take at least a day and a night to recover. Josie and Tom left their self-produced wedding with a four-hour drive ahead of them. When Tom opened his eyes just in time to see Josie almost nod off at the wheel, they decided perhaps it would be wise to get off the highway immediately and find a place to sleep.

See, your honeymoon is more about your wedding than it is about vacationing. You have to take that into consideration when you're planning it. You also have to think about who you are and try to predict what you might feel like doing right after you get married (good luck with that one). Those are the questions you want to ask yourself, not, "Where could we have our ultimate vacation?" Then plan the kind of trip that will be a treat, not a chore.

Don't choose someplace just because you think you should want to go there. Kathleen felt a lot of pressure from friends and family to go to Europe. "But we really didn't have any desire to. It didn't appeal to us. We wanted to go to a beach somewhere."

And don't plan on heavy-duty driving unless you really love being in a car. Gabi and Kevin went to a New England town that was twelve hours away because a bunch of people raved about it. The place was touristy and deserted because the season hadn't started, so the bride and groom were more than a little disappointed. Says Kevin, "It was boring, uncomfortable and emotionally overwrought. And that was just the drive."

Wedding Night–Mare

A good, solid piece of advice from more than one bride is to check out the place where you'll be spending your wedding night in advance. Not just the hotel, the room. Or if you're planning from a long distance, ask a trusted friend or relative to do it for you and to take some photos to e-mail or text. This is important.

Clarice didn't. "We made reservations at a little inn in Connecticut that my sister-in-law loves," she says. "But when we got there at eleven P.M., it turned out we were booked in the annex." So instead of being in a romantic, cozy canopy-bed room in a 19th-century farmhouse, she and Mitch ended up in a small adjoining modern building in what can only be described as an upscale motel room. They both were bummed out. Clarice felt depressed and decided to take a bath. When she got out of the tub and saw that her husband had fallen asleep, she started to cry. To make herself more miserable, she decided not to wake him up. "I sobbed for over an hour." Not a pretty picture.

Also, don't choose your honeymoon destination based on vague, general recommendations (i.e. "Oh, it's beautiful." "Oh, you'll love it." "Oh, I've heard it's very nice."). Not good enough. You need details so you can figure out if this is a place *you* will think is "beautiful" and "very nice." Based on my own crummy honeymoon, I suggest you consider going somewhere you already know and love. It takes a while to get used to even the nicest new place. But taking a chance that you might be disappointed is not worthwhile, because that gets blown all out of proportion when it's not just a trip but Your Honeymoon.

Your Hearts' Desire

Regina and Ted were planning on going to France, renting a car and staying in a different place every night. "As the wedding neared, we started to dread all that activity, so we decided just to bag it. We rented a place on St. Bart's and did nothing."

By the time their wedding happened, Mara and Patrick were totally wiped out. Their demanding jobs left them no time to enjoy the planning. Both were overwhelmed with work just before the wedding. Taking a big trip was out of the question; they figured they'd go on a honeymoon when things quieted down. Their postwedding plans were for a couple of days at an inn a hundred miles away. "We hardly ever get to spend time at home together," says Mara, "and that's all we really wanted to do." So that's what they did. They told all interested parties that they'd be gone until Wednesday, didn't answer their phones, watched a bunch of movies and just stayed in. "I never told my mother because I know she would think it was depressing to go home after your wedding," says Mara. "But for us, it was perfect."

"The best way for me to relax is to do something physical," says

Abby. If this is your sentiment exactly, plan your honeymoon accordingly. Of course, you have to take into account what your boyfriend likes to do. A week at an intense exercise-oriented spa might be his idea of hell. If you're both at the sedentary end of the scale, your honeymoon is *not* the time to turn over a new leaf and start biking thirty miles a day; if you like to veg, now you must veg. Embrace who you are and give that person a great time. Revamp later, maybe next January 1.

Money on Your Mind

Gail and Charlie had a modest but great honeymoon. They rented a housekeeping cabin in the mountains and spent the week "at home" in it watching TV, making microwave popcorn, going outlet shopping and eating at casual restaurants. Says Gail, "It was absolutely wonderful." After planning and paying for a huge party, an inexpensive, low-key vacation was exactly what they wanted.

It's smart to know when *not* to spend money. Part of my personal honeymoon anxiety came from the fact that we really couldn't afford to be away at all. So don't shoot your whole financial load if you won't be able to enjoy it. You have a lifetime of vacations together ahead of you. Susie and Tim booked a room in a very expensive hotel in New York. They weren't used to traveling, and didn't really know what to do with themselves. "All we could think about was that we were spending so much money on the room. We couldn't afford to go to shows or to nice restaurants. We would have been better off at home," says Susie.

What Goes Around Comes Around

Daphne and Rob decided to spend their honeymoon at a dude ranch in Phoenix. They're both athletic and were looking forward to a warm vacation full of activity. "Our friends had been there and loved it," says Daphne, "and we were excited about learning how to ride."

Months earlier, Daphne had argued with her father about the guest list for her wedding. She wanted to exclude the over-eighty faction of her extended family from the festivities. "I have about twenty-five living great-great-aunts and uncles who I don't even know and who can't get around on their own." (Her father, who was paying for the wedding, won the battle.)

Well, then, you can imagine how disturbing it must have been for Daphne, when she arrived at her honeymoon dude ranch, to discover that she and Rob were the youngest people there "by about forty years." Every activity at this ranch was a group activity, involving all fourteen guests. The manager apologized right away. It was a total fluke, never happened before. "The two couples we ended up hanging out with were in their sixties. They were the hippest people there." Ultimately, it was okay, because these couples were a lot of fun and talked endlessly to the newlyweds about the joys of marriage. And Daphne was duly awed by whatever force of spirit or nature took over her honeymoon to teach her a little lesson about respecting her elders.

Just a Sliver

—The Cake—

*D*o you know why wedding cakes cost a fortune?"

"No, but if you hum a few bars, I might be able to fake it."

Wedding cake prices are a bit of a joke. When in life would you ever consider spending that kind of money on a dessert product? Many of the wise brides and grooms I spoke to for this book found a way around quadruple-digit cakes. I personally lucked out in the cake department. My mother made me a magnificent three-tiered work of art covered with fresh flowers. (Now, years later, when I introduce friends to her, many follow "Nice to meet you" with "That cake was great!") It was by far the most opulent element of my wedding. Otherwise, it would have been Oreos all around.

Even if I'd had the money, I wouldn't have put it toward a cake. And most of the brides and grooms I spoke with agreed that a beautiful cake was not a top priority. Some talked about wanting a cake that *tastes* good or a specific *type* of cake, but no one said,

"Spend the money. It's worth it!" It is, after all, just a cake. Everyone looks for a few minutes and says, "Ooh, ahh, pretty"; then it gets hacked into paper-thin slices and it might as well be a Sara Lee. So why do bakers and caterers charge so much? Because they can.

"I'm embarrassed to tell you what I spent on my cake," says Jocelyn. "It was really pretty, just the way I wanted it, but it was certainly not an integral part of my happiness that day." In other words, she wouldn't have missed it if it hadn't been around. "And I only saw it for about a minute. It definitely was not worth the money to me."

At the very least, if you're spending a lot of dough (ha, ha) on your cake, treat it as part of the decorations. If the temperature and type of icing permit, have it on display for the whole wedding. That way everyone can enjoy it for four or five hours instead of just a couple of minutes.

"Also," complains Jocelyn, "I expected it to taste better. It had that 'wedding cake' taste, you know what I mean?" Yup. I know. Very sweet, mostly air. Says our cake expert, Maria, that's likely to be a simple ambrosia cake, which is light and high rising because it contains lots of baking powder. Bakers like it for wedding

BYOC

If you have your wedding at a restaurant or hall that handles the food, check into the possibility of bringing your own cake. The house cake is probably priced per person, like the rest of the food, so do the math and see what you'd be paying for the whole thing. You might be able to save yourself a bundle by buying one elsewhere.

cakes because fluffy equals stackable. And since many buy the dry ingredients premixed, there's an eerie worldwide sameness to the taste.

I'll Just Whip Something Up

If you're thinking pillars or spun-sugar roses, godspeed to you. "That's the stuff that makes professional wedding cakes expensive," says Maria, "labor-intensive decorations and assembly that require lots of expertise." But she firmly believes you can make a nice wedding cake at home (and she doesn't even know you!). According to Maria, if you use a recipe for ambrosia cake and don't aim too high, you can't screw up.

We're talking sheetcakes, stacked, with frosting between the layers—a simple, tasty cake that can be as big or as small as you need without any concern for gravity. And you don't have to worry about working with unwieldy quantities of batter, which can mess up a recipe. See how many people a layer feeds, multiply accordingly and make yourself a comfortable schedule. Bake one layer a night, if you like. Or one a week for four weeks. So many options! This whole plan is, of course, contingent upon adequate storage (i.e., a big freezer). Once the requisite number of layers are safely put away, you can forget about them. The day before or the day of the wedding, a dear and trusted helper will frost the cake with a very simple frosting. (That wall-of-icing look is hard to achieve. Settle for swirls—so easy, you can spread it with a paper knife!) He or she will then assemble the layers and transport the mighty object to the fridge at the reception site.

The cake will be made wedding-y at the last minute by how you decorate it. You can use fresh flowers, but be sure to get flowers that are grown without pesticides, or organic edible flowers, like nasturtiums, in fabulous colors. Some gourmet stores sell edible nasturtiums in fabulous colors. And candied violets are a beautiful decorating option; if you scattered these things on a whoopie pie it would look elegant. Now's the time to look at cookbooks, at magazines and online and steal someone else's easy cake-decorating ideas. Also, visit a good candy shop: Pick up some silver dragées or maybe little mound-shaped white chocolate truffles. There are lots of options inside those glass cases. (You'll be like a bride in a candy store!) Keep it very simple, and you can't go wrong.

I suggest a practice run of just one layer, plus icing, especially if you're not an experienced baker. One go-round will help you iron out a bunch of kinks. And then you can shock your friends one night by following a take-out meal with a delicious home-made confection.

Honey, Could You Pick Up Something for Dessert?

Marisa and Carlos had planned on making a wedding cake themselves—an apple spice cake they'd gotten the recipe for months earlier at a restaurant in Vermont. Marisa wasn't concerned so much about the visuals, but she did want a tasty dessert. "I was thinking, This would be a nice thing to have in winter at the end of a meal," says Marisa. Well, the week of the wedding rolled around, and it became clear that the homemade cake was not going to happen, so Marisa had some last-minute shopping to do. She found a pastry chef at a local restaurant who also freelances. Marisa had the chef make a small, two-tiered apple spice cake, frosted and with a little piping around the edges, but otherwise unadorned; that shaved some money off the price. Before the wedding, the bride decorated the cake stand with some extra pesticide-free flowers from the centerpieces. "It was perfect, inexpensive and so easy."

Having Your Cake

Two couples I talked to really wanted a carrot cake and were told by everyone they approached, "We don't do carrot wedding cakes." Is it some kind of ancient superstition? The bride should never feed the groom anything that contains root vegetables at the reception? No. Carrot cakes are dense. They don't stack so well. And they're dark, which makes them tough to cover with white icing. I talked to bakers who were willing to do a carrot wedding cake, but they charge a bit more for them. You'll find that some also charge more for chocolate cake, for the icing reason.

Never Say "Wedding"

Abby had a small wedding—sixty people. She called a funky bakery known for its delicious, beautifully decorated cakes. "When I said the words 'wedding cake' they said 'five hundred.' I said, 'Okay, I don't want a wedding cake. Give me the price of a cake.' And they said three-fifty.'" Are you starting to get the point here?

Name Your Price

"When I was calling around for prices for a cake that would serve 180, I was hearing figures like $1,800," says Naomi. "I didn't want to spend that kind of money on cake. So my first idea was to have a cake that was supposed to serve about sixty people and just have really skinny slices." Then Naomi decided to skip the cake altogether and just serve berries and cookies for dessert. "No one eats wedding cake anyway." Her mother, who had made no requests till this point, spoke up and insisted on a cake. "It was the only thing she'd asked for. So I found this photo on TheKnot.com—it was just a bundt cake with powdered sugar on top and a few roses stuck through the center hole. No icing." Naomi figured a three-tiered version (basically three bundt cakes, one smaller than the next) would be plenty. "I went to a local caterer and I said, 'Could you make this cake for me? I'm spending $550.' And she said okay. I told her I wanted a hazelnut orange cake, and she talked me up to $750." Naomi used long-stem roses for the center and cut the stems so the buds just peeked out the top.

Let Them Eat (Something Other Than) Cake

"I never like wedding cake, and I wasn't going to spend hundreds of dollars on one," says Jared. He thought it would be more appropriate for Gia and him to end their wedding lunch with their favorite dessert. So he contacted a local bakery and ordered mini cream puffs—three hundred of them (three for each guest). The giant mound o' treats, dusted with powdered sugar, was wheeled out instead of the cake, and the guests set upon them like vultures on carrion.

The Bridal Path

aybe you can hire a traffic cop to oversee your receiving line. ("Okay, move it along. Kiss the bride, kiss the groom, then step aside. Let's go, we don't have all day. Put the pedal to the metal there, gramps.") Yes, it can take a long time. So should you just skip it?

The consensus among my crowd of brides is that if you care about interacting with all your guests, you should either have a receiving line or "do the tables." Some people *don't* care. Barbara chose to do neither. "I think it's always weird when you talk to the bride at her wedding. She's off on some other planet and you can't have a real conversation with her, so I decided to do exactly what I wanted at my wedding. It's incredibly overwhelming, the fact of all those people, and to try and control it by making them line up to come see you seemed silly."

Pam is pro receiving line. You might be too if you had three hundred guests to deal with. "Once I did the official greetings, I considered the rest of the wedding my own," she says. She felt it saved her from having to do the tables or mingle all night. "I wanted to spend time with my friends, not with my father's business associates."

Marie says if you're going to have a receiving line, assign someone the task of organizing it. "Right after my ceremony I didn't have the presence of mind to say, 'Okay, we'll do the receiving line right here,'" she says. "I knew we had to do it, but we just hadn't planned it. It was a mess. There wasn't a line at all. The wedding party was scattered all over the sidewalk. It took forever."

The receiving line epitomizes what I hated about being a bride—all these people in one place who you'd love to talk to but who you can only interact with on a very superficial level. So I skipped it. We got sort of mobbed by the crowd after the ceremony. Then people came over to talk to us when they saw we were free. It was organic but a little awkward.

Sometimes having a receiving line is really important to the hosting parents. "My mother didn't know any of my husband's friends, so I'm glad we did it," says Noreen. "She was proud to be throwing the party, and she liked hearing that people were having a good time."

Regina's one regret about her wedding is that she *did* have a receiving line. "Our goal was to have the evening be unwedding-like in structure—a ceremony and just a big party." No traditional time frame, no formal everybody-watch-us-dance-with-our-parents segments. "But we ended up having a 'cocktail hour' because it took forty-five minutes to get everyone through the receiving line." And they did the tables anyway.

"It had a weird effect on me," says Dana of her receiving line. "I got kind of zombied-out, and then it made me relax." After smiling, thanking and turning to accept a kiss a hundred times, you too might attain a Zen-like calm. So maybe this assembly line of conviviality is a good idea. I can't think of a more efficient way to get the job done. But you might be able to speed it up by abbreviating the group a bit: just you, your new hubby and the parents. No wedding party, no grandma. Then you can finish up your hellos before your facial muscles cramp into a permanent smile.

Scattered Showers

From a bride's perspective, surprise showers are eerily similar to accounts of alien abduction. You're captured by calm, friendly beings and taken to an unthreatening environment, where you're placed in a central location, poked, prodded and observed. Your every move and utterance is recorded on advanced technological equipment. The beings give you unidentified items and document your reactions. They smile incessantly, never taking their huge eyes off you, and hush whenever it seems you are about to speak. They treat you like a less advanced, but extremely fascinating creature. You emerge unscathed, except for a few marks you can't identify (other women's lipstick) and a couple of spots that are tender to the touch (your left cheek, where your aunt pinched you; your ribs from overenthusiastic hugs).

It comes with the territory. You can't stop a surprise shower, so you might as well enjoy it, even if the thought of being taken off guard and fussed over gives you hives. Daphne discovered that a friend was planning a shower for her and that she was asking people for photos of Daphne's old boyfriends (a closer friend felt it was best to prepare Daphne, so she revealed the surprise). "Apparently she was working on some kind of presentation," says Daphne. "When I heard, I threw a little fit—in the privacy of my bedroom, of course."

When Colleen was on her way to her sister-in-law's shower, she secretly believed she was going to her own surprise shower. She laughs when she tells the story because it shows her as a ridiculously self-centered bride-to-be. "I thought they played this great trick on me—sent me an invitation to someone else's shower, but really it was my own. On the way over, I said so to my boyfriend. He kept denying it saying, 'No, it's really Cecilia's shower. I swear.' I didn't believe him until I got there and nobody shouted 'Surprise.'"

Amy told Penny she was throwing her a shower on June 3, and then surprised her by having it the week before. So Penny got the fun part of the surprise without the heart-stopping terror. And Amy got all the cooperation she needed from the bride (mostly in the form of names and addresses). Since Penny was moving across the country after her wedding, Amy asked each friend to bring, in addition to a gift, a photo of herself (for a collage) and a letter Penny could save and read when she arrived at her new home in Seattle.

When You're In on It

A planned shower can be a nice, intimate prewedding event if you talk diplomatically with the powers that be about your preferences. Feel the situation out. Does it seem cool to make a special request about what type of shower you have? There are plenty of themes besides the kitchen and the bedroom. If you have all the lingerie and housewares you need or want, think of something else.

"I felt uncomfortable about my friends having to buy me a shower gift *and* a wedding gift," says Gabi. But her mother wanted to give her a shower. Since Gabi had just moved into a new apartment and for the first time had southern exposure, she asked to make it a plant shower. That way guests wouldn't feel compelled to spend a lot of money, and Gabi would get something she wanted and would probably never buy for herself—a roomful of plants. "I named them after the people who gave them to me, which got kind of weird when a couple of the plants died. The ones that survived are my favorite presents, though." Talk about a gift that keeps on giving.

Sabrina makes quilts, so her sister threw her a fabric shower. Nicole had a book shower. Francine didn't want any gifts, so her friends planned a poem shower. Each person brought a poem she loved—or wrote—and over tea and sandwiches did a reading.

Boys and Girls Together

If the gender-segregating tendencies of conventional wedding activities bother you, lobby for a coed shower (pardon the pun). This immediately changes the whole feel of the event. For one thing, it's pretty much guaranteed that you won't be sporting a paper-plate hat by the end. But remember, when you double the potential guest list, you also cut the coziness quotient in half. Jeff helped his mother plan a wine shower for him and Molly. "It was fun, but it was overwhelming," he says. Because it was coed, it ended up being almost everybody from the wedding. "There was just too much going on there, too many people and too much happening."

We'll Just See Her at the Wedding

Marie's mother booked a restaurant for her shower. Six friends who were supposed to be coming blew it off at the last minute. "Everyone just took it very lightly," says Marie. "They didn't want to bother getting on the train on a Sunday afternoon and riding for forty-five minutes." So her mother ended up paying for meals no one ate. You might find that people don't always make the effort for the shower that they're willing to make for the actual wedding. Don't let this upset you or prompt you to reevaluate friendships you normally consider rock solid. Marie did. Three years later, she's still pissed off at her friends for their careless attitude.

You'll Sit Where I
Tell You to Sit

I didn't want to have table assignments at my wedding because I feel uncomfortable bossing people around. My husband reminds me that the *real* reason we didn't have table assignments was that we didn't exactly have enough seats. See how I blocked that out? Now that he mentions it, that does ring a bell. Right, not enough seats. We were counting on the sun to shine brightly and guests to mill about mostly outside and take turns sitting in natural shifts.

Well, at least the weather worked out. The "let the guests fall where they may" part was a problem. When people discovered that there was, in fact, no seating plan, a palpable tension filled the air. Then a quiet fight broke out between two rather assertive friends of mine, one of whom was holding a table for eight by herself.

Table assignments are a good thing. People like to be able to define their turf. They need a place to leave their sweaters or their bags. They want a home base at an event that's going to last four or five hours.

Max was at a recent wedding with no seating plan and 180 guests. "It was a nightmare," he says. "When they opened the dining room, it was like the running of the bulls at Pamplona. I ended up having to shove the bride's great-aunt so I could grab a table where all my friends could sit." Obviously, an atmosphere of fever-pitch competition is not conducive to a relaxed good time.

Please Be Seated

Well, it's all up to you . . . and your boyfriend and his parents and your parents. Just the six of you. (It's not that hard for six people to agree. Look at the Brady Bunch; they hardly ever fought.) Here's where politics come into play big time. Who's at the head table? Who's *near* the head table? Who's near the kitchen? We can't put Cousin Sadie with Cousin Matilda because they'll throw food at each other.

If you're not sure where to begin, look at the layout of the space and consider people's tolerance or lack thereof for loud music. The young 'uns can be near the speakers or the band; the older guests should probably be a comfortable distance away.

Family Matters

"Relatives sort of forget that somebody else is planning this wedding, and they bring all their grudges," says Lindsay. When one of her second cousins called with a negative seating request ("Don't seat me with so-and-so"), Lindsay threw in the towel. "I let my mother handle it, because if it were up to me, I wouldn't have honored any requests," she says. Her mother didn't mind the responsibility and, in fact, was glad to have the chance to avert potential disaster. Lindsay recommends passing the buck on seating the relatives. "It's one less thing for you to worry about the week before you get married."

Because there was a real danger of fisticuffs between Katie's and Jim's mothers about the seating plan, the couple insisted on handling that detail themselves. They let their mothers choose who would be at their own tables, and that was it. "We didn't even show them the final plan," says Jim. "It just got too ugly. They saw it when the guests saw it: the next day."

Colleen says her mother was "a real pain in the butt" about the seating plan. "She wanted to mix people up instead of putting them in the obvious places," says Colleen. That's kind of a bold move, but I respect it. Colleen didn't. She told her mother that people go to weddings to see people they know, not to make new friends. But, like a model bride, Colleen tossed her mother a crumb and let her experiment on a small scale. Her mother seated some relatives with a couple of her own friends, and placed the relatives' grown kids at another table. "I told her, 'Mom, they're not gonna want to sit there. They're gonna want to sit with their kids,'" says Colleen. "And what they did was they pulled chairs over and sat with their kids."

Musical Chairs

What do you do when you have a very solid group of ten friends and tables that seat eight? Well, you either make two people very angry, or you split the group approximately down the middle and fill in the two tables with some loose guests. You'd think your friends would be pretty mellow about where they sit, but this issue brings out the scorekeeper in a lot of people. Because where you place your friends supposedly reflects what you think of them, how much you love them and how seriously you take their role in your big event.

You may recall that Michelle caught a glimpse of a couple leaving her wedding about five minutes after everyone had sat down. "I found out later that they left because they didn't like where they were seated," says Michelle. "They wanted to be at one of the friends tables, but those were full, so I put them with my cousins." Such hypersensitive guests should detail their seating requirements on the reply card, or better yet, stay at home, where they can sit anyplace they like.

The Illustrious Head Table

This is like the lunchroom in junior high. Who gets to sit with the most popular couple in the school? If you have a wedding party, that's who gets to. But what about their dates? I'm only going to give one side of this argument. The dates have to be able to sit there too. Please! Greg, always a groomsman, never a groom, once had a bad experience in which the bridesmaid who he accompanied down the aisle somehow construed him as her date, even though they'd never met before. Greg attributes this largely to the fact that they were seated together. The bossy bridesmaid pressured him to dance with her and complained whenever he left the table. Needless to say, this was somewhat awkward for Greg's girlfriend, who was seated across the room at one of the friends tables. Look, if the head table isn't big enough for your party and their dates, figure something else out. Maybe just sit with the best man and maid of honor (plus companions) and a couple of other friends, and seat the rest of the attendants somewhere nearby. You'll make your bridesmaids and groomsmen miserable if you separate them from the people they came with.

If you don't have a wedding party, your guess for who to seat at the head table is as good as anyone's. Try to make it a cozy comfortable crowd for you. Maybe it's best to stick with one group of friends (if you and the groom have a mutual group you can agree on) rather than taking a couple from here and a couple from there. And if you think someone will be hurt to find out he or she is not at your table, it might be worth a phone call in advance. But anyone who gets mad about not being at the head table really does belong in junior high.

Like I Needed This?

—The Bachelor Party—

*I*t's funny (I wish I really believed that); just before you make a permanent commitment to a man, you get to see him at his absolute lowest and least appealing: wasted, drooling, slurring maudlin sentiments—post–bachelor party. Maybe that's the subliminal purpose of a bachelor party, to present a bride-to-be with a worst-case scenario. I want to believe there's some mysterious reason that such an antiquated activity persists; the traditional explanation (one last night of fun before being shackled to a ball and chain) is just too much for me to stomach.

If you have any trouble with the concept of the bachelor party and you think tension might ensue, make sure the party's not scheduled too close to the wedding. You may need time to have a fight and make up. And you don't want visions of your husband with a lap dancer in his face visiting themselves upon you as you head down the aisle.

Often the party is scheduled very close to the wedding because that's when all the buddy-boys come to town. If you are more evolved than I am, and you don't have any problems with the principles behind it and the activities involved, cool. But if you know you're going to fly into a feminist rage when you start hearing about the plans (or pointedly *not* hearing about them), insist that the party be at least a week before the wedding. Then maybe you won't have to associate that juvenile frat-boy behavior with the man you're supposed to spend the rest of your life with. There are also practical reasons to get it out of the way early.

"My husband's bachelor party was two days before our wedding," says Clarice. "The next day there were so many things still to be done, plus we had to get to the rehearsal in the afternoon." When Clarice woke up, she discovered her almost brother-in-law passed out on their couch, and a friend of the groom's comfortably

I Can Handle It . . . Then Again, Maybe I Can't

Obsessed with the implications of bachelor party behavior? The obvious solution is to go out with your own friends for a night of debauchery while said party is happening. This works for some women, but it didn't for Nicole, who can't even think about bachelor parties without smashing something. A week before her wedding, her boyfriend, Jamie, was taken out by his friends. The leader of the group was the best man (we'll call him Beelzebub), party boy of all party boys—the kind of guy who's disgusted that all his friends are "settling down" and who, when he was "temporarily engaged," spent far more time talking about his impending "bachelor weekend" than about his upcoming wedding. "I knew where they'd end up with him in charge," says Nicole. "It made me sick to think of my husband seeing other women dancing around naked! I don't think that's such a crazy way to feel." She tried to deal with it on her own, but she couldn't. She made plans with friends, then cancelled them. Finally she brought up the subject with Jamie. "He told me he had to do what the guys wanted, that it would be rude not to," she says. "Wasn't it 'rude' not to do what *I* wanted?" Once Jamie left the apartment, Nicole worked herself into a frenzy. An hour later, she called the bar where she knew the festivities were to begin and asked the bartender to find Jamie. (Not surprisingly, the groom's friends had confiscated his phone.) When she got him on the phone, she said, "You either come home now, or I'm not marrying you."

I think I'll leave this open-ended, like those after-school specials from the 1970s. Read it to a mixed group and discuss. Was Nicole being psychotic? Is Jamie too susceptible to peer pressure? Is Beelzebub really all that bad?

asleep on the hardwood floor, still in his coat. The groom himself was hungover and basically a lump. Clarice left to get a manicure and "run about a million errands," setting the alarm clock for ten (and a backup one on the groom's smartphone). When she came back at two in the afternoon, they were all still sleeping. Obviously no one had picked up the chairs for the reception, which was supposed to happen before noon. Needless to say, the boys were loudly awakened, and the rest of the day was less than pleasant.

Poor bachelor party timing contributed to Bonnie's prewedding nuttiness: "I was awake all of Thursday night worried about my husband, who had come home very drunk," she says. "Before he went to bed he took four ibuprofen to prevent a hangover and two allergy pills so he could breathe. I got paranoid that he might have taken too many drugs at once, so I stayed awake and kept an eye on him. He slept like a baby. I was a wreck the whole next day."

PHASE

3

· ·

How to Have Fun

*O*kay, now you're supposed to forget about everything that's been keeping you awake for the last several months. You'll become serene, pleasant, at peace with the universe. Ready, set, go! But wait! What about your caterer, whose cell phone is mysteriously not accepting voicemail messages? Or the ten inches of snow predicted for the weekend? Or that mysterious red abrasion between your eyebrows?

All valid concerns, but you must find a way to dismiss them. It's time to stop worrying and approach every seeming obstacle with a sense of relief. (As in, "Whew! The preparations are over. What a relief!") And if more significant disasters come your way this week, well, at least you've got your health.

So, do you think you're ready to enjoy the fruits of your labor? It's not as easy as it sounds. You have to *decide* to have fun, opt for it—not just put on a happy face, but find a way to somehow slip into a joyous disposition.

At her wedding, Gabi was never quite able to swing it. "I wasn't

The Countdown

One week before: You read a piece online about the rapidly escalating divorce rate in America. You turn off your tablet and turn on the TV. The topic on *Dr. Phil*: Suicidal Newlyweds. On the Oprah Winfrey Network: Infidelity in the 21st Century. You call your boyfriend at work and pick a fight.

Five days before: You are restless and unable to eat. You watch your boyfriend sleep peacefully. You get up at three A.M. and scrub the bathroom tiles with a toothbrush.

Three days before: The sleep-deprivation therapy finally pays off. You nod off at dinner and have to be carried to your bed. In your dream, you show up at the wedding in nothing but a bra and a pair of argyle knee-socks; Madonna is there, but you don't recognize any of the other guests.

Two days before: Your appetite has returned. You eat a whole box of Cocoa Puffs for breakfast, then go about your errands. You are confused by two items on your shopping list: off-white tights or pantyhose and a $30 lipstick. "Why would I need *these*?" you say aloud. You are in denial.

The day before: You bang your shin on your night table and don't realize you need a Band-Aid till hours later, when a woman on the bus complains that you're dripping blood on her shoes. Later you find yourself at a wedding rehearsal and it occurs to you: You must be getting married.

mentally prepared to have fun," she says. "We did so much of the work ourselves, and all through the wedding I kept making myself crazy over little things." She was overwhelmed by nervousness, exhaustion and the frustration of not being able to figure out how to have a good time.

Going into the big day with the right frame of mind can make all the difference, and getting into that mind-set requires some temporal distance from work. The more "do-it-yourself" your wedding is, the more time you need. April took a whole week off, "and it was the smartest thing I could have done," she says. Not everyone has that luxury, but if you do, take advantage. If it means making your honeymoon half as long as you'd hoped, well that's a little compromise. But you'll enjoy your wedding so much more if you have a little chill-out time before it.

Some brides are amazed at how *little* they have left to do the week of the wedding. If you're pretty much all set, and (more important) you're feeling fairly cool yourself, you may not need or want a week off in advance. All I can say is, err on the side of *more* time off, if you have the choice. This week is all about reaping what you've sown and experiencing as fully as possible a monumental, wonderful occasion. Take care to prepare yourself, so the big day can be as close to perfection as reality ever gets.

Decompression

—Care and Feeding of the Prewedding Bride—

*Y*our mission, should you choose to accept it, is to make the bride feel as good as possible, to indulge her in healthy ways, to repeat affirmations in her ear, if necessary. In short, to eliminate stress from her mind and body, and to erase signs thereof from her face. You have one week.

Here are some suggestions:

- **Go easy on the sugar and caffeine.** I don't care if you usually eat like a twelve-year-old whose parents are out of town; this week is different. You're going to be in a fragile emotional state, and a poorly timed cappuccino could really set you off.

- **Induce a good cry.** For the more guarded, this might mean watching say, *Terms of Endearment* on Netflix; for others, it could be as easy as looking in the mirror. Crying has tremendous release potential. (Have you ever seen an infant after a really intense fit of hysterics? Utter peace.)

- **Screen all calls.** Your phone will not stop ringing this week. And although all calls will be about the Big Day (which you are anticipating with unfettered glee!), they will not all be interesting, and some are likely to induce a fair amount of stress. This is when last-minute people cancel—at least the thoughtful ones. The others you'll hear from the morning of your wedding at seven, or never. It's when photographers forget the location; it's when you *still* haven't taken care of the cake/your shoes/the processional music, and your mother feels that the best way to motivate you is to call you the moment she wakes up, right before she goes to bed (she can't sleep anyway, worrying about this) and a dozen times in between.

- **Force yourself to smile.** Not a phony grin, a real smile, with your cheeks and eyes and everything. It's supposed to make you feel good, and it works. Try a minimum of two every four hours.

Customized Indulgence

A lot of people will throw the phrase "pamper yourself" at you this week, and you should. But not necessarily the way bridal magazines and wedding blogs tell you to. If you're not used to a massage and a pedicure, they might not be your idea of a rockin' good time. Newness can be anxiety-provoking. What you need are activities *you* consider indulgent. If your favorite form of release is a spinning class followed by a big brunch, go for it. Sit in the park and read a book. Play your iPod really loud. Watch a couple of episodes of *30 Rock*. See a mindless movie. Figure out what *your* idea of being spoiled is and then go for it. And remember, it's all supposed to result in an elated sense of relaxation (that would rule out gambling and all-night bar hopping).

A Little Meditation Never Hurt Anybody

One of the most common, most frustrating problems brides (and grooms) experience at their wedding is an inability to concentrate on what's going on, a difficulty being "in the moment." It can take hours to get a grip on what's happening. And then, what a bummer, because the wedding's almost over. So try giving a few minutes every day this week to focused relaxation. You won't be able to restructure your whole consciousness in one week, but if you make an effort to clear your mind a little (the effort is an end in itself), you might be able to relax, and that will carry over to the wedding. Meditating does not require that you chant "Om," sit in an agonizing position or attempt to transcend your earthly self (but you can if you want to). It can just be about breathing and releasing tension. Here's how to do it:

- Put your cat in another room or it will sit on your hair and spoil everything.

- Lie face up on the floor—use a towel if you haven't vacuumed this month. Let your legs be a comfortable distance apart. Put a softcover book about two inches thick under your head (hey, *this* book would be good!).

- Take a minute to really spread your body out. Use your hands to widen your back, so you can feel the floor with your spine. Fiddle around till you get comfortable, because you're going to try to lie still for a while.

- Close your eyes.

- Try to relax your weight into the floor, and listen to your breathing. Count ten natural breaths. Your breathing should become shallower.

- Next, mentally work your way up your body (starting at the feet), contracting muscles and then releasing them so they can relax. You don't have to follow these instructions exactly, just take your time and use every muscle group you can think of. And after each movement, count two breaths before you go on to the next one: Scrunch up all your toes, then release them (two breaths). Circle both ankles, then relax your feet (two breaths). Flex your feet so you feel your calves stretch, then release (keep breathing). Straighten your knees and lift your legs an inch off the floor, so you feel the tops of your thighs working, then drop them. Contract your buttocks, then release. Pull your abdominal muscles in, then let go. Make a fist and straighten your arms a couple of inches from the floor; relax and drop them. Hike your shoulders up to your ears, then release. Pucker your lips and bring all your facial features together. Then open your mouth wide. Then release.

- Spend a minute thinking about your face. Do a mental check to make sure every part of it is completely relaxed:

your jaw, your forehead, your sinuses, the muscles behind your eyes.

- Feel your weight dropping into the floor. Let your bones become so heavy that you couldn't move them if you tried.

- Visualize a blue sky with a few white clouds floating through it (the perfect weather you're anticipating for the weekend). Try to concentrate completely on the clouds.

- Every time an outside thought enters your mind, notice it, then let it float away with the next cloud.

"How long do I have to stay like this?" you ask. Oh, as long as you want. Twenty minutes would be good. But I don't want you to be aware of the clock (and you've already turned your phone to silent, right?), so stay for as long as you feel comfortable. When you've had enough, resist the temptation to stand up quickly. Instead, take a few deeper breaths, roll onto one side, and use your hands to push yourself up to a seated position, keeping the rest of your body pretty relaxed. Take a couple of deep breaths here, then get up and go about your bride-y business.

There's a possibility you'll fall asleep while you're doing this. That's okay. Sleep is *very* relaxing, and chances are, you're not getting enough of it this week.

To Do and Don't

Last-minute tasks to tackle or to avoid.

Do confirm absolutely everything. Sit down with your very organized I wedding binder (reinforcements on every page, no doodles on the cover) or spreadsheet, your phone and a pot of chamomile tea. Call and e-mail every person you're counting on for wedding help. Verify time, place, price and then every single specific detail you can think of. Pam did not make confirmation calls or send confirmation e-mails, and the day *before* her wedding, three limos pulled up in front of her parents' house. (The Better Business Bureau says that limo companies are among the most often complained about by brides and grooms.) If you're insecure about the reliability of any particular vendor, call and e-mail more than once; if you have special requests, verify those too. And don't forget to contact casual helpers—friends or relatives you're depending on—to talk over particulars too.

Don't take on too much. Paul and Krista decided to handle all the tux rentals for their wedding themselves; the tux wearers (fathers, grandfathers, groomsmen) were coming to Iowa from all over the country, and the meticulous bride and groom wanted all the tuxes to match exactly. (Is it just me, or do you smell trouble?) Of course, Paul and Krista were coming from Chicago and making the twelve-hour drive two days before the wedding. The men e-mailed their measurements to Paul, who rented the same double-breasted tux for each of them (a total of ten) in Chicago. Before leaving for Iowa, Paul went to pick up the tuxes, only to discover that the double-breasted style jacket runs very large. "Mine looked like a swing dress," he says. In addition to the fit problem was the fact of some missing items—one jacket (for the best man) and three pairs of shoes. "They finally found us a jacket, and we left for Iowa without the shoes."

When Paul and Krista arrived in Iowa, already harried from the tux experience, the men gathered to try on their perfectly matched penguin costumes; that's when the fun *really* began. The jackets for both the father of the groom and the father of the bride were huge. "They were the wrong size," says Paul. "Like, they were marked 42 long but they were really 50 regular or something." When Paul called to complain and beg for help, the Chicago tuxedo place threw its figurative hands up as if to say, "What can we do?" Krista took the phone and made a major stink, punctuated with expletives and threats. The morning of the wedding, the Chicago store FedExed some smaller jackets to Iowa. Says Paul, "On one, the sleeves were unhemmed."

Excuse me, but is this the kind of thing you want occupying your mind for the forty-eight hours prior to your wedding? You can't do everything. If there's a major wedding-week task you can't delegate, eliminate it. After such an ordeal, how much joy and satisfaction do you suppose Paul and Krista got out of those precisely matched tuxes? When they can bear to look at their wedding pictures (in which the groomsmen look like a bunch of fifth-graders dressed up in Daddy's suits), they'll let you know.

Do have a verbal run-through with your groom. Talk step by step through the day or evening, and make sure you agree about what's happening when. "My husband and I hadn't discussed what we were going to do before the ceremony," says Tasha. Since the couple was planning on walking down the aisle together, Tasha assumed they'd be hanging out together beforehand. "Just before the ceremony began, I was looking around for him, and I saw that he was outside greeting guests and palling around. Peering down on them, I felt like some princess trapped in an ivory tower." Tasha hadn't wanted to make an entrance all alone. "I would have been down there with him saying hello to everyone if I'd known that was what he was going to do. But we hadn't talked about it. We didn't make a plan."

Don't get your hair cut. You have to do this about two weeks in advance. Even if you're completely used to your hairdresser, your hair always looks better after a week or so; it's something about letting the wave settle (see every haircut article ever written). This is a particularly good piece of advice to pass on to your groom. Men often make the mistake of stopping off on the way to the most important event of their lives for a quick, unbelievably awful haircut. (My husband winces when he sees our wedding pictures, in which, thanks to his fresh haircut, he thinks he looks like Stan Laurel.)

Do have a "dress" rehearsal. Invite a friend, and put on your whole outfit, from undergarments to mascara. "I was nervous about operating my dress," says Lia. "There were dozens of hooks and tiny covered buttons that brought the train in to become part of the skirt." A little practice (plus a diagram uploaded to a friend's smartphone for the ceremony and reception) quelled her fears. Also, your new makeup needs breaking in, so take it out of the excessive packaging, and play dress up. Check it out in the right light. Maybe that lipstick has too much orange in it. Or, heaven forfend, that blush sparkles in sunlight! And make sure the cosmetics you need to keep with you at the wedding (powder, lipstick, and whatever else makes you feel secure) will fit into your little bag.

Don't starve yourself. You're not going to lose any weight this week. If you've been surviving on rice cakes for the past month, now's the time to start eating normally. Feed yourself the kind of diet you would feed, say, a ten-year-old princess who came to stay with you; that means something with more nutritive value than bagels and Diet Coke. And don't forget to have some protein every day.

Do prepare an emergency kit. Use an old handbag. Include safety pins, rubber bands, a needle and thread (black and white, or whatever colors you and the groom are wearing), a lint brush, hairpins (if applicable), makeup remover (for fixing that troublesome under-eye area after the ceremony and before the photo session, Advil (or your headache remedy of choice), saline solution (if applicable) and any pertinent replacement buttons. Entrust this to a reliable party or bring it to the reception site yourself and stash it in a potted plant.

Don't have anything on your face waxed, bleached or electrically removed. Cara got burned (quite literally) two days before her wedding. An eyebrow waxing left her skin red and slightly swollen. She iced down the swelling and covered the scarlet hue with some concealer. If you must do anything that can scar or bruise your pretty face, do it two weeks in advance to give yourself a chance to heal. Also, no facials less than three weeks before the wedding, unless you already have them weekly. Skin, like the fragile human psyche, does not react well to newness.

Do take absolutely the best care of yourself possible. Think positive thoughts. See your friends (only the ones who make you happy). Stay up till you're sleepy (to offset potential insomnia). Say no when you want to. And don't take any wooden nickels.

Seize Your Day

*I*t might seem easy but, like surviving a blind date, enjoying your wedding requires mental preparation, a sense of humor and perhaps a couple of weak drinks. The advice I collected for this section is the most valuable in the book, because even if you manage to get the ideal floral arrangements, the perfect food and a brilliant photographer, none of it matters if you don't have the time of your life.

Stage Fright

If throughout the planning you've had a difficult time being the recipient of so much uniquely bizarre attention, the wedding day could be the proverbial straw that breaks the bride's back. Says Greta, "Before the ceremony, I was in the bathroom crying because people were going to be looking at me, and I couldn't stand the attention, and I was going to have a breakdown. I was covered with a rash, sobbing. They had to pump me full of Benadryl."

If this is likely to be you, or even if it's a part of you, you have to find a way to overcome your self-consciousness. I'm not saying you'll have the stage presence of Katharine Hepburn. I'm just suggesting that *you* have the ability to talk yourself out of some of your fears. First, try to keep in mind that although a wedding is about the bride and groom, the guests spend much more time with one another than they do with you. And people *like* to go to weddings. For your friends, seeing you get married is fun, no matter how well you perform, no matter how little you're doing to justify their attention. They want to be there; they want to watch. And your wedding is also a chance for relatives to see one another and wish you well. What you're giving to everyone is a party they can enjoy and remember and refer back to ("Oh, that was right before Sheri's wedding, after Liz had her first baby.")

Don't let all the talk about it being "your day" weigh you down with guilt either. Of course it's not just your day. It's your husband's day and your parents' day and his parents' day too. And it's the guests' day. Says Clarice, "I always have a great time at my friends' weddings—much better than I had at my own. At mine I was riddled with guilt about being the center of attention, I was overcome with host anxiety and I was in a daze for most of it." But there are lots of happy brides, and many of them are not the exhibitionist type. Allison was nervous about being the woman in white who everyone was staring at, but she didn't allow her shyness to become crippling: "I thought, If you're ever going to have to be the center of attention, isn't this the best way to do it— surrounded by people who love you? And I kept reminding myself of that all day."

It's My Party, and I'll Do What I Want To

Once you settle in to your role, you have to make a decision to be a little selfish with your time at the wedding. Paul and Krista, who worked very hard on their wedding, made a promise to themselves. "We decided that we were going to do whatever we wanted," says Paul. "That if we felt like sitting in one place all night and letting everybody come to us, we would." They didn't, but it was a pleasure for them to know they were off the hook before the day even began.

Lia was surprised to discover as soon as her reception began that she just wanted to be with her new husband. "I didn't want to be apart from him," she says. So they spent nearly every minute beside each other. They visited each table together, slowly, for as long as they felt like; they sat with friends together; they danced together. "I tried to mingle, but it just wasn't fun. Maybe I felt a little overwhelmed, and I needed my best friend with me as a security blanket."

Pam had heard plenty of depressing stories from brides who didn't fully enjoy their weddings. "Everybody said to me, 'Oh, I don't even remember my wedding. I didn't eat the dinner. I didn't dance.' And I thought to myself, You know it's like a four-hour thing. It's over before you know it," says Pam. She realized that you have to teach yourself a little selfishness if it doesn't come naturally to you. "So months ahead of time I psyched myself into believing that the day was completely for me." It worked. "I remember the dinner, I remember dancing, I remember talking with my friends. I didn't put pressure on myself to talk to everyone who was there." Pam hung with the people she wanted to hang with and had a great time.

Some Very Grounded Advice

Have a sandwich before you get into your dress. "Someone will always make sure you have a glass of champagne in your hand, but no one will make sure you eat," says Josie. And champagne on an empty stomach can give you a nasty headache.

If you wear contact lenses, get an emergency pair. "After wearing lenses for nine years and never losing or ripping one," says Rachel, "I accidentally rinsed one down the drain just before my wedding rehearsal." Yikes! When your hands are shaking and your mind is off in the stratosphere somewhere, you do things you've never done before. Be prepared.

Don't duck or cover. There may be a point after the ceremony when guests are throwing things at you (I mean rice or birdseed, of course). Remember then that if you use your bouquet to protect your face, you will be Flower-Head in the photos of that special moment. If you have a veil you can pull over your face, use it. Otherwise endure the pelting with a smile.

Make use of other people's pockets. "I gave our best man a small tin of mints to hold for me," says Joanne. Of course, if you're having a dress specially made, you'll have a secret compartment big enough for a breath freshener, a lipstick and a light snack sewn right in.

Careful of that fragile stomach. If you're traveling around in a limo, don't ride backward. Says Darcy, "As we were driving to the reception, I looked at my new husband, who had turned pale and sweaty. He asked, 'Is it hot in here?' and changed to a forward-facing seat just before losing his breakfast."

And speaking of nausea . . . Moderation is the last thing you want to think about on your day of hyperbolic everything. If you're a practiced drinker, I don't have any advice for you. But if you have a low tolerance, too much celebrating could wreck your party and your dress. Jeff got goaded by his twentysomething cousin into doing shots of vodka. A mild beer drinker with a notoriously fragile stomach, Jeff found himself on the bathroom floor, apologizing profusely through the door after his fifth shot. It was the end of the wedding, so it wasn't a disaster. But it's a bummer that Jeff has no recollection of the last hour of his wedding—that's 20 percent of it. In dollars, that was 2,000 that he did not enjoy.

A thousand words. Ask friends who have digital cameras to bring them (everyone will already bring their smartphones) and send you their photos right after the wedding. Upload them to an album on Flickr or Picasa. Then you'll be able to look at them whenever you want, wherever you're headed.

Philosophical Tips

Leave the baggage of planning behind. It's not easy to slough off resentments you might have developed over the past months, especially if they're in your face on your wedding day in the form of, say, a best man you absolutely can't stand. But the only person who's going to ruin your wedding for you is you (does it sound like I interviewed your mother for this part, or what?). And resentment is useless. Plus it makes you break out.

Let go of the details. "The night before my wedding, I was having a little anxiety attack about the centerpieces," says Eva. A family friend took her aside and said, "You've done all you can do, so now just relax and enjoy every wonderful moment." Eva says that advice saved her and helped her have "a beautiful, fun, perfect day."

Embrace the mishaps. Robin says, in a loaded situation, always assume that three things will go wrong. "I did," she says, "and that took a lot of pressure off the wedding to be perfect." Marie happened on number one before her wedding even started. She stood outside her mother's house waiting for a limo that never came and ended up riding to the ceremony in a neighbor's Subaru. "I tried to lie down across the backseat so my dress wouldn't get all crinkled," she says. "It was very funny for my brother, but I failed to see the humor at the time."

If the wedding's going too fast, slow it down. "It's a dancer's trick," says Wendy. "When you're trying to do movement that feels too fast, you pretend you're doing it in slow motion." This little mind game can help you feel like the party isn't whizzing by.

Be the guest, not the host. "Until it's really happening, you just can't imagine what it's like to have every person you like and care about in one place focusing on you," says Gabi. "I felt responsible for anyone who didn't know a lot of people, or anyone I hadn't seen in a long time. And I really wanted to be with my closest friends, who are people I see almost every day, so I felt guilty about that." But Gabi knew this wasn't going to work, so she talked herself out of it. "I realized I had to be the one who was just appearing, and I couldn't be the one who was worrying about whether everyone was eating." Victoria says go into the day knowing that you won't be able to talk to everyone, and don't worry about slighting people. "I had a good time because I didn't let myself make it a day of obligations. I just made it a day of fun."

Exude joy. Says Tracy, "My boss had told me that he believes what makes or breaks a wedding is the mood of the bride and groom, so I sort of kept that in mind." She made a real effort not to get bogged down by the details and to allow herself to just feel happy. "Everyone panics, and it always works out, right?"

Take a mental picture. "At some point during the reception, get your husband and walk to the back of the room, and look at your party. Just watch for a minute," says Phoebe. "It's so beautiful— everyone all dressed up, dancing and laughing. It's an image you'll never forget."